REPRESENTAT[illegible] DIVINE IN ARA[illegible] POETRY

MW00396711

ORIENTATIONS 5

ORIENTATIONS

A multidisciplinary annual of the Dutch Association
for Middle Eastern and Islamic Studies

Editors
Gert Borg
(University of Nymegen)
Ed de Moor †
(University of Nymegen)

REPRESENTATIONS OF THE DIVINE IN ARABIC POETRY

Edited
by
Gert Borg
and
Ed de Moor †

Rodopi

Amsterdam – Atlanta, GA 2001

The paper on which this book is printed meets the requirements of "ISO 9706:1994, Information and documentation - Paper for documents - Requirements for permanence".

ISBN: 90-420-1574-8
©Editions Rodopi B.V., Amsterdam - Atlanta, GA 2001
Printed in The Netherlands

CONTENTS

INTRODUCTION

It seems that no region in the world has a density of prophethood as the Middle East. Prophets are the key figures in the Old Testament and from prophethood originated three of the worlds great religions: Judaism, Christianity and Islam.

In some cases the appearance of a prophet marks a major change in one of the societies that make up the Middle East and such was certainly the case in beginning Islam: the revelation by Mohammed coincided with the remarkable transition from a tribal Bedouin society to urban Islamic society in Mecca, which eventually evolved into the military, financial and political superpower of the Umayyad and Abbasid eras, the heirs to all previous Mediterranean cultures and societies.

The traces of prophethood that are scattered throughout Middle Eastern history and that mark the stages of growth of its intellectual and cultural identity show one important common feature: they are all recorded in words. Prophethood is a strongly textual activity, not only in itself, but also in its aftermath of interpretation and re-interpretation of accounts of the prophets' deeds and of the texts that were revealed to the people through these prophets. "In the Beginning was the Word..." is a suitable expression for a great stretch of Middle Eastern History.

In Islam the fascination for "the word" is as vigorous as in Judaism and in Christianity, but an extra dimension is, that the revealed text, the Koran, is considered to be verbatim the word of the Almighty Himself, thereby providing the Arabic language with just an extra quality. No wonder that throughout Islamic history the study of the word, the Koran, the prophet's utterances and the interpretation of both, has become the main axis of knowledge and education.

As a consequence the intellectuals – and also the poets in Islamic culture - were thoroughly familiar with religious terms and the phraseology of a language which was highly estimated because of the divine origin with which it was associated. No wonder therefore, that allusions to religious texts can be found throughout Arabic literature, both classical and modern.

The subject of this volume is the representation of the divine in Arabic poetry, be it the experience of the divine as expressed by poets or the use of imagery coined by religion.

PART I: CLASSICAL ARABIC POETRY

The first contribution takes us to the very brink of verifiable Arab history, facing what is for some the realm of pre-Islamic myth or constructed history: the poet Umayya ibn Abî al-Ṣalt, probably one generation older than Muḥammad, claimed to have been chosen to be the "prophet of the Arabs". Part of his poetry is clearly inspired by religious ideas and even aims at bringing a message to the people. There is no direct evidence in the text to suggest that it is not authentic; still the far-reaching consequences of its being authentice such that caution seems to be advisable.

It is with this warning for caution that the second contribution by James Montgomery takes over. The author discusses a passage taken from the work of Umayya concerning the Ark and the Flood. On the basis of this text Montgomery discusses the meaning of ships in the Koran in the context of early poetic references to seafaring. He concludes that there is hardly any reason to suppose, that Koranic references to seafaring bear any deep mythological meaning; probably they simply draw on early Arabic imagery, in which the terminology connected with ships and seafaring was well known and used incidentally.

Another instance of using religious terminology in poetry is discussed by Van Gelder. In his analysis of a poem by the 10th century AD poet Mudrik al-Shaybânî, he argues that an older judgement by Ullmann might well be eligible for revision. Whereas Ullmann considered this poem, which contains playful allusions to Christianity and Christian religious practice an example of bad taste, Van Gelder argues, that this highly original love poem for a Christian boy should be judged in its historical context, in which Islam was the dominant religion.

The realm of religion for which language is the appropriate vehicle *par excellence* is of course mysticism. Bachmann discusses two poems by the 13th century teacher of "mystical philosophy", Ibn al-ᶜArabî, one a traditional *qaṣîda*, in which the poet uses its tripartite structure to convey the idea of a mystical experience. The other poem Bachmann discusses is a *muwashshaḥ*, a strophic poetic structure often used for erotic themes, in which Ibn al-ᶜArabî describes the "erotic" relationship of creation to its creator.

On the basis of new manuscript evidence Scattolin offers a fascinating interpretation of a huge poem by the other great mystic of Islam, the 13th century Egyptian poet ᶜUmar Ibn al-Fâriḍ. The analysis of the *Tâ'iyya al-Kubrâ* shows how this great poet used poetic language to express his feelings of unity with his creator.

In his contribution Schippers discusses a number of poems from the *dîwân* of the 13th century Andalusian poet Ibn Sahl. After the boy Mûsâ, who serves as the addressee of the poets love poetry, this part of the collection is called the *mûsâwîyât*. The name of the boy (Moses) evokes a number of allusions to passages of mostly Koranic origin, all expressed within the typical thematic ambiance of Andalusian poetry: wine and song.

PART II: MODERN ARABIC POETRY

Wild sets out to show in general terms to what extent the Koran serves as a subtext in poetry by several modern Arab poets. He distinguishes between two ways of using the Koran for such purposes; one in which the Koranic idiom and wording is "borrowed" to intensify the religious impact of verse, the other in which this "borrowing" is used as an ironic, nostalgic or even destructive counterpoint to its poetic context. This functionalizing of the Koran may lead to such extremes as Ḥasan Ṭilib's parody of Koranic idiom.

The poetry of Arabs emigrated to the Americas, the *Mahjar*-poetry, contributed much to Modern Arabic poetry in the sense, that it speeded up developments which were already casting their shadows, like the breaking up of the traditional set of themes that the audience became used to. The effect of citizenship of a nation like the USA and the cultural shock it provoked against the background of the mixed Muslim-Christian society that most of these emigrated Lebanese and Syrians came from, resulted in vivid religious ideas and imagery. Nijland discusses these images in the works of Nuᶜayma, Gibran and Abû Mâḍî, three of the main writers in the North American *Mahjar* and also points out the unexpected religious inclinations that these poets developed in their private lives, such as Nuᶜayma's flirtation with Free Masonry and Gibran's pantheism.

Another breakthrough in Modern Arabic poetry was achieved by the 20th century poet Ilyâs Abû Shabaka; he was one of the first to frankly address themes like sin and sexuality, still unusual within Arabic poetry in the first part of that century. As Ostle shows in his contribution Abû Shabaka did so by using religious idiom and ideas, like repentance and confession, and by referring to Biblical passages.

In his contribution about Badr Shâkir al-Sayyâb De Moor discusses the historical circumstances in which this poet – one of the so called Tammuzian poets – started his career. One of the ambitions of these Tammuzian poets was to break the shackles of tradition and conformity and to bring about renewal in society and in literature. They introduced a set of themes and motives concerning rebirth and resurrection from ancient mythology and Christianity to combat concepts like "desert" and "barrenness" which they thought reigned Arab society in the fifties. In a closer study of two poems by al-Sayyâb De Moor analyses some of the most striking of these images and ideas.

Weidner discusses the presence of the Divine in the poetry of Adûnîs. It is not (a) God though, but more of a God-like creature: Adûnîs endows this protagonist with attributes, that would never fit the God of Islam nor Christianity. In other works of Adûnîs we find extensive allusions to religious and semi-religious texts. The poet even seems to go so far as to replace the Divine by the profane, using a Koranic passage as a subtext for a description with sexual connotations. Adûnîs tries to save the Divine "by inventing a modern shape for it".

As Allen shows, the prominent themes in the poetical works of the Christian-Palestinion poet Tawfîq Ṣâyigh are alienation, tortured love, exile and destructive despair. However in two of his poems that Allen discusses, there is a glimmer of hope, that is inspired by the return of Jesus Christ and the moment of consolation that Christ offers. Ṣâyigh often refers to Christian imagery and religious texts like the Psalms and the Gospel. As a Christian – as opposed to Muslim fellowmen – Ṣâyigh is able to communicate with the Divine, but his poetry is never confined to a Christian audience. Instead he uses the mythical potential of the Gospel to craft a combiantion of sacred and secular that appealed and still appeals to a larger audience.

Religion, God, the Divine and the texts that are associated with this realm of the sacred have never been absent from Arabic poetry. Indeed it seems to be and to have been one of the main themes around which the Arab poets' intention to stand up in the open and to speak – as is the role of Arabic poetry – has revolved. One can only be amazed by the plethora of images and themes that were actually used, a testimony of Arabic poetic ingenuity.

Ed de Moor organised the colloquium on the "Divine in Arabic Poetry" at the occasion of the 50th anniversary of the Institute of Arabic and Middle Eastern Studies at the Catholic University in Nijmegen. It is hard to say how much I regret, that he was not able to see the printing of this volume, which of course I dedicate to his memory.

Many thanks are due to those who made this colloquium possible and to the Institute of Arabic and Middle Eastern Studies that generously provided some of the financial means to assist in editing and printing this volume.

A NOTE ON TRANSLITERATION

The transliteration used for this volume is:
b,t,th, j, ḥ, kh, d, dh, r, z, s, sh, ṣ, ḍ, ṭ, ẓ, ᶜ, gh, f, q, k, l, m, n, h, w, y.
Initial *hamza* is not indicated.
The *hamza al-waṣl* is transliterated with *a*, even in the article.
Long vowels: â, î, û.
Diphthongs: ay, aw.

Nijmegen, December 2000
Gert Borg

Part I:

Classical Poetry

THE DIVINE IN THE WORKS OF UMAYYA B. ABÎ AL-ṢALT

BY

GERT BORG
University of Nijmegen

The discussions that concerned the work of the poet Umayya b. Abî al-Ṣalt are dominated by the question of its authenticity. Seidensticker[1] meticulously discusses this subject and reaches a disappointing conclusion: we first need an authorative edition of Umayya's work, before the discussion about this poet and his work can continue.

Of course we have every reason to be cautious in view of what is at stake: fragments of the work that is attributed to this poet show some kind of similarity with passages in the text of the Koran, so we are close to a minefield of historical and religious implications. Of course such implications cannot be the scope of this contribution; at this stage we can hardly do more than confine ourselves to less ambitious questions and propositions. The trap however is always there, so we are well advised to be careful to refer to a historical person "Umayya".

On the other hand: if - in accordance with Seidenstickers point of view - we accept, that the problem of the authenticity of Umayya's work should be solved first, before we could seriously discuss it, we are surely heading for a state of mute stagnation in our dealing with this poets work, because an authorative edition of it does not seem to be forthcoming shortly. Nonetheless: caution is the order of the day.

Authenticity is an ambiguous and often unruly problem. To illustrate this, we can refer to the following example: Seidensticker[2] argues against the authenticity of one poem ascribed to Umayya[3]. In this poem the archangel Gabriel is made responsible for breathing Jesus into Mary's breast through her garment, which Seidensticker states is consistent with - later! -

---

1. Seidensticker, T., The Authenticity of the Poems ascribed to Umayya Ibn Abî al-Ṣalt *in* Tradition and Modernity in Arabic Language and Literature (J.R. Smart ed.), Richmond, Surrey, 1996, 89-96
2. Seidensticker, op. cit., 91.
3. al-Ḥadîthî, B. ᶜA., *Umayya Ibn Abî al-Ṣalt Ḥayâtuh wa-Shiᶜruh*, Baghdad, 1975, (Dîwân:) 292.

Islamic *tafsîr*, whereas in the Koran (Q. 66,12) God himself performed this creative act. At first glance this seems a convincing argument to shed doubts on the poems authenticity, but we cannot definitely rule out the possibility, that ideas about Gabriels involvement in Jesus' conception circulated in the area before Koranic revelation, especially so, because in Christian tradition Gabriel plays an important role in this process as well. Seidenstickers argument is sound and he is probably right, but a different state of affairs cannot be excluded.

Normally the way out of the authenticity problem would be to historically assess the biographical data of Umayya b. Abî al-Ṣalt himself, that is to say, the little we know about him, but this does not seem to bring us closer to any solution, because almost everything about this man is enigmatic.

Just as an example we could look at the end of his life: he is believed to have died around the year 631, that is 9 of the Hijra, and did *not* convert to Islam, although most sources regard him as an extremely religious person. Some sources - for what they are worth - describe a meeting, Umayya had with the prophet Muhammad in person. After hearing some of Umayya's poetry Mohammed states, that Umayya actually almost was a muslim[4].

The main reason that al-Ḥadîthî gathered from his sources for Umayya's non-conversion is, that he apparently believed himself to be the chosen prophet of the Arabs[5]. Arab historians consider him to have been a *ḥanîf* - but we don't know what a *ḥanîf* exactly is. Does the word merely indicate that someone is monotheistic? Or does it also refer to actively preaching some form of religious ideas as perhaps in Umayya's case[6]?

4. Al-Iṣfahânî, *Kitâb al-Aghânî*, Cairo, 1963, IV, 129; al-Ḥadîthî, op. cit., 66-7
5. He is described as travelling to Iraq and entering a church. After some time he reappears, in total shock, but he and his party continue their journey to Iraq. On the way back Umayya enters the same church and after a while comes out as shocked as he was before. When asked for the reason of his anguish he claims to have heard at his first visit, that he was to become the prophet of the Arabs, which seems a good reason to become nervous. The second time, however, he has learned, that God decided against him and would not grant him this honour. See al-Iṣfahânî, *al-Aghânî*, IV, 123
6. An interesting point might be, that the same root in Hebrew (ḤNP) is associated with profaneness, polution, desacration; could this be a case of adopting an honorary soubriquet?

The first source to turn to for an answer to these questions would be the diwan of this poet, but as we have seen things are not made any easier for us there, because the main part of his diwan seems to be lost, and some of what remains of it, is under severe suspicion of not being authentic. As for Umayya's identity the essential question might be: How does Umayya present himself? The answer is simple: he is a poet. I know of no literary texts in *saj*ᶜ or in any other prose that are ascribed to him.

All sources ascribe to him some traditional *marâthî* and some *madiḥ*-poetry, so we may at least assume, that he knew and practised some of the literary conventions of the time.

The poetry, that was collected in a *Dîwân Umayya* the main part of which is nowadays lost, and that has been gathered from several sources consists of poems of four kinds:

- tiny fragments (one verse or even only half verses) without any context, that can hardly be analised
- longer fragments, that stand on their own, because they cannot technically be connected to other fragments
- longer fragments, that according to their rhyme and metre, may or may not belong to other fragments
- shorter and longer poems, that seem more or less unaffected by the ravages of time, because they show some kind of thematical development or at least have some kind of beginning and end.

Thematically his poetry can be divided into two categories:

- traditional poetry, consisting of *madîḥ*, *fakhr* of his own tribe Thaqîf and a few *marâthî*
- religious poetry, which - as I hope to show - partly has a vigourous public character, partly a distinctive personal character

The very fact, that Umayya composed other poetry than the usual kinds that we know from *jâhilî* and *mukhaḍram* poets is in a way nothing unusual: as Jacobi has shown[7], the poets of the era just before Islam tended to experiment within the framework of the traditional genres, like for instance in love poetry, but tried out some new ideas as well. On the other hand we

7. Jacobi, R., *Die Anfänge der arabischen Ġazalpoesie: Abû Dhu'aib al-Hudhalî in Der Islam*, 61, 1984, 219 ff.

know of no other poet of this early age who took religious ideas as a theme for his poetry. In this respect Umayya seems to be standing quite alone.

Looking at the same phenomenon from an opposite point of view makes it even more intriguing: if we suppose, that in that very age some individuals dwelled on religious topics or even acted as vagant preachers - I have not been able to find any proof of such practices - they might have used ordinary language or even *saj*ᶜ as their vehicle - in the latter case continuing the tradition of the *kuhhân* - but to use *poetry* as a means of expression for these purposes seems to be quite unusual, because of its status in expressing the traditional core of poetic themes. On the other hand it can be argued, that poetry is the logical vehicle for preaching religious thought, if we think of poetry as the only "media" of the time.

It may be, that this thematic originality had some influence on the quality of Umayya's poetry. From a technical point of view, in terms of mediaeval Arabic literary theory, Umayya probably was not a very strong if not weak poet: he often uses enjambement, reiterates rhyme words easily, uses strange and sometimes even obscure wording, a partly non-Arabic vocabulary[8] - and his themes are of course contrary to the normal stock and pile that a pre-Islamic audience would expect.

Let us now turn to the texts:
Some notes on the text of poem 21:

In line 1B al-Hadîthî reads: *wa-lâ majdu*, but I prefer to read with Schulthess: *wa-amjadu*, because the last reading would be metrically correct.

In line 4B I suggest to read: *mu'abbadu* in stead of *mu'ayyadu*, a reading in line with the *al-Zahra* manuscript, edited by Vallaro[9]; al-Ḥadîthî calls it a case of *taṣḥîf*.

Vallaro's edition of the *Kitâb al-Zahra*, written by Abû Bakr Muḥammad bn Dâwud al-Ẓâhirî who died in 297 A.H., contains a second part of the same poem.

Translation of the first part:

---

8. See for instance Ibn Qutayba, *al-Shi*ᶜ*r wa-al-Shu*ᶜ*arâ'*(Beyrout, s.d.), I, 370-1
9. Al-Ẓâhirî, *Kitâb al-Zahrah*, Parte Seconda (ed. M. Vallaro), Napoli, 1985, 14-6

1. Praise to You and Grace and the Kingdom, O Lord, Nothing is higher than You and more praiseworthy
2. King on the Throne of Heaven, a Ruler, to whose Glory the faces bow and [people] kneel down
3. Over Him is the veil of light, the light surrounds him and rivers of light burn around him
4. No man rises towards him with a look of his eyes and beyond the veil of light are immortal (strong?) beings
5. Angels with their feet in His earth and their necks rising over the Heavens
6. Among them those who are bearing one of the legs of his Throne with their hands and if that were not so, they would become exhausted and fall to the ground (?)
7. Standing on their feet bowing under it (the Throne), their shoulderblades trembling from fear
8. They are with a Lord whose command they observe, they prick their ears to the Inspiration, standing still
9. Among them are his secretaries, the Holy spirited Gabriel and the strong spirited Michael, the steady one
10. Angels who will not stop being servants, Cherubs, some of them kneeling, others prostrated
11. The prostrated ones never raise their heads, they praise their Lord above them and glorify him
12. And the kneeling ones bow their backs to Him in fear, repeating Gods benefactions and praising him
13. And amongst them are those who fold their heads in their wings and whose heads are almost sweating at the very thought of their Lord
14. out of fear, not tiring from serving Him and they do not consider it a burden to serve Him longtime
15. Behind them are the guards of Heavens gates, standing near them, with their keys, watchful
16. Good servants they are, chosen for his command; behind them stands a strong, well equipped army
17. Under the water masses in the deep soil there are angels who descend and rise
18. And between the layers of the earth under its inner parts there are angels who go to and fro on His command
19. Praise be to the One whose power his creation does not know and Who is on his throne, alone and unique

20. The One Whose reign is not contested by his creatures and Who is unique even though his servants do not hold Him for that
21. King of the strong heaves and the earth below; there is nothing above us that will bend
22. He is God, the Creator of creation, and all of his creatures, male and female, are his servants in obedience
23. How can creation be like its Creator, Who is forever and eternal, whereas the created will vanish
24. The created has no access to the act of creating; who then can be eternal against the course of fate
25. So [the created] will vanish and only the overpowering One will stay, who produces Life and Death eternally and will not weaken
26. The birds concealed in their hiding praise Him and behold: they ascend in the open air of heaven
27. And out of fear of my Lord thunder above us praises him and the trees and wild animals, forever
28. The whales praise him and the sea, swirling, and all that it encloses and holds together

What we see in the first part of the poem is an exalted vision, in which Umayya tries to present Gods transcendency; He is an unapproachable ruler of Heaven with a strong command over his angels; they have the task to serve him, uphold his throne and praise him continuously and their main motivation to do so, is fearful respect for their Lord.

Further away from Heaven, under the earth and sea, his angels are seen running errands on his command. (17-18)

What kind of place is this Heaven? What strikes us first of all is that Umayya never mentions any room for the souls of the righteous in this perfectly organised fortress: obviously they will have no share in Heavens glory, which in itself is a strange image for Umayya, because elsewhere in his poetry he articulates, that the sinners will be punished in hell, whereas the righteous will dwell in the comfort of Heaven.

Furthermore it seems, that what inspires Umayya to present this kind of Heaven, looks like the very ideal of an *earthly* court: it is strongly organised with God at the head of its hierarchy assisted by his secretaries Gabriel and Michael. They appear to be some kind of middlemen between God and his angels, although this is not mentioned explicitly: probably it would not be fitting to put anyone in a commanding or even subcommanding position in the presence of the Lord and in such a kind of organisation.

It is strange to see, that humans are hardly mentioned in this part of the poem, but Umayya of course implies them in the whole of creation. In verse 20 Umayya refers to failing belief in the Oneness of God, and this must necessarily be a reference to human failure to do so.

Umayya stresses the difference between the Almighty who is one and eternal, whereas all of his creation is mortal and cannot possibly reach His overwhelming state of being.

Finally he presents a pastoral scenery in which several creatures in nature - even thunder -, by the essence of being what they are, praise their Creator.

One of the remarkable things is the epithet of God that is missing: in this text God is never mentioned as being *raḥîm*, an epithet Umayya uses frequently in other poems, at one time even for the prophet.

The second poem that I would like to discuss can in my view only be interpreted correctly if we assume that it was actually performed before a live audience.

Translation:

1. In front of (in the face of?) the Owner of the Throne, before Whom THEY will be shown, the One Who knows what is in the open, and also the hidden word
2. on the day WE will come to Him - he is a merciful Lord - what he promised always came true
3. on the day YOU[10] will come to Him, as He said: INDIVIDUALLY when He will not forget righteous nor sinner
4. Will I be blessed? It is blessing I hope for[11]; or will I be blamed for what I obtained in a shameful way
5. My Lord: *If* you forgive me, forgiveness is *all I can hope for* (?) or if you punish me, You will not punish an innocent

---

10. According to al-Ḥadîthî (op. cit., 314: *yawma na'tîhî*) the translation would run: "on the day WE will come to him".
11. It was suggested to me by Mike Carter to read a *mafᶜûl muṭlaq* here: "Will I be blessed in the way I hope to be blessed ...". This is a good solution, but I still prefer my own translation because of the parallel construction in 5a.

6. If I will be blamed for what I have committed, then I will surely face an abominable punishment ----------
7. My Lord, You have destined for everyone to descend to the fire of hell, you have imposed a book, firm in its judgement
8. My Lord, do not withhold from me eternal paradise but be merciful, my Lord, and forgiving to me

In this poem Umayya also starts with a reference to God Almighty, an opening with which Umayya seems to legitimize his performance. As if in soliloqui he then refers to humanity as a whole by using the personal pronoun THEY. He does so, however, in front of an audience, in which everyone knows - or is supposed to understand - that he or she will be among those who will be judged.

In verse 2 he knits a bond between his audience and himself by using the first person plural WE, a bond that seems even more intimate when he describes God as a merciful Lord: the thought behind it is: we are united and we can be assured of Gods steadfastness.

But in verse three he is pointing a finger at YOU, meanwhile opposing a Lord of wrath and vengeance to the merciful one in verse 2. He even goes so far as to stress the individual judgement: *fardan*

Now we come to an important question: Whom does Umayya mean by “I”, bearing in mind, that Umayya is performing for an audience. He is enacting a person adressing God and asking to be forgiven. We might even go as far as to assume, that the “I” here stands for every individual in his audience: the “I” is every individual for him- or herself, or - to put it another way - the “I” is the person for his audience to identify with. A modern equivalent might be the “I”, that a priest will use in praying during service: if he prays for “his” salvation, it is not only his own personal salvation - although it's not excluded -, but the individual salvation for everyone present. The “I” in this context might be used by Umayya as a rhetorical device, for which I was not able to find an appropriate technical term, but “identificational I” comes close to what I think would be appropriate.

With this in mind we may be able to understand the rather peculiar expression *fa-al-muᶜâfâtu ẓannî* in verse 5, which I translated provisionally as *forgiveness is all I can hope for.* A better translation would perhaps be: Forgiveness is what I'm guessing at, what I'm counting on. To grasp the full meaning of this passage we probably have to suppose that here Umayya does not speak for himself, but for the individual, who will think in everyday life, that things won't be that bad after all, that everything will be all right in the end.

In the remaining part of this poem Umayya enacts the repenting individual, almost falling to his knees in awe, begging to be forgiven. In short I think, that this poem can be characterized as a sermon that gradually becomes a prayer.

If we now return to the second part of the first poem, we will find that it also is a kind of prayer:

[29. Oh you, heart of mine, dwelling on desire, how long will you be so stubborn
30. Oh verily the world offers sufficiency to live, and whilst a man may become a respected sayyid in it
31. Behold! It will turn away from him and its loveliness will cease and he will have made from the dust of graves his cushion
32. He will be split from his soul that lived in his body and be a neighbour to corpses whose property proved to be unstable
33. Which man have you seen before me, living forever, who posessed in ancient times that what could keep him alive
34. Whom Fate torments with stumbling, will keep stumbling and the fates of time are unstable
35. The earth will not be well, even if its inhabitants will think it to be well: fate may always reveil itself
36. Have you not seen in what has passed a warning for you? Stop now! Don't be, heart of mine, [like] a blind man, erring to and fro
37. Because guidance has come that knows no doubt and only a liar will reject the truth
38. Be fearful of death and of resurrection after it and do not belong to those, who are deceived by today or tomorrow
39. Because you are in a world that decieves its inhabitants; in it there is an enemy, full of hate, who kindles a fire
40. who lives in the regions of heaven above the air and is without the knowledge of what is hidden, he will be completely without sleep [?]
41. If not for the bond with God, we would be wandering and lost and it would make us happy to be thrown to the ground to be burried alive
42. In this bond you will see the stories of ages passed and the stories of what is hidden, will be clear at resurrection
43. [There is nothing in them except the dog nearby and their booty and the ones in the cave are weakened?] (a reference to the *Ahl al-Kahf*)

44. *(missing)*
because my Lord said to the angels: bow down
45. for Adam when God completed his creation and they threw themselves down for him in obedience, prostrated, and they stayed that way
46. And Gods enemy spoke out of pride and evil nature "is it a piece of loam (?) on the fire of the hot winds? Go ahead: Make it your master!"
47. Thus disobedience drove him (Adam) away from the best of dwellings and that was what caused in ancient times his wrath
48. with us (primordial sin?); we will spare ourselves no folly nor trick to lead it (our soul) to a fire, that will be brought to it (?)
49. A hell that is burning and will not be made lukewarm for one moment and its heat will not become cold until the end of time
50. You have no example of how the devil and hell will be when you are being burned in the fire; you will be lost
51. He (the devil) is a leader, always calling you to the Fire, to bring us near it, without going there himself
52. You will have no excuse nor the (false) obedience of the sinner and you will have no influence on the fire when you are burning in it.]

Although this is a kind of prayer, it completely lacks the vigour and rhetoric devices of text 140. Nonetheless it is rather personal in tone, because the poet starts by adressing his own heart. Umayya soon however turns to a number of *ḥikam* on the transitory nature of rank and personal glory and of all earthly possessions. His observations of the ruling of Fate are at least still very much inspired by pre-Islamic concepts: a verse like 34 for example would easily fit in any pre-Islamic poem.

In verse 36 Umayya starts to urge his heart to turn away from idle disbelief and follow new guidance, that has come. The word used in verse 37 for "guidance" is *hudâ*, but it is hard to see what he means by it. Does it refer to the new mission by Mohammed, or to what Umayya's concept of the *dîn al-aḥnâf*? The preceding verse 36 and the following verses 41 and 42 may give a clue: Umayya points to a warning from the past, with which he probably means the history of the prophets and he explicitly mentions the bond with God. From verse 44 onwards we can also notice an orientation towards stories from the Old Testament: creation, paradise and the primordial sin, so my best guess would be, that it is not early Koranic revelation, that is at stake here, but Biblical inspiration, unless of course this message of his is inspired by the corresponding Sura's, and he semi-quotes them, so to say.

As usual Umayya ends his poem with vivid images of eternal punishment in hell, the destiny of all sinners.

If we compare these two poems we can point at the following differences

- The longer poem 21 consists of two very different parts: I would call the first part a hymn to God, whereas the second part might best be described as a personal prayer
- This poem, nr 21, is rather formal in character, shows some connections to pre-Islamic poetry and, as far as Umayya's religious ideas are concerned, it refers mainly to the Old Testament
- Its religious perspective is rather rigid, because it mainly focuses on two ideas: God is almighty and the individual, confronted with this glory, should repent.
- Apart from resurrection, when the hidden will be revealed, it holds no promise whatsoever for us humans
- Seen this way the poem creates an enormous distance between God and us, mortals, if only for the ranks of servants who are put in between and who, though more lofty than we are, are seemingly only motivated by fear. In other words: in this vision we, humans, are hardly more than worms

In contrast to this, the shorter poem nr 140

- shows many more features of a vivid performance, mainly by its quick changing of personal pronouns
- this makes it sound much more as an act of preaching in front of a live audience
- it offers us humans much more of a perspective to share in the glory of God
- it does so by clearly making a distinction between the righteous and the sinners
- in verse 7 it clearly refers to the Koran
- in short: this poem offers a perspective op hope

Based on the comparison of these two poems, I would be tempted to put an earlier date to the longer of the two, although it is clear, that Umayya in both of these texts acts as a *nadhîr*.

This relative dating, if convincing, can be a contribution to the question of the authenticity of Umayya's work: if we can detect a development in religious convictions that would run parallel to a possible development on a personal level, and to a development in historical facts as we know them, we would have a strong indication for the intertextual authenticity of these poems.

Anyone might argue the other way around: that the shorter poem preceded the longer and I would be curious for the arguments given. I can even think of some arguments myself, but in the end, the result would be the same, in the sense, that the difference between the two can be attributed to mental change or development and would be an indication for changing religious attitudes.

I argued earlier that Umayya b. abî al-Ṣalt should first of all be seen as a poet. We can now modify his position some more: he probably started as a conventional pre-Islamic poet, but in the religious poetry that he started to make, he is a *nadhîr* who uses poetry as a medium for his religious message. This offers a curious parallel, because as far as I am aware the prophet Mohammad started off the same way: as a *nadhîr*.

Texts

Poem 21

1. *Laka al-ḥamdu wa-al-na*ᶜ*mâ'u wa-al-mulku rabbanâ*
*fa-lâ shay'a 'a*ᶜ*lâ minka jaddun wa-lâ majdu*
2. *malîkun* ᶜ*alâ* ᶜ*arshi al-samâ'i muhayminun*
*li-*ᶜ*izzatihi ta*ᶜ*nû al-wujûhu wa-tasjudu*
3. ᶜ*alayhi ḥijâbu al-nûri wa-al-nûru ḥawlahu*
wa-anhâru nûrin ḥawlahu tatawaqqadu
4. *wa-lâ basharun yasmû ilayhi bi-ṭarfihi*
wa-dûna ḥijâbi al-nûri khalqun mu'ayyadu (mu'abbadu? B.*)*
5. *malâ'ikatun 'aqdâmuhum taḥta 'arḍihi*
*wa-'a*ᶜ*nâquhum fawqa al-samawâti ṣu*ᶜᶜ*adu*
6. *fa-min ḥâmilin 'iḥdâ qawâ'imi* ᶜ*arshihi*
bi-'aydin wa-lawlâ dhâka kallû wa-balladû
7. *qiyâmun* ᶜ*alâ al-'aqdâmi* ᶜ*ânîna taḥtahu*
*farâ'iṣuhum min shiddati al-khawfi tar*ᶜ*adu*
8. *fa-hum* ᶜ*inda rabbin yanẓurûna li-'amrihi*
*yuṣîkhûna bi-al-'asmâ*ᶜ*i li-al-waḥyi rukkadu*

9. *'amînâhu rûḥu al-qudsi Jibrîlu minhumâ (minhumû? B.)*
wa-Mîkâlu dhû al-rûḥi al-qawîyu al-musaddadu
10. *malâ'ikatun lâ yaftirûna ᶜibâdatan*
karûbîyatun minhum rukûᶜun wa-sujjadu
11. *fa-sâjiduhum lâ yarfaᶜu al-dahra ra'sahu*
yuᶜaẓẓimu rabban fawqahu wa-yumajjidu
12. *wa-râkiᶜuhum yaḥnû lahu al-ẓahra khâshiᶜan*
yuraddidu 'âlâ'a al-'ilâhi wa-yaḥmadu
13. *wa-minhum muliffun fû janâḥayhi ra'sahu*
akâdu li-dhikrâ rabbihi yatafaṣṣadu
14. *mina al-khawfi lâ dhû sa'matin bi-ᶜibâdatin*
wa-lâ huwa min ṭûli al-taᶜabbudi yajhadu
15. *wa-ḥurrâsu 'abwâbi al-samâwâti dûnahu*
qiyâmun ladayhi (ladayhâ? B.) bi-al-maqâlîdi ruṣṣadu
16. *fa-niᶜma al-ᶜibâdu al-muṣṭaffûna li-'amrihi*
wa-min dûnihim jundun kathîfun mujannadu
17. *wa-taḥta kathîfi al-mâ'i fî bâṭini al-tharâ*
malâ'ikatun tanḥaṭṭu fîhi wa-taṣᶜadu
18. *wa-bayna ṭibâqi al-'arḍi taḥta buṭûnihâ*
malâ'ikatun bi-al-'amri fîhâ taraddadu
19. *fa-subḥâna man lâ yaᶜrifu al-khalqu qadrahu*
wa-man huwa fawqa al-ᶜarshi fardun muwaḥḥadu
20. *wa-man lam tunâziᶜhu al-khalâ'iqu mulkahu*
wa-'in lam tufarridhu al-ᶜibâdu fa-mafradu
21. *malîku al-samâwâti al-shidâdi wa-'arḍihâ*
wa-laysa bi-shay'in fawqanâ yata'awwadu
22. *huwa allâhu bârî al-khalqa wa-al-khalqu kulluhum*
'imâ'un lahu ṭawᶜan jamîᶜan wa-'aᶜbudu
23. *wa-annâ yakûnu al-khalqu ka-al-khâliqi alladhî*
yadûmu wa-yabqâ wa-al-khalîqatu tanfadu
24. *wa-laysa li-makhlûqin ᶜalâ al-khalqi juddatun*
wa-man dhâ ᶜalâ marri al-ḥawâdithi yukhladu
25. *fa-yafnâ wa-lâ yabqâ siwâ al-qâhiri alladhî*
yumîtu wa-yuḥyî dâ'iman laysa yamhadu (yahmudu? B.)
26. *tusabbiḥuhu al-ṭayru al-kawâminu fî al-kafâ*
wa-'idh hiya fî jawwi al-samâ'i taṣaᶜᶜadu
27. *wa-min khawfi rabbî sabbaḥa al-raᶜdu fawqanâ*
wa-sabbaḥahu al-'ashjâru wa-al-waḥshu 'abbadu

28. *wa-sabbaḥahu al-nînânu wa-al-baḥru ẓâkhiran*
wa-mâ ḍamma min shay'in wa-mâ huwa muqlidu
...
29. *alâ 'ayyuhâ al-qalbu al-muqîmu ᶜalâ al-hawâ*
ilâ 'ayyi hâdhâ al-dahri minka al-taṣaddudu
30. *a-lâ 'innamâ al-dunyâ balâghun wa-bulghatun*
wa-baynâ al-fatâ fîhâ mahîbun musawwadu
31. *idhi 'nqalabat ᶜanhu wa-zâla naᶜîmuhâ*
wa-'aṣbaḥa min turbi al-qubûri yuwassadu
32. *wa-fâraqa rûḥan kâna bayna ḥayâtihi*
wa-jâwara mawtâ mâluhu mutabaddadu
33. *fa-'ayya fatan qablî ra'aytum mukhalladâ*
lahu fî qadîmi al-dahri mâ yatazawwadu
34. *[not in al-Zahra] wa-man yabtalîhi al-dahru minhu bi-ᶜathratin*
sa-yakbû lahâ wa-al-nâ'ibâtu taraddadu
35. *wa-lan taslama al-dunyâ wa-'in ẓanna [al-Zahra: ḍanna] 'ahluhâ*
bi-ṣuḥbatihâ wa-al-dahru qad yatajaddadu
36. *'a-lasta tarâ fîmâ maḍâ laka ᶜibratan*
fa-mah lâ takun yâ qalbu 'aᶜmâ taladdadu
37. *fa-qad jâ'a mâ lâ rayba fîhâ mina al-hudâ*
wa-laysa yaruddu al-ḥaqqa illâ mufannadu
38. *fa-kun khâ'ifan li-al-mawti wa-al-baᶜthi baᶜdahu*
wa-lâ taku fî-man gharrahu al-yawmu aw ghadu
39. *fa-'innaka fî dunyâ gharûrun li-'ahlihâ*
wa-fîhâ ᶜaduwwun kâshiḥu al-ṣadri yûqidu
40. *[not in al-Zahra] wa-sâkinu 'aqṭâri al-raqîᶜi ᶜalâ al-hawâ*
wa-min dûni ᶜilmi al-ghaybi kullu musahhadu (?)
41. *[not in al-Zahra] wa-law-lâ wathâqu llâhi ḍalla ḍalâlunâ*
wa-la-sarranâ 'annâ nutallu fa-nû'adu
42. *[not in al-Zahra] tarâ fîhi akhbâra al-qurûni allatî maḍat*
wa-'akhbâra ghaybin fî al-qiyâmati tanjudu
43. *[not in al-Zahra] wa-laysa bihâ illâ al-raqîmu mujâwiran*
wa-ṣaydahumû wa-al-qawmu fî al-kahfi hummadu
44. [the ᶜajuz is damaged in my xerox of al-Ḥadîthî; this version taken from al-Zahra]
mina al-ḥiqdi nîrâna al-ᶜadâwati baynanâ
li-'an qâla rabbî li-al-malâ'ikati 'sjudû
45. *li-Âdama lammâ kammala Allâhu khalqahu [al-Zahra: ḥaqqahu]*
fa-kharrû lahu ṭawᶜan sujûdan wa-kaddadû

46. *wa-qâla ^{c}aduwwu Allâhi li-al-kibri wa-al-shaqâ*
'a-ṭînun [al-Ḥadîthî: li-ṭînin] ^{c}alâ nâri al-sumûmi fa-sawwadû
47. *fa-'akhrajahu al-^{c}iṣyânu min khayri manzilin*
fa-dhâka alladhî fî sâlifi al-dahri yaḥqadu
48. *^{c}alaynâ wa-lâ na'lû khabâlan wa-ḥîlatan*
li-nûridahâ nâran ^{c}alayhâ sa-yûridu
49. *jaḥîman talaẓẓâ lâ yufattaru sâ^{c}atan*
wa-lâ al-ḥarru minhâ 'âkhira al-dahri yabrudu
50. *fa-mâ laka fî al-shayṭâni wa-al-nâri 'uswatun*
'idhâ mâ ṣalîta al-nâra bal 'anta 'ab^{c}adu
51. *huwa al-qâ'idu al-dâ^{c}î 'ilâ al-nâri lâbithan*
li-yûridanâ minhâ wa-lâ yatawarradu
52. *fa-mâ laka fî ^{c}udhrin wa-ṭâ^{c}ati fâsiqin*
wa-mâ laka fî nârin ṣalîta bihâ yadu

Poem 140

1. *^{c}inda dhî al-^{c}arshi yu^{c}raḍûna ^{c}alayhi*
ya^{c}lamu al-jahra wa-al-kalâma al-khafîyâ
2. *yawma na'tîhi wa-hwa rabbun raḥîmun*
'innahu kâna wa^{c}duhu ma'tîyâ
3. *yawma ta'tîhi (al-Ḥadîṯî: na'tîhi) mithla mâ qâla fardan*
lam yadhar fîhi râshidan wa-ghawîyâ
4. *'a-sa^{c}îdun sa^{c}âdatan ana arjû*
'am muhânun bi-mâ kasabtu shaqîyâ
5. *rabbi 'in ta^{c}fu fa-al-mu^{c}âfâtu ẓannî*
'aw tu^{c}âqib fa-lam tu^{c}âqib barîyâ
6. *'in 'u'âkhadh bi-mâ 'jtaramtu fa-'innî*
sawfa 'alqâ mina al-^{c}adhâbi farîyâ
7. *rabbi kullan ḥatamtahu wârida al-nâ **
ri kitâban ḥatamtahu maqḍîyâ
8. *rabbi lâ taḥrimannanî jannata al-khul **
di wa-kun rabbi bî ra'ûfan ḥafîyâ

SALVATION AT SEA?

SEAFARING IN EARLY ARABIC POETRY [1]

BY

JAMES E. MONTGOMERY
University of Cambridge

The issue of the (ir)religious character of pre-Islamic poetry has been approached in a variety of ways. Chief among explications is the excision, by Muslim transmitters, of *Jâhilî* religiosity, in an attempt to accentuate the miraculousness and divine origin of the Koran. An alternative response is the interpretation of this poetry as a relentlessly mundane (in the sense of this worldly) expression of the human, nomadic vision of life. This paper reviews, in the context of pre-Islamic poetry and the Koran, the quest for that ancient, Near Eastern and Semitic religious symbol, the ship of souls.

The mysterious and controversial pre-Islamic 'religious' poet Umayya b. Abî l-Ṣalt is in so many ways pivotal because of his promise. This poet was a member of the Thaqîf tribe of al-Ṭâ'if, related, through his mother to the Meccan aristocracy, with whom he enjoyed a close affinity, if his panegyrics on several notables and his threnody for the Meccans slain at Badr are genuine. Umayya's existence has never been questioned (he is lauded in a poem by the Umayyad Surâqa b. Mirdâs) although every aspect of the traditional picture of him has been subjected to sceptical scrutiny.

This picture is given by Ibn Qutaybah, *Kitâb al-Shiʿr wa-l-Shuʿarâ'*, 279 as: "he had read the ancient scriptures of the scriptures of Allâh and loathed the worship of effigies ... In his poetry he would tell tales (*qiṣaṣ*) of the prophets and produce many terms unfamiliar to the desert Arabs which he

1. A fuller treatment of the same material, from the standpoint of the thematic potential of the movements of the *qaṣîdah,* is to be found in J.E. Montgomery, *The Vagaries of the Qaṣîdah. The Tradition and Practice of Early Arabic Poetry*, Warminster 1997, Chapter Six. Versions of this paper have been given at New York University (Center for Middle Eastern Studies) and Cambridge University (Divinity Faculty). I am grateful to my patient listeners for their instructive remarks.

had derived from the ancient scriptures and stories which he had derived from those of the People of the Book". Some 900 of his verses are extant. T. Seidensticker in an article published recently [2] argues "that there might well be some authentic material" (p. 96) among them.

Five elements should feature prominently in an assessment of what may plausibly be expected of Umayya's poetry: the religio-cultural environment of al-Ṭâ'if, Umayya's traditional identification as a *ḥanîf*, his dealings with Muḥammad, the fragmentariness of his poetic remains and the motives for falsification. Umayya was a contemporary of Muḥammad and they were reputedly hostile rivals: this would preclude influence on the latter by the former. Umayya's non-traditional, so-called 'religious' verse (if genuine) may attest to the circulation, in Mecca and its environs, if not throughout the peninsula, of the *qiṣaṣ* elements of the Koran. There is at times considerable divergence between Umayya's poetic version of a tale and that in the Koran. Legendary material contained in the *Tafsîr* works is often adduced as a source, though this material must itself have a source, and Hirschberg's championing of pre-Islamic Haggadic material remains an attractive fund of information for Umayya.

Koranic echoes and ideas in Umayya's poetry should be reassessed in the light of the research into such features of the poetry of the Mukhaḍramîn which I have carried out (see Chapter Seven of *The Vagaries of the Qaṣidah*), and might necessitate a revision of Umayya's *floruit* and his (spurious?) laudation of the Prophet. Only snippets of his verse have survived and although some long poems have been reconstructed, it is impossible to draw any conclusions as to their narrative style and techniques and also to determine whether the legendary 'religious' material ever formed part of a (traditionally conceived) polythematic *qaṣîda*. Schulthess [3] thought that he could discern in the clumsiness of Umayya's versification proof that he had taken his narrative materials from prose versions. Any emotional or character analysis of Umayya on the basis of such shakily attested texts is unwise.

---

2. "The Authenticity of the Poems Ascribed to Umayya Ibn Abî al-Ṣalt" in J. Smart (ed.), *Tradition and Modernity in Arabic Language and Literature*, Richmond 1996, pp. 87-101.
3. *Umajja ibn Abi ṣ Ṣalt*, Leipzig 1911, pp. 5-6.

There are a number of pre-Islamic, poetic versions of the story of Nûḥ, the authenticity of which needs careful consideration [al-A^{c}shâ (ed. Ḥusayn) Cairo 1950: Poem 79.28-9, Umayya b. Abî l-Ṣalt (ed. Schulthess) Leipzig 1911: Poem 28.10-13, 29.1-8, 30.6-8, 10-11, 32.24-36]. If they are forgeries, it should be noted that on occasion the forger displays an intimate acquaintance with the language and imagery of pre-Islamic and early Arabic seafaring (see Umayya Poem 30.11, for example).

The following piece is a reconstruction (effected by the scholar Schulthess [1911: Poem 29] from fragments contained in two medieval works) [4] of a poem describing the Ark and the Flood. The various quotations are marked by asterixes.

1. And she floats therein and crosses the sea with her sails <as fast as> the arrow of the <archer> who competes in an archery contest. [5]

***

2. The birds and land animals inside her cry out along with the mighty beasts of prey and the elephants,
3. Since she contains a couple of all that lives, amid humped waves <as big as> mountains.

***

4. Allâh, Our Lord, Master of Might and Blessings, listened to the son of Âdam, Nûḥ, [6]

---

4. The works in question are the *Kitâb al-Ḥayawân* of al-Jâḥiẓ and al-Zamakhsharî's *Asâs al-Balâghah*. I have not had access to other editions of Umayya's poetry.
5. The phrase *fa-hya tajrî fî-hi* is similar to Koran 30.46 (*wa-li-tajriya al-fulku bi-amri-hi*, so that the ships may sail by His command). The contest is one of long-distance shooting.
6. It is unlikely that the text means that Nûḥ is the son of Âdam. The phrase *ibn âdam* is similar to Banî Âdam, a koranic sobriquet (which occurs six times in the Koran: 7.26, 27, 31, 35, 17.70, 36.60) for 'mankind'. See 5.27 for the dual *ibnay âdama* (of Cain and Abel, who are not named). The catalogue containing Âdam and Nûḥ in 3.33 is largely chronological but does not imply any familial connection between the two. The phrase *rabbu-nâ dhû al-jalâlati wa-al-afḍâli* is not found in the Koran, although the following similarities should be noted: 55.78 (*tabâraka 'smu rabbi-ka dhî al-jalâli wa-'l-ikrâmi*) and 55.27 (*wa-yabqâ wajhu rabbi-ka dhû al-jalâli wa-'l-ikrâmi*) where the context (24-27) is nautical -- it is a sign of Allah's blessings that the ships sail on the deep and do not sink; *wa-'llâhu dhû al-faḍli al-^{c}aẓîmi* (2.105 = 3.74 = 8.29 = 57.21 = 57.29 = 62.4). The divine epithets are carefully and appropriately chosen:

5. When He fulfilled His promise to Him of the Dove (i.e. Nûḥ), [7] as the people were all, on His ark, like a <hungry> family, [8]
6. Locking the hold upon them (?), <in the form of> a messenger from among the light, swift doves, <as white as a> statue: [9]
7. For He had rewarded it, for acting as a messenger, <by giving it> a collar and by dying <its plumage> dark, a sign which would not wear away
8. And it brought him (i.e. Nûḥ) the truth, when He had rewarded it, a plucked branch,[10] <heavy> with dates, when it came <back> the next morning.

***

Verse 1 depicts the Ark as it rises with the Flood and sets sail upon the watery deep. Verses 2-3 depend, for their interpretation, upon the meaning of the verb *ṣarakha*, either 'to cry out loudly' or 'to call for help'. The first would suggest a description of the animals at the outset of the Ark's voyage, the second sense would provide a natural introduction to Nuḥ's

---

Allâh's power is manifest in His control of the Deluge, His favours are shown to Nûḥ by preserving him from death and in his salvation. G. von Rad remarks upon the anthropomorphism of Yahweh at this point in the Genesis account (*Genesis*, trans. J.H. Marks, London 1972, 117-18 & 128), although Noah does not appeal to Yahweh before the Flood but merely acts in accordance with His will. Nûḥ's appeal to Allâh is a prominent feature of the Arabian version.

7. For the phrase *dhû al-ḥamâma*, see *dhâ al-nûn* (Koran 21.87) of Yûnus, where the protagonist of a tale is identified by means of the creature which features in the tale.
8. The implication in *ka-al-*^{c}*iyâli* is that they are dependent on Him for food and sustenance.
9. The phrase *ḥâbisan jawfahu* ^{c}*alayhi* is not at all clear. It may refer to Allâh 'staying the open sea for him', i.e. preventing the Ark from being sunk. See Koran 11.81 (*yaḥbisuhu*, Allâh's withholding of the punishment of the unbelievers). Cf. Genesis 7.16, "And God shut him in": von Rad remarks "that Yahweh himself shut up the ark behind Noah is again one of those surprising statements of the Yahwist, almost hybrid in its combination of near-childlike simplicity and theological profundity" (1972: 120). The syntax of verses 5-6 is obscure. The *timthâl*, "statue" (lit. 'image'), is presumably synonymous with *dumya*, 'icon', made from marble, gold or ivory, with which the white complexion of the *ḥabîb* is often compared in pre-Islamic verse. See S. Fraenkel, *Die Aramäischen Fremdwörter im Arabischen*, Leiden 1886: 271-2.
10. The *wa* in the second hemistich may be epexegetic: the plucked branch is the form which the truth (*ṣidq*) takes, or it may be metri gratia. *Rashâ* usually means 'to bribe', a meaning inappropriate to the context.

prayer answered in verse 4. In verses 4-8 Allâh's response to Nuḥ's prayer assumes two forms: the dove is altered from the white dove (?) to the collared turtle-dove,[11] as a reward, and this alteration in its physical appearance is a sign from Allâh to Nûḥ, as is the bunch of dates brought by the dove to him. Both signs taken in conjunction are incontrovertible evidence that Allâh has heard Nûḥ's prayer and has granted salvation.

It is interesting to note the specifically Arabian details of the story of the metamorphosis of the collared turtle-dove and the substitution of the Biblical olive-branch by a (Ḥijâzî) date-branch. The remainder of Schulthess's reconstituted poem is concerned with Abraham's sacrifice of Isaac.

In the Koran there are, on first reading, three types of reference to ships and seafaring. There is the enigmatic ship (*safîna*) which the mysterious companion of Mûsâ, identified as al-Khaḍir, scuttles, for an equally enigmatic reason, the Ark of Nûḥ and the ships which are a sign of Allâh's kindness to man.

Mûsâ and the Mysterious Companion

Koran 18.71 and 79.

71. So they set off until, when they had put out <to sea> on the ship, he scuttled it.
79. The ship belonged to some paupers who laboured on the sea. I wanted to render it defective as there was a king behind them who commandeered every ship by force.

11. There is an aetiological legend involved here, accounting for the markings of the collared turtle-dove of the Ḥijâz. It is evident from al-Nâbighah's *Mu^{c}allaqa* (in *The Divans of the Six Ancient Arabic* Poets, ed. Ahlwardt, London 1870): Poem 5: 38 that the Meccan fondness for doves (see F. Viré, "Ḥamâm", *EI*2, iii, 109-10) was also a pre-Islamic phenomenon. The verse also suggests that the Ḥaram and the Ka^{c}ba were a sort of bird sanctuary, perhaps implying that the *ḥamâm*, by virtue of its role in the Flood, was viewed as especially favoured by Allâh. Viré considers these birds to be "domestic pigeons deriving from the rock-dove".

The only other instance of *safîna* in the Koran is 29.15: *fa-anjaynâ-hu wa-aṣḥâba al-safînati*, so We rescued him and those on board the Ark. This *âya* draws on the notion of Allâh's beneficent guidance of sea-going vessels and suggests that the tale of Nûḥ and the Ark, which becomes, in the Koran, the prototype, indeed the archetype, of all sea-going ships, validates this religious conception of seafaring: all safely arrived ships are manifestations of the archetypical Ark and owe their safe arrival to the beneficence of Allâh. [12] In 18.79 the Companion scuttles the ship because, according to this concept of seafaring, the use of ships against the will of Allâh is not to be tolerated.

Nûḥ

Three of the major Qur'anic accounts of Nûḥ will be discussed, in an attempt to shed more light on the early Islamic attitude to seafaring.

Koran 11.36-49.

36. Nûḥ was inspired, "Only those of your people who have believed will be safe, so be not doleful at what they do.
37. Make the Ark under our guidance (lit. in our eyes) and inspiration but do not address Me about those who have done wrong, for they will be drowned". [13]

---

12. J.P. Lewis, *A Study of the Interpretation of Noah and the Flood in Jewish and Christian Literature*, Leiden 1968 provides a valuable survey of exegetical interractions with the Biblical Noah and the Flood. Of the apocryphal *Book of Wisdom* he refers to "God's providence, which manifests itself in guiding sailors in wooden ships, which wood could just as readily have been used to make an idol, earlier manifested itself at the flood" (1968: 23). For Rabbinic exegesis, the dimensions specified for the Ark constituted a blue-print for ship-builders.
13. Here the Koran differs completely from the Gilgamesh and Biblical Floods: "the god Ea did not reveal the coming of the Flood to Utnapishtim directly, because of fear of the other gods, but only in a dream did he order him to build a ship. The same motif – construction of a ship without knowing why – was conceived by the Yahwist as a test of faith and obedience" (von Rad 1972: 124). H. Speyer, *Die Biblischen Erzählungen im Qoran*, Hildesheim 1961, 92-3, sees in this an allusion to the nautical specifications imposed by Yahweh upon Noah in the construction of the Ark, and interprets the phrase *bi-aᶜyuni-nâ* as a public remonstrance to mankind and an exhortation to repentance.

38. As he was making the Ark, whenever a gathering of his people passed him by, they would scoff at him. He said, "Though you scoff at us, we shall scoff at you as you <now> scoff.
39. You will know to whom a confounding chastisement will come and upon whom a lasting chastisement will alight".
40. <This continued> until when Our behest arrived and the oven boiled, [14] We said, "Load it with two of every pair and your family (except for those to whom word has already gone) and those who have believed" – scarcely a few had believed with him.
41. He said, "Sail upon her in the name of Allâh, whether she be afloat or at anchor, for my Lord is Clement, Merciful".
42. She floated with them through waves like mountains, and Nûḥ called upon his son who had withdrawn aside, "My son, sail with us and do not be one of the Unbelievers",
43. But he replied, "I shall take refuge in a mountain which will protect me from the water", and he said, "Only those to whom He is merciful will today be protected from the behest of Allâh" but the waves came between them and he was one of the drowned.
44. It was said, "Earth, swallow your water! Sky, cease!" The water receded and the behest was effected. She came to rest on al-Jûdî and it was said, "Gone are the wrong-doing people!"
45. Nûḥ called on his Lord and said, "My Lord, my son was one of my family, but your admonition is binding, for your are the most just of those with jurisdiction".
46. He said, "Nûḥ, he was not one of your family. An impious deed! Do not ask about that of which you have no knowledge, for I admonish you lest you become one of the immoderate".
47. He said, "My Lord, I beg Your pardon for asking about that of which I have no knowledge. If you are not clement and merciful to me, I shall surely be one of the lost".

---

14. The flood of fire became a prominent Christian eschatological obsession: see Lewis 1968: 15 (the *Book of Adam and Eve*), 26 (the *Book of Enoch*), 33-4 (the *Jewish Sybil*). Speyer (1961: 103) traces the motif of a flood of blazing fire to Rabbinic sources, suggesting a Hebraic, as well as Aramaic, etymology for *tannûr*. Both Rabbinic and Christian sources feature Noah as a warner to his people who deem him insane: Lewis 1968: 32-4 (the *Jewish Sybil*), 37, 102-3, 135. See further Speyer 1961: 93-7.

48. It was said, "Nûḥ, descend <from the Ark> in peace from Us, with blessings upon you and upon communities <descended> from those with you – communities which We shall allow to find gratification but which will then be touched by a painful chastisement from Us".
49. Those are some of the accounts of the unknown with which We inspire you. Neither you nor your people knew them previously. Show restraint, for the reward is for those who fear Allâh.

This passage is full of the techniques of Qur'anic rhetoric; ring-composition, both verbal (*w-ḥ-y*: 36, 37 & 49) and thematic (37 & 45: Nûḥ's address concerning his son), punning (*s-kh-r*: 38, *ḥ-k-m*: 45), construction through leitmotif (the roots *'-m-n*, *'-m-r*, *ʿ-dh-b*, for example), grim irony (the waves as big as mountains, the equation manifest in early Arabic poetry, highlight the error of Nûḥ's son who seeks refuge on a mountain-top), word-play (the apobaterion is a derivative of *j-w-d* a root which designates generosity and fertility; [15] the *jahl* [46] which Nûḥ comes close to showing contrasts with the *ṣabr* [49] to which Muḥammad is exhorted). It is clear that Allâh instructs Nûḥ in the fabrication of the Ark, for which Nûḥ is subjected to the mockery of his folk. [16] This suggests that Allâh teaches Nûḥ the art of ship-building, not merely that the Ark had to be constructed to divinely inspired specifications, so as to withstand the torrential assault from the heavens and the boiling deluge unleashed from the earth: [17] most pre-Islamic ships did not have decks but were open. In *âya* 41, Nûḥ invokes Allâh's name to protect the Ark whether it be at sea or in the harbour. After his altercation with Allâh, in which Nûḥ displays his all

---

15. The pun is entirely lost on Speyer 1961: 107. Streck, "Djûdî", *EI2*, ii, 574, notes that the Koran is presumably referring to Mount Jûdî in Arabia "which was probably considered the highest mountain of all".
16. Other reasons are given for this mockery in al-Ṭabarî: building the Ark on dry land and a self-proclaimed prophet working as a carpenter. See al-Ṭabarî *Annales*, ed. Barth, Leiden 1879-81: 186 & 189 (= F. Rosenthal, *The History of al-Ṭabarî. Volume 1. General Introduction and From the Creation to the Flood*, Albany 1989, 356 & 359). Building the Ark on dry land is seen as a test in the Biblical version: "to Noah the command must have seemed strange and incomprehensible. A ship on dry land! ... That was a test of his obedience and faith" (von Rad 1972: 120). For Jewish and Christian parallels, see Speyer 1961: 98-101.
17. This notion finds expression in the phrase *wa-sakhkhara la-kumu al-fulka li-tajriya fî 'l-baḥri bi-amrihi* (14.32). See further 22.65, 45.12.

too human fallibility (as Mûsâ does in his quizzing of the Companion), Allâh showers His blessings on Nûḥ and his descendants.

Koran 23.23-30.

23. We sent Nûḥ to his people and he said, "My people, worship Allâh, with no gods but Him. Do you not fear Allâh?"
24. The gathering of his people who were unbelievers said, "This is but a man like you who wants superiority over you. If Allâh wished, He would send down angels. We have heard nothing about this <message> from our primeval fathers.
25. He is merely a man who is possessed. Wait for him <to prove himself> for a while".
26. He said, "My Lord, assist me for they have called me a liar". [18]
27. So We inspired him, "Make the Ark under our guidance (lit. in our eyes) and inspiration. When Our behest arrives and the oven boils, then guide on board two of every pair and your family, except for those of them to whom word has already gone, but do not address me about those who have done wrong, for they will be drowned.
28. When you and those with you are settled on the Ark, then say, 'Praise be to Allâh who rescued us from the wrong-doing people!'
29. And say, 'My Lord, harbour me in a blessed harbour, for You are the best of harbourers!'"
30. In that there are signs. We put <man> to the test. [19]

This version of the Nûḥ tale stresses the instructions received by him from Allâh, as to the fabrication of the vessel and his comportment while sailing it. [20] As equally relevant as the verses narrating the story of Nûḥ are the verses which immediately precede them, viz. 12-22. The *Sûra* begins with a variation on the theme of Paradise for the believers (1-11) and proceeds with an eleven verse disquisition on the role of Allâh as Creator: as Creator

---

18. Speyer (1961: 102) assigns this motif of the request for punishment a Christian provenance.
19. My translation of verse 29 and 30 is heavily indebted to Arberry, *The Koran Interpreted* (Oxford 1986), 345.
20. In al-Ṭabarî's version of the fabrication of the Ark, Allâh commands Nûḥ also to plant the tree from which the Ark is to be built: al-Ṭabarî (Barth) 1879-81: 185 (= Rosenthal 1989: 355).

of Man (12-14), as Resurrector of the Dead (15-16) and as Creator of the Cosmos (17-22). In this latter role, Allâh creates the heavens (17) and the oceans from rain (18). From the rain also come the gardens and oases with their life-sustaining fruit (19-20) and finally cattle from which man gains sustenance: "and on them and on the ships are you carried" (23.22).[21] This reference to *al-fulk*, with its ambiguously indeterminate number, leads immediately into the tale of Nûḥ, a tale which functions contrapuntally to verses 12-22, as the rain turns into a deadly chastisement with which Allâh annihilates mankind. The narrative of Nûḥ, however, also works as an illustration to verse 22, depicting the manner in which Allâh gave knowledge of seafaring to man.[22]

Koran 54.9-15.

9. Before them the people of Nûḥ thought it lies. They thought our slave a liar and said, "Possessed" and so he was thrust away.
10. So he called on his Lord, "I am bested, so assist me".
11. Therefore, We opened the gates of heaven with a flood of water
12. And We made springs burst open on the earth, and the water <from both sources> met in accordance with a behest which had been determined.[23]
13. We carried him on <a ship> with timbers, oakum and pegs,[24]

---

21. This notion is of frequent occurrence: 17.70, 40.80, 43.12.
22. In Sûra 7, the account of Nûḥ (59-64) is preceded by two verses in which Allâh controls the winds and sends rain to revivify dead lands, an anticipation of His resurrection of the dead from their graves.
23. Arberry (1986: 553): "for a matter decreed". "The heavenly ocean ... which is above the firmament ...., empties downward through latticed windows ... According to the Priestly representation we must understand the Flood, therefore, as a catastrophe involving the entire cosmos. When the heavenly ocean breaks forth upon the earth below, and the primeval sea beneath the earth, which is restrained by God, now freed from its bonds, gushes up through yawning chasms onto the earth, then there is a destruction of the entire cosmic system according to biblical cosmogony. The two halves of the chaotic primeval sea, separated – the one up, the other below – by God's creative government ..., are again united; creation begins to sink again into chaos. Here the catastrophe, therefore, concerns not only men and beasts as in the Yahwistic account but the earth ... – indeed, the entire cosmos" (von Rad 1972: 128).
24. A standard exegesis of *dusur* as 'iron nails' was intended to enhance the miraculous nature of the Ark since it was widely held throughout the ancient world "that there

14. Floating under our guidance (lit. in our eyes), as requital for him who had been disbelieved. [25]
15. We have left it (the ship) behind as a sign, but is there anyone who remembers?

In this account, Allâh explicitly assumes full control of all stages of the narration. Verse 15 is an unequivocal declaration that all ships are but manifestations of the archetypical Ark, constructed and steered by Allâh. In the light of these statements, the common Qur'anic declaration of the ship as a sign assumes extra significance.

A number of these declarations include the associated notion of Allâh's deliverance of seafarers from the storm and their subsequent ingratitude.

Seafaring as a Blessing from Allâh

A succinct expression of this notion is Koran 31.31:

31. Do you not see that the ship floats on the sea through the grace of Allâh that he might show you of his signs? [26] Therein are signs for every thankful, temperate <man>.

An elaboration on this is Allâh's rescue of seafarers in a storm:

Koran 10.22-23.

22. He is the One who transports you by land and sea so that, when you are on the ships and they float with them, with a favourable wind, and they rejoice in them, and a tempestuous wind comes to them (the ships) and the waves come to them (the travellers) from every place and they think that they are enclosed, they call on Allâh, devoting their religion entirely to Him, <saying that> "if We rescue them from this, then we shall be among the thankful".

---

were magnetic rocks (loadstones) in the sea, which drag iron-fastened ships to their doom" (G. Hourani, *Arab Seafaring*, Princeton 1995: 95).

25. The phrase *bi-a*^{c}*yuninâ* implies that Allâh pilots the Ark. In the Apocryphal *Book of Adam and Eve*, the navigation is effected by an angel: Lewis 1968: 38.
26. Further examples: 42.32, 55.24-5. An extension is fishing: 2.164, 16.14, 35.12.

23. So when He has rescued them, behold they act excessively on the earth, with no right to. You people, your excess is but against your own souls, a commodity of the lower life, but then to Us will you return and We shall inform you of what you used to do.

This passage is conspicuous for its *iltifât* and for the complexity of its syntax. While the diction employed to describe the storm differs from the Deluge (this is a gusty and not an aqueous disaster), the term *fulk* and the root *j-r-y* together with the depiction of the waves and Allâh's soteriological action associate this with the Ark (other examples are: 6.63, 17.67, 29.65, 42.32-3). The shift from second to third person in verse 22 is very effective, because of the indefiniteness of the referent of the third person: who are 'they' – the wrong-doers or the representatives of mankind on the Ark? It makes excellent oratorical sense not to be any more specific. In Sûra 69, in a catalogue of cataclysms (4-5: Thamûd; 6-8: ^{c}Âd; 9-10: Fir^{c}awn; 11-12: the floating ship), followed by some eschatological catastrophes (13-16) and depictions of Paradise and Damnation (17-37), the second person plural pronominal suffix *kum* is used amphibologically:

11. When the water swelled, We carried you on the floating <ship>
12. That we might render it a memorial for you and that comprehending ears might comprehend it.

The apostrophized and the delivered are undifferentiated, past and present are blurred. Heinrich Speyer understood this passage as designating the Ark but was somewhat puzzled:

> The designation of the Ark as *tadhkira* can, according to Mohammed's views, mean that succeeding generations ought to learn from the punishment of the Flood. *Tadhkira* is used in connection with an object in this single instance in the Koran; it elsewhere refers to things of a general nature, such as the Koran itself or Judgement Day. It is, however, conceivable that Mohammed was urged by a legend of the actual existence of the wreck of the Ark to remind men of the amazing miracle (1961: 104).

The Ark, and not its wreck, was, for Muḥammad and the early Islamic community, still in existence: in the form of the ships which plied their trade in the Red Sea and the Indian Ocean, an abiding testament to Allâh's compassion, to His act of faith in humankind.

Koran 17.66-69:

66. Your Lord is the one who propels for you the ships on the sea that you might crave His bounty, for He is Clement to you
67. And when the scourge touches you on the sea, those on whom you call go astray except for Him. When He has rescued you <and brought you> to land, you turn away and mankind disbelieves.
68. Are you safe from Him causing you to be engorged at the land's edge or from His sending a sand-storm against you? You will not find anyone to stand surety for you then.
69. Or are you safe from Him sending you on to it (the sea) one more time, letting loose a typhoon, and drowning you for your unbelief? You will not find anyone to follow you out onto it (the sea) against Us then.

This passage is followed by a declaration of Allâh's conveyance of man by land and sea (verse 70). The blurring of past and present, the difficulty of distinguishing coterminous seafaring from man's rescue in the Ark, are at their most acute here. Traditionally, verses 66-7 are understood with present significance, although they could easily be translated as past tenses. This atemporality, in which the past is re-enacted constantly in the present, is a feature of the Koranic vision of history. This point is made clear in the succeeding verses in which a second deluge is threatened (verse 69), in conjunction with a revisitation of the catastrophe which wiped out the people of Lûṭ (68).

A cognate expression is the following:

Koran 24.39-40.

39. The deeds of those who disbelieve are like a mirage in a desert which the parched <traveller> thinks is water, until, when he comes to it, he finds that it is nothing but finds Allâh is with him there and He pays him his reckoning in full – Allâh is swift of reckoning;
40. Or are like darknesses on an open sea covered in waves upon which are waves upon which are clouds – darknesses piled one upon the other – when <the traveller> stretches forth his hand he is almost

> unable to see it: those to whom Allâh gives no light will have no light.

In these *âyas*, the topos of storm is adapted to denote the deluded error of the Unbelievers. The dark sea, clouded over, is associated with the deceptiveness of the mirage, in a manner reminiscent of the comparisons of litter-bearing camels, travelling in the folds of a mirage, with ships at sea. They rest upon the notion contained in, for example, *Sûra* 27.63:

> 63. Is He who guides you through the darknesses of the land and the sea
> and who sends the winds as joyous tidings heralding His clemency –
> is there a god with Allâh? Allâh is Exalted above your polytheism.

The tale of Muḥammad and ʿIkrimah b. Abî Jahl, as narrated by al-Ṭabarî, told in ʿIkrimah's own words, sheds further light on the religious conception of seafaring:

> ʿIkrimah b. Abî Jahl fled to the Yemen. His woman, Umm Ḥakîm bint al-Ḥârith b. Hishâm embraced Islam and beseeched the Messenger of Allâh for his safety, which he granted him. She left in search of him and brought him to the Messenger of Allâh (*ṣ-l-ʿ-m*). ʿIkrimah, so they recount, used to tell that the reason for his returning to Islam, after he had gone to the Yemen, was <the following> told in his own words: "I wanted to ride out to sea to join the Abyssinians, but when I came to the ship to embark upon it, its captain said, 'Slave of Allâh, do not ride on the ship before you have declared the uniqueness of Allâh and have divested yourself of all idols, save for Him. For I fear lest we perish on board, if you do not do this'. I replied, 'So no-one rides out to sea without declaring the uniqueness of Allâh and divesting himself of all but Him?' and he said, 'Yes, no-one rides on her (the ship) without devoting himself entirely'. So I said <to myself>, 'Why should I part from Muḥammad, for this is <the message> which he has brought us, by Allâh – that our God on the sea is our God on the land' and then I recognised Islam – it entered into my heart" (al-Ṭabari, *Annales*, ed. de Jong, Leiden 1882-85: 1640-1).

Barthold ("Der Koran und das Meer, *ZDMG* 83 [1929], 43) commented that Muḥammad borrowed this concept from the Christians "who were afraid to bring the wrath of God upon themselves and their ships, should a godless heathen be found among them". The narrative is, however, entirely consonant with Qur'anic notions furnished by and exemplified in the tale of Nûḥ and the Ark. Whatever the Arabian origin of this tale, there is no need to seek justification for the religious conception of seafaring anywhere else.

Early Arabic Poetry.

Two Expressions of Loathing for Sea-Travel

An Anonymous Bedouin (Th. Nöldeke, *Delectus Veterum Carminum Arabicorum*, Berlin 1890, 62-3).

1. I said, when the ship was well out at sea, and Tyre was distant, having been close,
2. And a wind blew strongly, the waves roaring, the sea under the ship bellowing,
3. "I wish that my salary and military stipẹnd were purely for them (i.e the sailors?), and that my lot were swift camels in reins and a saddle!
4. What a decision it was which led me to a ship and to a dark <valley, i.e. sea>, with its middle turbulent, in commotion:
5. Its surface looks flat when the wind is at rest, but if it blows, the flats become rugged, uneven.
6. Ibn Bilâl, you summoned me and led me astray, though men like me are not easily led astray.
7. If my feet ever touch terra firma again and the time comes for the men on the ship to disembark,
8. If I am ever saved from waves which loom as large as Mount Ḥirâ' and Mount Thabîr,
9. Then, on the parade ground, a group can pass my name under review – but only if the return is easy!
10. <I did have> a pleasant dwelling in the vicinity of al-Sharabba and a life with abundant conversation.
11. I wish I knew whether I shall ever say to <a group of> braves, when the sunrise is at hand,
12. 'Let the bright <camels> be brought near to al-Sharabba', as one returning home, tossed hither and thither on the waves of the sea".

This playful piece of late Umayyad verse (dated to the reign of al-Walîd b. Yazîd [d. 744]) reiterates the sentiment of Ibn Barrâq's four line aversion to the sea. In verses 4-5, the topos of sea = desert is taken, for once, at its face value, and questioned by a son of the desert, while the topos of waves = hills or dunes (see also, e.g., Koran 11.42) receives the same treatment, though this time the hills are two of the holy mountains of Mecca, associated with the career of the Prophet Muḥammad. In verse 2, camel terminology is appplied to the sea, to contrast with the poet's longing for a nomadic existence in 3 and 10-12. The point of the second hemistich of verse 12 is that the poet doubts whether he will ever survive the outward voyage, let alone see his homeland again: this voyage is, of course, an aqueous raid in the Bedouin style. The Koranic echo of Nûḥ and his family on the Ark in verse 7 (Koran 29.15) is also used to good effect.

Ibn Barrâq al-Hudhalî (Wellhausen, *Skizzen und Vorarbeiten 2. Letzter Teil der Lieder der Hudhailiten*, Berlin 1884): Poem 238.1-4 (= *Ash*^{c}*âr al-Hudhaliyyîn*, ed. Farrâj and Shâkir, Cairo 1965-6: p.878).

1. Oh, will worries go away, will I escape from sailing the sea?
2. Will a hump-backed <ship>, in the darkness every evening, rush with us through the dark depths,
3. Its prow cleaving the water, persevering, on dunes of stinging brine,
4. The <waves> tossed by the swell like ewes grazing beside other ewes?

This terse piece is a fine example of the mistrust of the sea felt by the early Arabs, and sheds emotional light on the description of nautical affairs in terms of the desert.

2. *Ship, Camel or Horse?*

The sixth century AD pre-Islamic poet Bishr b. Abî Khâzim of the tribe of Asad, a rather implausible jacktar, records his own memorable sea voyage, though unfortunately he does not mention points of departure or destination.

Bishr should be allocated a middle- to late-*Jâhilî* floruit (J.E. Montgomery, "The Deserted Encampment in Ancient Arabic Poetry: A Nexus of topical Comparisons", *JSS* 40 [1995], 296-7). Von Grünebaum ("Zur Chronologie der frühdarabischen Dichtung", *Orientalia* 8 [1939], 345) gives his date of birth as c. 535 AD, although others have insisted on a somewhat later date (see F. Sezgin, *Geschichte des arabischen Schrifttums*, Volume 2, Leiden 1975: 211). His poetry, it can be argued, bears traces of influences, stylistic and lexical, found in the compositions of poets associated with the court circles of al-Ḥîra, although given Bishr's dates, it is equally plausible to see in this the influence, poetic and otherwise, exerted over the peninsula by the Lakhmid capital.

Bishr's poetry found great favour among the anthologists. His poetry is an interesting mixture of styles: at times heavily reminiscent of his fellow tribesman and precursor ᶜAbîd b. al-Abraṣ; at times innovative, forward looking and progressive, with some of the techniques, devices and treatments which are also to be encountered in the poetry of, for example, Labîd b. Rabîᶜah. [27]

The poem under discussion here is unusual in that it describes a sea-voyage made by Bishr, a not inconsiderable feat for a son of the desert.

1 *taghayyarati al-manâzilu min sulaymâ*
bi-râmata fa -'l-kathîbi ilâ buṭâḥi
2 *fa-ajzâᶜi al-liwâ fa-birâqi khabtin*
ᶜafat-hâ al-muᶜṣifâtu mina al-riyâḥi
3 *diyârun qad taḥullu bi-hâ sulaymâ*
haḍîma al-kashḥi jâ'ilata al-wishâḥi
4 *layâliya tastabîkâ bi-dhî ghurûbin*
yushabbahu ẓalmuhu khaḍila al-aqâḥî
5 *ka-anna niṭâfatan shîbat bi-miskin*
hudû'an fî thanâyahâ bi-râḥi
6 *salî in kunti jâhilatan bi-qawmî*
idhâ mâ al-khaylu fi'na mina al-jirâḥi
7 *naḥullu makhûfa kulli ḥiman wa-thaghrin*
wa-mâ baladun nalîhi bi-mustabâḥi
8 *bi-kulli ṭimirratin wa-aqabba ṭirfin*
shadîdi al-asri nahdin dhî mirâḥi
9 *wa-mâ ḥayyun naḥullu bi-ᶜaqwatayhim*
mina al-ḥarbi al-ᶜawâni bi-mustarâḥi
10 *idhâ mâ shammarat ḥarbun samawnâ*
sumuwwa al-buzli fî 'l-ᶜaṭani al-fayâḥi

---

27. Bauer (*Altarabische Dichtkunst*, Volume 1, Wiesbaden 1992, 220) remarks upon the influence exerted upon Labîd by Bishr.

11 *ᶜalâ luḥuqin ayâṭiluhunna qubbin*
yuthirna al-naqᶜa bi -'l-shuᶜthi al-ṣibâḥi
12 *wa-muqfiratin yaḥâru al-ṭarfu fîhâ*
ᶜalâ sananin bi-mundafaᶜi al-ṣudâḥi
13 *tajâwabu hâmuhâ fî ghawratayhâ*
idhâ al-ḥirbâ'u awfâ bi -'l-barâḥi
14 *wa-kharqin qad qaṭaᶜtu bi-dhâti lawthin*
amûnin mâ tashakkâ min jirâḥi
15 *muḍabbaratin ka-anna al-raḥla minhâ*
wa-ajlâdî ᶜalâ lahaqin layâḥi
16 *wa-muᶜtarakin ka-anna al-khayla fîhi*
qaṭâ sharakin yashibbu min al-nawâḥî
17 *shahidtu wa-muhjarin naffastu ᶜan-hu*
raᶜâᶜa al-khayli tanḥiṭu fî 'l-ṣiyâḥi
18 *bi-kulli kasîbatin lâ ᶜayba fîhâ*
aradtu tharâ'a mâlî aw ṣalâḥî
19 *bi-irqâṣi al-maṭiyyati fî 'l-maṭâyâ*
wa-takrimati al-mulûki wa-bi -'l-qidâḥi
20 *wa-khaylin qad labistu bi-jamᶜi khaylin*
ᶜalâ shaqqâ'a ᶜijlizatin waqâḥi
21 *yushabbahu shakhṣu-hâ wa -'l-khaylu tahfû*
hufuwwan ẓilla fatkhâ'i al-janâḥi
22 *idhâ kharajat yadâhâ min qabîlin*
uyammimuhâ qabîlan dhâ silâḥi
23 *ujâlidu ṣaffa-hum wa-la-qad arâ-nî*
ᶜalâ qarwâ'a tasjudu li -'l-riyâḥi
24 *muᶜabbadati al-saqâ'ifi dhâti dusrin*
muḍabbaratin jawânibuhâ radâḥi
25 *idhâ rakibat bi-ṣâḥibihâ khalîjan*
tadhakkara mâ ladayhi min junâḥi
26 *yamurru al-mawju taḥta mushajjarâtin*
yalîna al-mâ'a bi -'l-khushubi al-ṣiḥâḥi
27 *wa-naḥnu ᶜalâ jawânibihâ quᶜûdun*
naghuḍḍu al-ṭarfa ka -'l-ibili al-qimâḥi
28 *fa-qad ûqirna min qusṭin wa-randin*
wa-min miskin aḥamma wa-min silâḥi
29 *fa-ṭâbat rîḥuhunna wa-hunna jûnun*
ja'âji'uhunna fî lujajin milâḥi

TRANSLATION

1 Sulaymâ's dwellings in Râma and al-Kathîb as far as Buṭâḥ have changed <beyond recognition>

2 As too have the slopes of al-Liwâ and the stony runs of Khabt – effaced by violent winds:

3 Abodes where Sulaymâ used to halt, slender-waisted, her sash loose-<fitting>,

4 During the nights when she would hold you captive with a <mouth> of sharp teeth, its lustre like bedewed camomiles,

5 As if, in the dead of night, drops of water had been mixed with musk and wine in her incisors.

6 Ask if you are uninformed about my people when the horses return from the inflicting of wounds!

7 We halt in the <most> fearsome spot of every protected grazing-ground and mountain pass and no territory close to us can be ravaged,

8 On prancing mares and noble stallions, lean-bellied, strongly-built, with prominent withers, brisk and energetic.

9 When we halt in the very heart of a tribe's territory, it receives no respite from fierce, constant warfare.

10 When war girds herself, we arise like full-grown camels in the wide enclosure

11 On lean-flanked, tight-bellied <horses> that kick up dust on the tousled <braves>, fair of face.

12 A desolate waste, where a man's gaze becomes confused, on a track in Ṣudâḥ where the torrent rushes,

13 In the hollows <on either side> the owls answer one another, when the chameleon stands erect in the open plain,

14 And an open desert have I crossed on a fleshy, strong <she-camel>, secure <in its footing>, uncomplaining of <its> wounds,

15 Compact and sturdy: the saddle and my limbs seemed to be set upon a gleaming, white <bull oryx>.

16 A battle-ground where the horses are like sand-grouse in a snare, leaping on <all> sides

17 Have I taken part in, and a sanctuary have I defended against a motley group of horse, snorting and neighing amid the clamour.

18 With every blameless possession have I been minded to increase my wealth or my well-being

19 By means of making my beast amble among other beasts, of honouring kings and of the gaming-arrows.
20 And horses have I confounded with a squadron of horse, on a wide-legged <mare>, enormous, hard of hoof
21 Whose appearance, when the horses race and gallop, is like the shadow of <a bird in flight>, its wings outstretched:
22 When her legs have left one tribe behind, I direct her to another tribe, bearing arms,
23 Attacking their lines. And I have found myself on a high-humped <ship>, prostrating herself before the winds,
24 The gaps <in her timbers> caulked, tied with oakum and pegs, with compact and sturdy boards, heavily laden.
25 When she rode out on a watercourse with her captain, he bethought himself of his faults
26 <As> the waves passed under wooden <ships> lying low on the water, their timbers soundly fitted,
27 While we sat on their boards, averting our gaze like camels refusing to drink –
28 They had been laden with *qusṭ* and myrtle, with black musk and weapons –
29 But then their wind turned favourable, and they showed black, their prows on the briny deep.

In verses 23-9, Bishr concludes his magnificent boast with his finest achievement - a voyage by sea. This section is introduced with the words *wa-la-qad arânî*, stamping this as a continuation of the *mufâkhara*, being of the reflection, in old age, of past achievements variety. These lines are a good example of the comparison of ship with camel, a not uncommon feature of pre-Islamic nautical descriptions, they offer parallels for the Qur'anic depiction of nautical activities, and are remarkable for the anthologist-cum-commentator Ibn al-Shajarî's wilful interpretation of this passage as a horse description (i.e. the *lafẓ* pertains to ships, the *maʿnâ* pertains to horses). [28] The information which it, if genuine – and I have little

28. Ibn al-Shajarî is not alone in his attempts to deny poetic ships veridicality, although he is perverse in his adaptation of the ship to the martial demands of *mufâkhara* by wilfully seeing horses in almost every verse. Moreover, the other early Arabic ships which have been denied veridicality, have also been denied it on the grounds of convention, as they each occur in a variation of the litter-bearing camels = ships

doubt on that score – offers on pre-Islamic maritime activity must be very cautiously evaluated: unfortunately, much remains conjectural.

The structure of this poem resembles that of a poem by al-Nâbigha al-Dhubyânî which I discussed in an article published in *Edebîyât* in 1994 ("Arkhilokhos, al-Nâbighah al-Dhubyâni and A Complaint Against Blacksmiths. Or, A Funny Thing Happened to Me"), and of a number of other poems. It is formally bipartite (*aṭlâl / nasîb* [1-3a, 3b-5] and *mufâkhara* [6-29]), with the paratactic justificatory arrangement used so skilfully by al-Nâbighah in Poem 23, and also, in a *qaṣîda* with a tripartite structure, by ᶜAntara in his *Muᶜallaqa*. Just as al-Nâbigha teases his audience's poetic expectations with his curtailed oryx / onager episode combination, so too Bishr takes the ship / camel equation attested in solitary instances and within the compass of single lines and expands it to a length of seven lines, thereby toying also with the structural properties of the *waṣf al-nâqa*, on which al-Nâbigha ends his poem. In verse 15, he also teases audience expectation by apparently launching into a *waṣf al-nâqa* which is abruptly terminated by verse 16. The audience must wait until verse 23 for their vigorously transmogrified *waṣf al-nâqa* movement.

The first six verses of the poem are precisely divided between *dhikr al-aṭlâl* (1-3a) and *nasîb* (3b-5). The *mufâkhara* movement contains both tribal and personal vaunting: tribal military might (6-11), personal bravery manifested in traversing desert wastes (12-15), personal military might (16-17), personal achievements (18-19), personal military might (20-23), personal bravery in sailing the briny deep (23-9). The standard *mufâkhara* transition of *wâw-rubba* occurs in verses 12, 14, 16, 17, and 20. Despite its apparent paratactic structure, the poem is manifestly hypotactic, as it is concluded with Bishr's crowning achievement.

---

equation proper to the *nasîb*. Al-Sukkarî, in his commentary on the *dîwân* of al-Akhṭal, interprets the Umayyad eulogist's ships as camels (see Montgomery 1997: 187-8, no. 1i), while Rhodokanakis follows Ibn al-Sikkît's lead in viewing Ibn Qays al-Ruqayyât's ships with suspicion (see Montgomery 1997: 194, no. 3d) (see E. Wagner, *Grundzüge der klassischen arabischen Dichtung*, Volume 2, Darmstadt 1988, 114-5). Both poets move directly to the maritime vehicles and omit reference to the terrestrial. Bishr's camel / ship, whilst part of the *mufâkhara*, has the structural properties of the *waṣf al-nâqa* movement, and Ibn al-Shajarî's scholiastic activity is thus further unique.

For Fraenkel (1886: 209-32), the references to nautical affairs prove that seafaring was common among the pre-Islamic Arabs. That seafaring was not unfamiliar to a number of pre-Islamic and early Islamic Arabs, notably the Mesopotamian and eastern sea-board poets, would be a more accurate assessment: there is no indication that Arab ships are referred to, though this is perhaps a justifiable assumption in some cases. The Mesopotamian provenance of a number of poetic maritime passages belies the assertion that they are clichés which have found their way to the highlands of Najd and upper reaches of the Ḥijâz. The issue of personal acquaintance with the sea (an issue raised by H. Kindermann & C.E. Bosworth, "Safîna", *EI*2, viii, 808-9) is irrelevant for most poetic instances, except for the poems by Bishr, Ibn Barrâq and the anonymous nomad, in which the involvement of the poets in an epic sea-voyage is portrayed as genuine – at least, therefore, it is not necessary to assume that all references to the sea are poetic figments or empty clichés, though the majority do imply that the poets watch the ships on the open sea or sailing up and down the Tigris or Euphrates.

Much has been made of the Koranic references to seafaring, which have led a number of Western scholars to conclude that Muḥammad himself must have ventured on to the briny deep at some point in his life. Pre-Islamic poetic references to seafaring attest to the existence in *Jâhilî* Arabia of a sophisticated nautical vocabulary, on which the Koran may have drawn: the quest for justification in biography is unnecessary.

In two pieces, Ilse Lichtenstädter ("Origin and Interpretation of some Koranic Symbols" in *Studi Orientalistici … Giorgio Levi Della Vida*, Volume 2,1956, 58-80 & *Introduction to Classical Arabic Literature*, New York 1974), taking issue with this quest for biography in Qur'anic marine descriptions, has developed a more challenging argument, suggesting that in these maritime references

> the poets are not just trying to turn a beautiful phrase by this motif. They are making use, in their poetry, of some ancient religious symbolism which survived because it was no longer understood as such, and escaped the purge of later generations because it was beyond reproach since it was embodied in the Koran (1956: 75).

The same applies to the Koran:

> Just as in ancient Egypt the boat journey is symbolic for death and birth, the fright of the sailors in the Koranic ship stands for the fear of death and the terrors of Judgement Day, their survival for Resurrection (1956: 77).

To say that the poets no longer understood the proper meaning of their nautical passages is to misunderstand the poetic use to which these passages are put in the context of the poems of which they form part. The poets do not reflect upon the wider, mythological, significance of these references, not because they found them obscure but because they intended them for an exact poetic function, to which mythologizing was not appropriate. Of the thirty or so poetic instances which I have collated, only the short pieces by Ibn Barrâq and the anonymous nomad and the ambitious delineation limned by Bishr could conceivably meet Lichtenstädter's description and in the case of the latter, it would be strange of Bishr to boast to his beloved of his resurrection, since his boat-trip does end safely. For the nomad, the return is distinctly terrestrial and not eschatological, being an Islamic example of homesickness, *al-ḥanîn ilâ al-awṭân*. Only the obscure Ibn Barrâq in a four line 'morsel', then, could conceivably bear the meaning which Lichtenstädter demands of pre-Islamic shipping. Furthermore, this interpretation of the Qur'anic ship does no justice whatsoever to the complexity and variety of its religious denotations, both as the Ark of Nûḥ, its coterminous embodiment and a perdurable witness to the power and beneficence of Allâh. [29]

29. Few would accept her outlandish emendation of the Koranic *falak* (in 21.33 and 36.40) to *fulk*: 1956: 76-7. The root *s-b-ḥ* is not used of shipping, the idea involved is one of rotation, precisely like the wheel of a spindle perpetually revolving, and *falak* is a prime example of a Koranic quibble, evoking, but not invoking, *fulk*.

MUDRIK AL-SHAYBÂNÎ'S POEM ON A CHRISTIAN BOY

BAD TASTE OR HARMLESS WIT?

BY

GEERT JAN VAN GELDER
University of Oxford

In his masterly monograph on poetry in *rajaz* metre, Manfred Ullmann briefly discusses the poem by Mudrik al-Shaybânî, given in the Appendix to this contribution:

> In der *Murabbaᶜa* reimen jeweils vier Verse. Der im 10. Jahrhundert lebende Mudrik b. ᶜAlī aš-Šaibānī (GAL S I 132) machte in dieser Form ein päderastisches Gedicht von genau 200 Versen (Yāq. Irš. VII 153, 2 ff.). Besonders geschmacklos sind die Verse, in denen er auf den christlichen Glauben seines Geliebten ᶜAmr b. Yūḥannā anspielt, so, wenn er p. 154, 7 sagt:
>
> *yā laitanī kuntu lahū qurbānā*
> *alṯimu minhu ṯ-ṯaġra wa-'l-banānā.*
>
> Das Gedicht weist im übrigen keine sprachlichen Schwierigkeiten auf.[1]

We are all aware not only of Manfred Ullmann's unsurpassed philological knowledge of Arabic language and poetry, but also of his acute critical and literary insight into this poetry, demonstrated in his book on *rajaz* and many shorter erudite monographs. When he calls a poem *besonders geschmacklos*, "particularly tasteless", one should not lightly ignore or brush aside his judgement. After all, there are plenty of poems in Arabic that, in spite of their wit and technical merit, even I myself, one generation after Ullmann, would not hesitate to call tasteless and repulsive, -- one could think of many passages by Jarîr and his rivals, of poems by the infamous Ibn al-Ḥajjâj, or the *rajaz* poem by al-Aghlab al-ᶜIjlî on the "false prophets", Musaylima and Sajâḥ, which Ullmann rightly calls "coarse and filthy".[2]

---

1. Manfred Ullmann, *Untersuchungen zur Rağazpoesie. Ein Beitrag zur arabischen Sprach- und Literaturwissenschaft*, Wiesbaden, 1966, p. 52.
2. "... in grober und unflätiger Weise ...", ibid., p. 22.

Here I intend to have a closer look at the long poem by Mudrik al-Shaybânî mentioned by Ullmann, a poem in which the sacred and the profane, the human and the divine, are closely intermingled. Not much is known about the author. Yâqût tells us that he was born a Bedouin, from the region around Basra, that he settled in Baghdad when still a child, and became skilled in Arabic and *adab*.[3] No years are given; but from an *isnâd* in *Kitâb al-Aghânî*[4] it appears that he was a contemporary both of its author, Abû al-Faraj al-Iṣfahânî (d. 356/967 or later) and Abû al-ᶜAnbas al-Ṣaymarî (d. 275/888), so he must be placed in the late 9th and the first half of the 10th century AD; elsewhere, he is mentioned as being involved in a quarrel with Jaḥẓa al-Barmakî, who died in 324/936.[5] He made a name as a poet; Ibn al-Nadîm lists him among "poets who were not *kâtib*s and lived after 300 (AD 912)", his poetry filling 200 folios.[6]

We are told that Mudrik used to keep a literary "salon" or gathering *(majlis)* that was attended by youths. Whenever an elderly, respectable person would turn up, Mudrik would tell him that mixing with young boys was not becoming to him, and sent him away. Then a certain Christian boy called ᶜAmr Ibn Yûḥannâ attended his lectures and Mudrik became infatuated with him. When the other boys became aware of this, the boy felt ashamed and came no more. After that, Mudrik used to frequent the monastery called Dayr (or Dâr) al-Rûm,[7] east of Baghdad, where the boy came from. He made many poems on him, apparently in vain, for he began to suffer from the usual symptoms of love-sickness: emaciation and madness, became bed-ridden, and died from his love.[8]

The story is touching but somewhat trite, to those who are at home in the history of Arabic literature and culture. The long poem (see Appendix),

---

3. Yâqût, *Muᶜjam al-udabâ'*, Cairo, 1936-1938, xix, 135-46.
4. Cairo, 1927-1974, xxiii, 198 -- here he is called Mudrik Ibn Muḥammad al-Shaybânî, as he is in Ibn al-Nadîm's *Fihrist* (Leipzig, 1871-1872, p. 168); in al-Khaṭîb al-Baghdâdî's *Târîkh Baghdâd* (xiii, 273) his name is Mudrik Ibn Muḥammad Abû al-Qâsim al-Shaybânî, whereas the other sources call him Mudrik Ibn ᶜAlî al-Shaybânî.
5. al-Qifṭî, *Inbâh al-ruwât*, ed. Muḥammad Abû al-Faḍl Ibrâhîm, repr. Beirut, 1986, ii, 252-53.
6. See the note 4.
7. cf. Translation, stanza 6, note.
8. The story in Ibn al-Sarrâj, *Maṣâriᶜ al-ᶜushshâq*, Beirut, n.d., i, 242-43, ii, 258-59, Yâqût, *Muᶜjam al-udabâ'*, iv, 122-26; xix, 135-36, 145-46, Dâwûd al-Anṭâkî, *Tazyîn al-aswâq*, ed. Muḥammad Altûnjî, Beirut, 1993, pp. 65-66, Ṣafî al-Dîn al-Ḥillî, *Dîwân*, Beirut, n.d., pp. 441-42, Ibn Ḥijja al-Ḥamawî, *Thamarât al-awrâq*, ed. Muḥammad Abû al-Faḍl Ibrâhîm, Cairo, 1971, p. 319-20.

too, is not particularly original, as I shall demonstrate. But first, let us cast a glance at the poem itself. Ullmann is right in calling the poem "paederastic" if we take that word in its original sense: "relating to the love of boys". In modern European languages, however, the word has usually acquired the sense of "relating to sexual intercourse with boys" or "unnatural intercourse, sodomy". It is possible, even likely, of course, that Mudrik's intentions went in that general direction; after all, homosexual relationships were far from abnormal in mediaeval Muslim urban society, even though they were forbidden by orthodox Islam. What concerns us here is rather the fact that the poem is chaste in this respect. The boy has not been violated: the poet's hands have committed no crime, as he says in stanza 2, and there are no overt references to sexual organs or intercourse, unlike numerous poems by Abû Nuwâs and many others, which are either outright obscene or at least speak lovingly of the boy's attractive behind. Obviously, when Ullmann calls the poem *besonders geschmacklos*, he refers above all to the mixing of the sacred and the profane.

Arabic poets not rarely used sacred imagery and terminology in love lyrics;[9] here it derives not from Islam but from Christianity, which might be considered tasteless by Christians if they think that the poet is irreverently mocking what is holy to them, or blasphemous and heretical by Muslims if they believe that the poet seriously reveres un-Islamic things. Thus the poet risks being condemned both for his seriousness and for his jesting. I should like to argue that he is neither mocking Christian belief nor seriously thinking of abandoning Islam, and that neither Christians nor Muslims have reason to condemn the poet and reject the poem, unless they reject the conventions of Arabic poetry. The offending passage begins in stanza 7, after we have learned in stanza 5 that the beloved boy is a Christian. The fourth line of stanza 7, one of the less easy lines of the poem, seems to identify the boy as the human side of the Trinity *(ka-annahû nâsûtuhû ḥîna ttaḥad)*. The tenth stanza is a crucial one in the poem: the poet argues, with the logic of poetry, that the boy should relent if he keeps aloof only because of the difference of religion, for Mudrik has all but stopped being a Muslim; he has neglected the basic duties of the believer, praying and fasting. He suggests that this is not really his own fault: it is the boy's beauty that is responsible.

9. On this, see e.g. Johann Christoph Bürgel, "Die Profanierung sakraler Sprache als Stilmittel in klassischer arabischer Dichtung", in *Ibn an-Nadīm und die mittelalterliche arabische Literatur. Beiträge zum 1. Johann Wilhelm Fück-Kolloquium (Halle 1987)*, Wiesbaden, 1996, pp. 64-72.

Hence, "forbidden things are lawful for his sake" (stanza 10). The rest of the poem is an elaboration of this.

The poem pretends to be a love-letter,[10] with a fairly clear basic structure: "From a lover (1) to a Christian gazelle (5)"; then an excursus on his beauty and cruelty, with a series of impossible wishes (5-17), followed by an address to the beloved: "To you is my complaint (18)". The writer briefly reverts to the third person (22) and then again addresses ᶜAmr, introducing his request with a long series of oaths (23-48), which ends with another address ("You, whose manners are refined"). Finally he states his plea at the end of the poem (49-50) while offering the prospect of a rich reward in prose and verse. No idle boast this, for the name of ᶜAmr, son of John, is immortalized in the poem and the prose account in which it is embedded. Note that, although the writer of this love-letter is Mudrik the poet, he wishes to be the pen in ᶜAmr's hand (stanza 13), suggesting that he is in fact merely the pen, since ᶜAmr is the true inspirer, the only begetter of the ensuing poem.

Among the possibly original features of the poem is its form: neither in monorhyme nor in paired rhyme, as was often done in *rajaz* metre, but in stanzas of four lines. Brockelmann has suggested that this was an imitation of Christian popular verse, which was in its turn based on the more artful stanzaic forms of Syriac religious poetry.[11] The round number of fifty stanzas is hardly a coincidence. The poet Ibn Wakîᶜ al-Tinnîsî, who died in 393/1003, may have imitated Mudrik with his *rajaz* poem in four-line stanzas, forty-five of which are quoted in al-Thaᶜâlibî's *Yatîmat al-dahr.*[12] This is also a love poem, a complaint in the form of a letter to a Christian boy called George (Jirjis, see stanza 44). It contains allusions to matters relating to Christians and their religion: the girdle or *zunnâr* (st. 16), the Gospels (24-25), the Psalms (26) and various dignitaries (30, 32-33, 38-39), but not nearly as insistently as Mudrik. Al-Thaᶜâlibî also quotes twelve stanzas of a *murabbaᶜa*, said to be "very long", on a boy by an otherwise unknown Andalusian poet, Fâtik al-Shahwâjî.[13] This poem too takes the form of a letter;

10. For a poem in the form of a love-letter, see e.g. al-ᶜAbbâs Ibn al-Aḥnaf, *Dîwân*, Beirut, 1965, pp. 15-16.

11. Carl Brockelmann, *Geschichte der arabischen Litteratur*, Leiden, 1937-1949, Suppl. I, 438.

12. ed. Muḥammad Muḥyî al-Dîn ᶜAbd al-Ḥamîd, Cairo, 1947, i, 356-63.

13. *Yatîmat al-dahr*, ii, 18-19. Ullmann, *op. cit.*, p. 52 describes it as "eine lange päderastische Urǧūza murabbaᶜa" and calls it "berüchtigt"; but it is wholly free from obscenity.

there are no indications that the boy was a Christian. Then there is a poem in stanzaic *rajaz*[14] by the Damascene grammarian Abû al-Faraj al-Ḥusayn Ibn Muḥammad al-Mastûr, who died in 392/1002.[15] Only nine stanzas are preserved, but again it is said to have been long. It is not only made on a Christian boy, but it actually contains a series of oaths similar to those in Mudrik's poem: "By Jerusalem and the Holy Land ... By the monastery and the monks, by the Eucharist, by Paul, that great man ... By Mount Sinai, by the Psalms ... by the Messiah, by the sacrificed boy; by Easter" etc.

All these poems are obviously inspired directly or indirectly by Mudrik's poem. In some cases the inspiration is stated explicitly. Al-Muᶜâfâ al-Jarîrî (d. 390/1000), on whose authority the text of Mudrik's poem is quoted in the oldest source, says in his interesting collection *al-Jalîs al-ṣâliḥ al-kâfî* that in his youth he made a stanzaic poem *(musammaṭa)* "in the style of the poem on ᶜAmr the Christian by Mudrik al-Shaybânî". He quotes a couple of stanzas, but then asks God's forgiveness for dwelling on things that distract from worshipping God.[16] Elsewhere, he says that he has actually seen ᶜAmr, the Christian, who lived to have his hair turned grey.[17] Several centuries later, the well-known poet Ṣafî al-Dîn al-Ḥillî (d. 749/1349) made a *mukhammasa* out of Mudrik's poem. Normally, a poet would add lines of his own composition to each line of an existing *qaṣîda* in monorhyme, thus producing a *mukhammasa* with stanzas of five lines *(aaaab ccccb ddddb ...)*;[18] but in this case the procedure is reversed, for al-Ḥillî only had to add single lines, with a common rhyme, to each of Mudrik's stanzas.[19] Dâwûd al-Anṭâkî (d. 1008/1599), the author of *Tazyîn al-aswâq*, quotes this version, adding a commentary on some of the Christian terminology, in which he accuses both Mudrik and afî al-Dîn of ignorance of Christian matters, but demonstrates considerable confusion on his own

14. dimeter instead of Mudrik's trimeter.
15. Ibn ᶜAsâkir, *Tahdhîb Târîkh Dimashq*, repr. Beirut, 1987, iv, 362-63, Yâqût, *Muᶜjam al-udabâ'*, x, 164-66. See Brockelmann, *Geschichte*, S I, 438.
16. al-Muᶜâfâ Ibn Zakariyyâ al-Jarîrî, *al-Jalîs al-ṣâliḥ al-kâfî*, Beirut, 1993, i, 223-24, Ibn al-Sarrâj, *Maṣâriᶜ al-ᶜushshâq*, i, 138. Note the use of the term *musammaṭa*, even though Mudrik's composition lacks a common rhyme throughout the poem (cf. G. Schoeler, art. "Musammaṭ" in *EI²*).
17. Ibn al-Sarrâj, *Maṣâriᶜ al-ᶜushshâq*, ii, 170, quoted in al-Tanûkhî, *Nishwâr al-muḥâḍara*, ed. ᶜAbbûd al-Shâljî, [Beirut,] 1971-1973, iv, 275, Yâqût, *Muᶜjam al-udabâ'*, xix, 136, Ibn Ḥijja, *Thamarât*, p. 320.
18. See G. Schoeler, art. "Musammaṭ".
19. al-Ḥillî, *Dîwân*, pp. 441-48; strophes 7-23 are lacking (purged by the editor?).

part.[20] The poem by Mudrik remained popular, it seems; thus in the collection of tales in the style of *The Thousand and One Nights* called *al-Ḥikâyât al-ᶜajîba wa-'l-akhbâr al-gharîba* a few of the more memorable lines are quoted anonymously in the course of a love story.[21]

The "sacred", "Christian" elements in Mudrik's poem are contained, with one exception,[22] in two sections, the first elaborating the theme of "would that I were" (stanzas 11-15), the second being the series of oaths (stanzas 24-48). The first theme is an ancient erotic topos. "I wish I could be / a white-glowing lily / so you might take me / in your hands ..." said a Byzantine poet called Theophanes probably in the sixth century.[23] An anonymous Greek poet said, "I wish I were the wind, and you, / walking along the seashore, / would uncover your breasts and let me / touch them as I blow."[24] In Arabic we find several lines predating Mudrik, such as when al-ᶜAbbâs Ibn al-Aḥnaf (d. c. 188/804) makes his beloved Fawz say:

> ᶜAbbâs, would that you were my shirt *(sirbâl)*[25] on my body, or would that I were a shirt on ᶜAbbâs!
> Or would that he were a wine and I were to him some rainwater, forever together in a cup![26]

or :

> I wish I were her toothbrush in her hand, forever smelling the fragrance from her teeth,
> Or would I were a shift on her, so that I could enjoy the softness of her skin and of her clothes ...[27]

---

20. Dâwûd al-Anṭâkî, *Tazyîn al-aswâq*, ii, 66-88 (no stanzas omitted)
21. Hans Wehr (hg.), *Das Buch der wunderbaren Erzählungen und seltsamen Geschichten*, Wiesbaden - Damascus, 1956, pp. 501-2 (parts from stanzas 11, 12, 15, with some additions). See pp. 274-76, 278 for similar poems with "Christian" oaths.
22. stanza 7.
23. tr. Peter Jay, in *The Greek Anthology and other ancient epigrams, a selection in modern verse translations*, ed. with an introd. by Peter Jay, Harmondsworth, 1981, p. 366 (*Greek Anthology*, xv, 35).
24. tr. Barriss Mills, *ibid.*, p. 324 (*Greek Anthology*, v, 83).
25. or "trousers", for *sirbâl* and *sirwâl* are obviously related, both deriving from Persian *shalwâr*.
26. *Dîwân*, Beirut, 1965, p. 180, cf. al-Sharîf al-Murtaḍâ, *Ghurar al-fawâ'id*, ed. Muḥammad Abû al-Faḍl Ibrâhîm, Cairo, 1954, ii, 64, al-Ḥâtimî, *Ḥilyat al-muḥâḍara*, ed. Jaᶜfar al-Kattânî, Baghdad, 1979, ii, 230.

Women employed the conceit too, such as a certain Umm Khâlid:

> O, I wish I were a shadow where he appears,
> O, I wish I were a mantle for him when he protects himself with it against the bitterly cold east wind, or his sandal ...[28]

And Khadîja, al-Ma'mûn's daughter:

> O, would that I were his dove, or his sparrowhawk, while he could do with me whatever he wishes.[29]

A closer parallel to Mudrik in this respect is offered by a line by the poet-caliph al-Walîd Ibn Yazîd (d. 126/744); I quote the poem in which it occurs in its entirety:

> Your heart, Walîd, has become stricken by a passion which, of old, used to hunt pretty girls,
> By the love for a tender girl showing bright teeth, who appeared to us while going to church on a feast day.
> I kept looking at her with the eyes of a tender lover, until I saw her kissing the wood:
> The wood of the Cross. Ah, woe to me, having seen a cross thus revered.
> I asked my Lord if I could be in its place, and then serve as fuel in Hell's blaze.[30]

Al-Mu^{c}âfâ al-Jarîrî tells us that the girl in question was called Safrâ (or Sufrâ) and gives some details about how the two met. He adds the following remark on the poem:

> Mudrik al-Shaybânî did not quite reach this degree of shamelessness (or depravity, *khalâ^{c}a*) in what he said on ^{c}Amr the Christian: "Would that I were a crucifix to him (...)" Al-Walîd has produced more of this kind of shamelessness, licentiousness *(mujûn)* and foolishness in religious matters *(sakhâfat al-dîn)*, too much to

27. *Dîwân*, p. 73.
28. Ibn Abî Ṭâhir Ṭayfûr, *Balâghât al-nisâ'*, Beirut, 1987, p. 331.
29. *al-Aghânî*, xvi, 16.
30. al-Mu^{c}âfâ al-Jarîrî, *Jalîs*, ii, 317, Ibn al-Sarrâj, *Maṣâri^{c} al-^{c}ushshâq*, ii, 168, Francesco Gabrieli, "Al-Walīd ibn Yazīd, il califfo e il poeta", *RSO* 15 (1935) 1-64, see p. 42 (from Sibṭ Ibn al-Jawzî, *Mir'ât al-zamân*, with some variants and lines 1b-2a lacking).

> quote here. We have rebutted some things that he said in his poetry, which contains his feeble error and his unbelief.[31]

The learned and pious *qâḍî* al-Jarîrî obviously had mixed feelings about such shamelessness. In his youth he went as far as to imitate Mudrik, but, although he renounces his juvenile folly and uses strongly condemnatory terms about al-Walîd, he is not ashamed to mention it and to quote al-Walîd's poem, and he would have quoted more but for its length, as he says.

Mudrik may have emulated al-Walîd; more likely he followed an even more famous and greater poet, Abû Nuwâs, who sings of many Christian boys and says in one poem, recently translated and discussed by James Montgomery and before him, more briefly, by Ewald Wagner and Andras Hamori:

> O I wish I were the priest or the metropolitan of his Church! No, I wish that I were the Gospel and the Scriptures for him!
> No, I wish that I were a Eucharist which he is given or the chalice from which he drinks wine! No, I wish I were the very bubbles <of the wine>! (tr. J.E. Montgomery)[32]

The extensive use of Christian oaths is another element that Mudrik may have taken over from Abû Nuwâs. Numerous instances have been collected by Ewald Wagner in his monograph on the poet.[33] A whole series of these oaths occurs in a poem by Abû Nuwâs on a Christian boy, quoted in al-Shâbushtî's *al-Diyârât*.[34] If the rhyming hemistichs of the first line are anything to go by, it would seem that the oaths stand at the beginning of the poem:

---

31. *Jalîs*, ii, 318; he adds that he may come back to the topic in a following chapter *(majlis)* of his book; but he fails to do so.
32. Abû Nuwâs, *Dîwân*, ed. Aḥmad ʿAbd al-Majîd al-Ghazâlî, Beirut, 1984, p. 333; James E. Montgomery, "For the Love of a Christian Boy: A Song by Abū Nuwās", *JAL* 27:2 (1996) 115-24, see pp. 118-19. See also Ewald Wagner, *Abū Nuwās. Eine Studie zur arabischen Literatur der frühen ʿAbbāsidenzeit*, Wiesbaden, 1965. p. 201, Andras Hamori, *On the Art of Medieval Arabic Literature*, Princeton, 1974, pp. 119-24.
33. Wagner, *Abū Nuwās*, pp. 195-203.
34. al-Shâbushtî, *al-Diyârât*, ed. Gûrgîs ʿAwwâd, repr. Beirut, 1986, pp. 204-206 (the editor points to the parallel with Mudrik's poem).

By the Baptism in the Old Monastery, by the Metropolitan *(muṭrînî)*[35] and the Patriarch *(jâthalîq)*,
By Simon, by John, by Jesus, by Mâsarjîs (Sergius), the friendly priest,[36]
By the birthday of the Messiah, by Epiphany, by the penitential prayers *(bâᶜûthâ)*,[37] by the fulfilment of duties,
By Ashmûnâ and the seven that she let go first -- none of them swerved from the (right) path,[38]
By Lady Mary, by Easter Day, by the Eucharist with the old wine,
By the crosses that are lifted upon lances, which glitter when they light up as if with lightning,
By your pilgrimage to Mâsarjusânâ, the monasteries of Nawbahâr and Fîq,[39]
By the building of God's church -- may it be ransomed -- and the priests that have come from afar,
And by the clapper *(nâqûs)* in the churches, in which prayers are performed at sunrise,
By Mary, by Christ and by every priest *(ḥabr)*, disciple *(ḥawârî)* in a strong religion,
By the monks in their cells, on their heights, who stay there in exertion and misery,
By the Gospel of Palm Sunday *(injîl al-shaᶜânîn)* -- may it be ransomed -- and the recitation *(shamᶜala)*[40] of the Christians on the road,[41]
And by the great crosses when they appear, and by the girdle *(zunnâr)* round a slim waist,
And by the beauty placed in you: have mercy on my burning and my dry mouth!
Ah, by closeness after remoteness, (I swear) the oath of a man in love with his killer:
You have become the adornment of every monastery and a feast, in spite of your harshness and recalcitrance.
All your lovers announce that they are renouncing Islam and will go to the Christians.

This poem is particularly close to Mudrik al-Shaybânî's poem, in theme and structure. Abû Nuwâs went a good deal further than Mudrik in offending

---

35. An unusual form.
36. Compare the version in Wagner, *Abū Nuwās*, p. 196.
37. Hava: "Prayers said on Easter Monday"; cf. Wagner, *Abū Nuwās*, p. 200, Georg Graf, *Verzeichnis arabischer kirchlicher Termini*, Louvain, 1954, pp. 19-20.
38. A reference to the mother and her seven sons that died as martyrs in the story of Maccabees II, 7 (Ashmûnâ: cf. the dynasty of the Hasmoneans or Maccabees).
39. cf. Wagner, *Abū Nuwās*, p. 199.
40. See Mudrik's poem, stanza 30.
41. cf. the version in Wagner, *Abū Nuwās*, p. 200.

religious sensibilities, not only here when he says jokingly but explicitly that he will abandon Islam, but also, for instance, in a poem in which he maintains that Christian religious authorities, while disparaging intercourse with women, had recommended sexual relationships with boys.[42] Such cynicism is absent from Mudrik's poem. Of course, a Muslim should not swear Christian oaths; but the poem should not be read theologically but rhetorically and poetically.[43] It is obviously far more effective, when addressing someone, to swear by things that are holy to the addressee than by things that he would reject or find meaningless.

There is yet another precursor of Mudrik al-Shaybânî. The Kufan minor poet Bakr Ibn Khârija lived in the first half of the ninth century, was admired by al-Jâḥiẓ (d. 255/868-9) and Di^{c}bil (d. 264/860), and was noted as a drunkard. He is said to have been enamoured of a Christian boy called ^{c}Îsâ Ibn al-Barâ' al-^{c}Ibâdî, on whom he made "a poem in paired rhyme *(qaṣîda muzdawija)* in which he mentions the Christians, their religious customs and their feasts, naming their monasteries, and preferring them (to others)".[44] The poem has not been preserved. The term *muzdawij* refers, in principle, to poems rhyming *aabbccdd*, but Mudrik's poem has also been called a *muzdawija*,[45] so it is possible that Bakr Ibn Khârija's poem consisted of a series of monorhymed quatrains, and that Mudrik adopted his example.

From all this it is clear that Mudrik's poem stands in the middle of a well-established tradition of "transconfessional" Muslim poems on Christian boys, which make ample use of Christian terminology and allude to Christian customs and beliefs. It is also obvious that, although ostensibly the poem is a love poem, and Mudrik's love was, by all accounts, sincere, yet the main point of the poem is precisely this ostentatious display of

42. Wagner, *Abū Nuwās*, pp. 202-203.
43. One could quote once again the well-known statement of ^{c}Alî ^{c}Abd al-^{c}Azîz al-Jurjânî (d. 392/1001), *qâḍî*, poet and critic: "If bad religious beliefs were a reason for dismissing a poet, the name of Abû Nuwâs would have to be deleted from the records ... But religion is to be kept separate from poetry." *(al-Wasâṭa bayn al-Mutanabbî wa-khuṣûmihi*, ed. Muḥammad Abû al-Faḍl Ibrâhîm & ^{c}Alî Muḥammad al-Bajâwî, Cairo, n.d., p. 64). For a less frivolous use of Christian oaths (because not in the context of boy-love), see the poem by the Persian poet Khâqânî (d. 595/1199), discussed in V. Minorsky, "Khāqānī and Andronicus Comnenus", *BSOAS* 11 (1945) 550-78 (I owe this reference to Dr Anna Livia Beelaert, Leiden).
44. al-Iṣfahânî, *Aghânî*, xxiii, 189. See on Bakr Ibn Khârija *Aghânî*, xxiii, 188-92, al-Shâbushtî, *Diyârât*, pp. 242-43.
45. e.g. Yâqût, *Mu^{c}jam al-udabâ'*, xix, 136, al-Anṭâkî, *Tazyîn*, ii, 66.

knowledge (or misinformation, on several occasions) of Christian terms, names and concepts. The long series of strange and often un-Arabic words and names has a somewhat humorous effect, which I am sure is at least partly intended, even though being funny was obviously not Mudrik's primary aim. Some poets -- al-Walîd Ibn Yazîd, Abû Nuwâs -- clearly meant to outrage the pious, but Mudrik is not one of them. His poem is certainly not meant as a form of disrespect either towards Christianity, by mocking it, or towards Islam, by seemingly abandoning it. Mixtures of the sacred and the profane are normal in Arabic panegyrical and amatory verse, in which the patron and the beloved are often quasi-blasphemously raised to nearly divine status. The mediaeval critics, though they may not wholeheartedly approve of this, do not seem to mind very much as long as it is found in poetry and is capable of being taken as metaphorical. It is different when the divine status is taken seriously and literally. Thus al-Thaᶜâlibî expresses scorn for those philosophers who maintain that the divine spirit rests in a worldly ruler, and for those mystics who believe that God's beauty and His light reside in a pretty boy or beautiful girl; but when the same motif is used in non-mystic poetry by Ibn Nubâta al-Saᶜdî or al-Ḥâtimî, he seems to find it unobjectionable.[46]

The image that evoked Ullmann's scorn, Mudrik's wishing to be the Eucharist taken by the boy, is central in the poem. The key word is *qurbân*, also "offering, sacrifice, communion" and derived from the root *QRB*, implying "nearness". The very first line anticipates the theme in speaking of remoteness and proximity, and the penultimate stanza epitomizes it in using the word *taqrîb* in a sense that is ambiguously sacred and profane, translated here as "communion".[47] To any Muslim the word *taqrîb* would necessarily evoke the *muqarrabûn* mentioned several times in the Koran, "those brought near", viz. to God, be they angels or human beings. One should note that, on the one hand, the boy is revered almost as a deity, which is found in Arabic love lyrics since the time of the ᶜUdhrite poets and al-ᶜAbbâs Ibn al-Aḥnaf.[48] The boy is said to look like God incarnate in stanza 7, a stanza in which he is depicted as animal, human (yet inhuman), and divine. On the other hand, the poet also raises himself to divine status, in Christian terms at least, by imagining himself as being the Eucharist. He

46. al-Thaᶜâlibî, *Âdâb al-mulûk*, ed. Jalîl al-ᶜAṭiyya, Beirut, 1990, pp. 36-37.
47. The root occurs also in stanzas 11, 41, 48.
48. e.g. Jean-Claude Vadet, *L'esprit courtois en Orient dans les cinq premiers siècles de l'Hégire*, Paris, 1968, pp. 249-56, Susanne Enderwitz, *Liebe als Beruf: al-ᶜAbbās Ibn al-Aḥnaf und das Ġazal*, Beirut - Wiesbaden, 1995, pp. 150-56.

suffers without sin for his love (stanza 2 and *passim*), just as Christ suffered, and offers himself as a sacrifice, or Eucharist, to this God-like boy. It is the perfect union: the poet, Christ-like, gives himself to the boy, who is also Christ. Since the poem, in the shape of a love-letter, is both an offering to the boy and a means to immortalize him, it may not seem too far-fetched, in this context, to compare the poem itself to the Eucharist. Of the trinity Poet -- Poem -- Beloved, it is only the Poem that still exists on earth, the other two living on only through it.

It is an interesting speculation what Muslim and Christian critics, in the past and the present, would have had to say about Christian poems extolling Muslim boys in terms of Muslim rites and customs, had such poems been made. The Muslims, being religiously and politically dominant, could afford to play with religious motifs pertaining to the other group, especially if the poet and lover is the dominant and active partner (who conventionally decribes the passive beloved as being dominant). It is, of course, unthinkable that the tables could ever have been turned.

Appendix: the poem on ^{c}Amr the Christian

basic text: Ibn al-Sarrâj, *Maṣâri^c al-^{c}ushshâq*, ii, 170-75

sigla:
A: Dâwûd al-Anṭâkî, *Tazyîn al-aswâq*, Ḥ: Ṣafî al-Dîn al-Ḥillî, *Dîwân*, IḤ: Ibn Ḥijja, *Thamarât al-awrâq*, IS: Ibn al-Sarrâj, *Maṣâri^c al-^{c}ushshâq*, T: al-Tanûkhî, *Nishwâr al-muḥâḍara*, YB: al-Yâqût, *Mu^{c}jam al-buldân*, YU: Yâqût, *Mu^{c}jam al-udabâ'*

variants:
1. *juthmân: jismân* (sic, l. *jusmân*) YU; **2**. *aḍnâhû: ablâhû* Ḥ IḤ; **3**. *aḥârat: ajâdat* A YU; *nâṭiqatin ... staraqqâ: dhâba ilâ an kâda yafnâ ^{c}ishqâ / wa-^{c}an daqîqi al-fikri suqman daqqâ* IḤ, Ḥ the same with *^{c}anhu* for *suqman*; **4**. *tuṭfîhi: tuṭfi'u* YU, *yukhmidu* Ḥ, *ka-annahâ: munhallatan* A; **5**. *^{c}idhâra ... ḥayârâ: fuḍḍila bi-'l-ḥusni ^{c}alâ al-^{c}adhârâ / kullu al-warâ mundhu nashâ ḥayârâ* Ḥ; **6**. *bi-dâri: bi-dayri* YB A, *^{c}an: min* YU; stanzas **7-23**: Ḥ-; **9**. *faqdî: faqrî* YU A; **10**. *dînî: dhanbî* YU IḤ A, *naqḍihî: naqṣihî* YU A; **11**. *akûnu minhu abadan: mu^{c}allaqan fî ^{c}unqihî* ḤA **12**. *bal: yâ* YU T I A, *althimu ... al-banânâ: yamzujunî bi-rîqihî liyânâ* ḤA; **14**: *^{c}ûdha, maqdhûdha, ma'khûdha, manbûdha: ^{c}ûda, maqdûda, maḥdûda, mashhûda* A, *barkatan bi-ismihî:*

birkatan bâsimatan A; **26**. *rîq: rûḥ* Ḥ **27**. *yashfî wa-yubrî akmahan wa-abraṣâ: wa-mubri'an min akmahin wa-abraṣâ* Ḥ; **28**. *wa-bâ^c^ithi al-mawtâ mina: bi-'l-nafkhi fî al-mawtâ wa-fî* Ḥ **29**. *mâ: man* YU IḤ A; **31**. *mârat: mârî* T YU Ḥ IḤ A; **32**. *min abîhi: ^c^inda llâhi* YU A, *min mawlâhu* IḤ; **33**. *khûṣ: nakhl* Ḥ IḤ; **34**. *mar Mârî: mâ Mârî* YU; **35**. *Ash^c^ayâ: Sha^c^yâ'a* YU; **37**. *dujâ: hudâ* IḤ *ṣârû: sârû* YU A; **38**. *min muḥkam: min munzal* IḤ; **39**. *Murqus: Mâr ^c^Îd* YU IḤ, *Mar ^c^Abdâ* A, *al-shafîqi al-nâṣiḥ: al-taqiyyi al-ṣâliḥ* IH4, *bi-ḥaqqi Yûḥannâ ... al-ṣaḥâṣiḥî: wa-'l-shuhadâ'i bi-'l-falâ al-ṣaḥâṣiḥî / min kulli ghâdin minhumû wa-râ'iḥî* IḤ, *Yûḥannâ al-ḥalîm: Yamlîkhâ al-ḥakîm* YU A; **41**. *âḥâd: a^c^yâd* YU IḤ, *wa-ṭûli tabyîḍika: wa-ṭûli taftîtika* YU, *wa-ṭûli taqṭî^c^ika* A (and reversing the order of verses 3 and 4), *bi-ṭûli taqṭî^c^ika* Ḥ (reversing 3rd and 4th line); **44**. *dayrânî: ghufrâni* Ḥ; **45**. *salîm: salîḥ* T A, *masîḥ* YU IḤ Ḥ (Ḥ reversing the order of vss. 3 and 4), *bi-mâ: wa-mâ* YU IḤ Ḥ; **46**. *mighfar: mafriq* YU IḤ; *wa-ḥaqqi kulli barkatin wa-maḥramî: wa-ḥaqqi kulli kâhinin muqaddamî* YU, *bi-ḥaqqi kulli kâhinin muqaddamî* IḤ; Ḥ has a different text: *bi-kulli nâmûsin lahû muqaddamî / yu^c^allimu al-nâsa wa-lammâ ya^c^lamî / bi-ḥurmati al-ṣawmi al-kabîri al-a^c^ẓamî / wa-mâ ḥawâ al-mîlâdu li-bni maryamî*; **47**. *dhî: fî* Ḥ IḤ, *dhabḥ: dinḥ* T, *al-mudhhibi li-'l-nifâq: al-ibrîzi lâ al-awrâq* Ḥ IḤ; **48**. *al-khamîsi al-nâsî: khamîsi al-nâsi* IḤ; the stanza missing in Ḥ; **49**. *raghibta: sa^c^ayta* Ḥ

form:

aaaa bbbb cccc .... (50 strophes); metre *rajaz*, three feet per verse: *NNSL NNSL SLL* (or *LLL* or *NLSL*, *S* standing for a short syllable, *L* for a long one and *N* for one that is either short or long). The translation employs an iambic pentameter of ten or eleven syllables, not unlike the original as far as the comparison goes. In order to fill the line, occasional slight padding or curtailing was necessary, without much affecting the meaning. Thanks are due to my colleague Dr G.J. Reinink, who gave a number of useful comments and suggestions concerning the poet's allusions to matters of Christian belief and ritual.[49]

translation:

1. From a far lover, whose fond love is near,
With telling tears and with a silent tongue,
Someone whose heart is bound, his body loose,
Tormented by rejection and forsaking,

49. In the following notes I shall indicate my indebtedness by the addition of "[GJR]".

2. Without a crime committed by his hands
Except a passion which his eyes betrayed,
That yearned to see the one that caused his grief,
(A "cure" by him who made him waste away?)

3. -- Woe to a lover for what he must suffer
From tears that flow in streams unstintingly,
Speaking, although they make no proper speech,
Telling of love that can enslave a man;

4. Nothing remains of him save eyes that weep
With tears that are like pearls strung on a string,
Extinguished by the fires of love, or kindled,
Resembling drops that fall from heaven above --

5. To a gazelle, one of the Christian tribe *(Banî al-Naṣârâ)*,
Whose cheek-down *(ᶜidhâr)* captivates all virgin girls *(ᶜadhârâ)*,
And leaves wild lions in bewilderment,
Imprisoned in the snares of love for him;

6. A fawn from the Greek House,[50] who wants *(rîmin bi-dâri al-Rûmi râma)* to kill me
By means of coal-black eyes *sans* added kohl,
And locks that make my reason fly away,
And with a pretty face and ugly deeds.

7. Which lion was not hunted with this fawn?
He kills with looks, fearing no tit for tat.
When he says "Here!" his looks say "That's enough!"
He seems His human nature, when He's One *(ka-annahû nâsûtuhû ḥîna ttaḥad)*.

8. No fairer full moon, or a fairer sun,
Nor fresher branch was ever seen by people

---

50. See YB on *Dayr al-Rûm*: a Nestorian monastery in Baghdad, so called because in the time of al-Mahdî a number of Byzantine prisoners of war were lodged on the site before the monastery was established. YB quotes this stanza, reading *bi-dayr* instead of *bi-dâr*.

Than ᶜAmr -- I would give my life for ᶜAmr,
Gazelle that with his eyes pours wine for me.

9. Now look at me: I'm shattered by his stature *(bi-qaddihî maqdûdû)*
And tears have carved out furrows on my cheeks.
Nothing impairs him whom I sorely miss,
But that rejecting me sullies his deeds.

10. In case he thinks my crime[51] is that I'm Muslim,
My sins have done their utmost to undo this,
For I have been remiss in prayer and fasting:
Forbidden things are lawful for his sake.

11. Would that I were a crucifix *(ṣalîb)* to him,
So that I could always be close to him!
Then I could see his beauty, smell his perfume,
Fearing no slanderer nor any spy.

12. Or that I were a Eucharist *(qurbân)* to him,
And thus could kiss his mouth and fingertips;
Or else a Patriarch *(jâthalîq)*, an Archbishop *(muṭrân)*,
So that obeying me would be his creed.

13. Or that I were a Holy Book *(muṣḥaf)* to ᶜAmr,
So that he'd read my letters every day,
Or else a pen with which he would write down
Some moral entertainment, well-composed.

14. Or that I were a talisman *(ᶜûdha)* to ᶜAmr,
Or else a vestment *(ḥulla)* that he wears, well-cut,
Or else a benediction[52] in his name,
Or else a church *(bîᶜa)*, abandoned, in his country (?)[53]

---

51. reading, with YU, A, IḤ, *dhanbî* for *dînî*.
52. *barka*, a variant of *baraka* (see Dozy, *Supplément aux dictionnaires Arabes*, s.v.).
53. A has different rhyme-words; *ᶜûda* (for *ᶜûdha*) could mean "piece of wood", "stick", perhaps "piece of incense". Instead of *manbûdha* "abandoned, derelict", A has *mashhûda* "well-attended"; but the poet may have preferred to be alone with his beloved. As for the use of charms, see H. Gollancz, *The Book of Protection, Being a Collection of Syriac Charms*, London, 1912, Ph. Gignaux, *Incantations magiques syriaques*,

15. Or that I were his girdle *(zunnâr)*, so that he
Could wrap me round the circle of his waist,
Until, when night folds up the day, I would
Become an under-garment for his loins *(izâr)*.

16. He has -- by Him who'll spare him for me! -- killed me;
He robbed me, clothed in weakness, of my wits:
An antilope who, whether far or near,
Sits in my body in my spirit's place.

17. O heartbreak for his ruddy, blood-red cheeks!
O heartache for the gap between his teeth!
There's nothing like his large and deep-black eyes
To take away one's piousness and scruples.

18. To you is my complaint, human gazelle,
About my desolation after cheer.
O you whose face is my new moon and sun:
A life cannot be killed but for a life.

19. Grant me your gracious love, as I[54] have done;
Do it for old time's sake, as I now do.
Reject, as I reject, your long rejection,
For there's no passion for you like my passion.

20. Look, I am drowning in a sea of passion,
Drunken with love for you, not sob'ring up,
Burning although not touched by burning fire,
Commiserated by my foes and friends.

21. I wish I knew if you would pity me
For my long sickness and debility,
Or is there still a way to reach you yet
For any lover with a skinny body?

22. He gives me pain and sickness in each limb,

Louvain, 1987 [GJR].

54. Reading *judtu* instead of *judta*.

And eyes that weep, shedding both tears and blood,
From love for this full moon, this sun, this idol:
To him, about his wrongs, is my complaint.

23. I say, while he plays havoc with my heart,[55]
"O ᶜAmr, you who fills *(ᶜâmir)* my heart with grief,
I swear by God an earnest, solemn oath:
A man favoured by you is truly favoured.

24. O ᶜAmr, I implore you now by Christ *(al-Masîḥ)*:
Please listen to these words so eloquent,
That tell you of the speaker's wounded heart,
Revealing all the torments he endures.

25. O ᶜAmr, by the truth of God Divine *(al-Lâhût)*
And by the Holy Spirit *(Rûḥ al-quds)* and God Human *(al-Nâsût)*,
Who, lying in a cradle carved of wood,
Was given speech instead of being silent,[56]

26. By God as Man *(Nâsût)*, who, placed in Mary's womb,
Resembled the saliva in her mouth,
And then became hypostasis eternal *(qanûm al-aqdam)*,
And then addressed mankind, while not yet weaned;

27. By Him who, after death, was shrouded in
A cloth cut to His size and measurement --
He was God-fearing and to God devoted;
He used to heal and cure the blind and leprous --

28. By Him Who brought to life the forms of birds,[57]
And Him Who raised the dead out of their graves,
To Whom all things must in the end revert,[58]
He Who knows all there is on land or seas;

---

55. Lit. "he stands up and sits down with my heart".
56. A reference to Koran 3:46, 5:110, 19:29-33.
57. cf. Koran 3:49 and 5:110 (both places making mention also of Christ's curing the blind and the leprous and his raising the dead).
58. In the Koran the "reverting", a very common idiom, is always to God, not to Christ as here.

29. By those who pray in their high-tow'ring cells *(ṣawâmiᶜ)*,
Either prostrate before their Lord or kneeling,
While every sleeper weeps before he sleeps
For fear of God, his tears flowing in streams;

30. By those who shave their pates, and all their lives
Apply themselves to suff'ring misery,
Who strike the clapper *(nâqûs)*[59] in their church, and chant,
About to worship Jesus, busily;[60]

31. I swear by Holy Mary *(Mârat Maryam)* and by Paul *(Bûlus)*,
I swear by Simon called the Rock *(Shimᶜûn al-Ṣafâ)*, and Peter *(Buṭrus)*,[61]
I swear by Daniel *(Dânîl)* and I swear by Jonah *(Yûnus)*,
Ezekiel *(Ḥizqîl)*, and by Jerusalem *(Bayt al-maqdis)*,

32. By Nineveh *(Nînawâ)*,[62] who once prayed to his Lord,
When he had purified his heart from evil,
Asking God's pardon, Who forgave his sin,
Obtaining from his father[63] what he wanted;

33. I swear by all the medicine that cures
A madman, in the flask of holy chrism *(mayrûn)*;[64]
By all the blessings of palm leaves and olives
That are reported in the deeds of Simon;[65]

---

59. Also "church-bell"; but normally in Muslim territory the Christians were forbidden the use of bells and employed clappers or rattles instead.
60. *mushamᶜilîn*: the verb, according to the dictionaries, means "to disperse", "to run swiftly"; al-Fîrûzâbâdî's *al-Qâmûs al-muḥîṭ* connects it with "the reciting [of the Holy text or prayers] of the Jews". Abû Nuwâs speaks of *shamᶜalat al-Naṣârâ* (al-Shâbushtî, *Diyârât*, p. 206) and verses of the Psalms sung *(mushamᶜal)* in various modes (Wagner, *Abū Nuwās*, p. 195).
61. *sic*.
62. Alluding to the story of Jonah, "Nineveh" apparently stands for "the people of Nineveh", but the syntax (verbs in 3rd person masculine singular) shows that the poet thought of a person rather than a collective.
63. Some sources have, instead of "his father", "God" or "his Lord".
64. Greek *múron*, Syriac *mûrûn*. Dâwûd al-Anṭâkî (*Tazyîn*, ii, 77) explains it as "hermit"; he is able to do so because he interprets *qulla* "flask" as "monk's cell" (apparently confusing it with *qilliyya*). Subsequently, however (ii, 79), he seems to understand it correctly.

34. And by the splendid feast days of the Cross *(ᶜîd al-ṣalîb)*,
The feast of Simon, and Breaking the Fast *(ᶜîd al-fiṭr)*,
And by the much-respected Palm Branch feast *(shaᶜânîn)*,
And that of the exalted Holy Mari *(Mar Mârî)*;[66]

35. And by Isaiah's *(Ashᶜayâ)* feast, and by the Temples *(al-hayâkil)*,[67]
And incense *(dukhun)* in the hands of pregnant women,
Which cures the madness of a lunatic
And every hidden sickness in the limbs;

36. And by the seventy of God's servants,[68] who
Spread God's religion in the several lands,
And guided people to the Guidance, so
That those who strayed were led upon the Path;

37. I swear by the twelve nations *(umam)*,[69] who departed
For different lands, reciting words of wisdom,
Until, when dawn had unveiled darkness, they
Went to their God and reached a blessed state;

38. And by the well-established Gospel text *(muḥkam al-Injîl)*
With interdictions and commandments firm,
And stories of exalted tidings, told

---

65. The allusion is not clear; it could refer to the story of Jesus in the house of Simon the leper, Matth. 26:6 ff. [GJR].
66. Mari is the apostle who is reputed to have brought Christianity to Parthia; cf. J.B. Abbeloos, *Acta Sancti Maris*, in *Analecta Bollandiana*, 4, Paris, 1885, pp. 43-138 [GJR].
67. *haykal* (Syriac *hayklâ*) may have the sense of "church" [GJR] or "chancel, place where the altar stands" (Graf, *Verzeichnis*, p. 117).
68. Obviously referring to the "seventy evangelists" mentioned in Luke 10:1, 17. The Nestorians had a feast devoted to them [GJR]. Dâwûd al-Anṭâkî (*Tazyîn*, ii, 80), however, identifies them as those chosen ones who ate from "the table". Either he is thinking of the story in St. Matthew 14 (The feeding of the five thousand), a version of which is also told in the Koran (the sura of al-Mâ'ida "The Table", 4:112-15), or he refers to the Last Supper.
69. Clearly referring to the twelve apostles. The choice of the word *umam* is odd; perhaps it alludes to the lands to which the apostles were assumed to be sent, or to the twelve tribes from which they were chosen; cf. F. Haase, *Apostel und Evangelisten in den orientalischen Überlieferungen*, Münster, 1922 [GJR].

By generation after generation;

39. I swear by Mark *(Murqus)*, the kind admonisher,
I swear by Luke *(Lûqâ)*, doer of pious deeds,
I swear by gentle John *(Yûḥannâ)*, the excellent,[70]
And all the martyrs on the barren plains;[71]

40. And by the baptism *(maᶜmûdiyya)* of spirits, and
The altar *(madhbaḥ)*, celebrated everywhere,
And those attending, dressed in coarse monk's frocks *(amsâḥ)*,
Worshipping God, while weeping and lamenting;

41. By your taking the Eucharist *(taqrîb)* on Sundays,
Your drinking wine as red as mulberry,
Your breaking[72] of the hearts, all of the time,
By means of the black pupils of your eyes;

42. And by Isaiah's *(Shaᶜyâ)* sanctifying Him,[73]
With praise of God, above all things transcendent,
And by Nestorius *(Nasṭûr)* and what he teaches
About the learned doctrines of the Law:

43. Two great authorities and men of learning,
Pillars of piety and gentleness,
Who never spoke without intelligence,
Whose death meant life to their antagonists;

44. And by the Bishop *(usquf)* and the Archbishop *(muṭrân)*,
And the most learned and most holy Primate *(jâthalîq)*;
I swear by Priest *(qass)* and Deacon *(shammâs)* and by Friar *(dayrânî)*,
By the great Patriarch *(baṭrak)* and all the monks *(ruhbân)*;

45. And by the hermit [prisoner? *maḥbûs*] on the mountain top,
And by Saint Nicholas *(Mâr Qûlâ)*, who humbly prayed;[74]

---

70. Among the variants of this stanza, some sources (Yâqût and al-Anṭâkî) have Mar ᶜAbdâ and "Yamlîkhâ the sage" for Mark and John, respectively.
71. The reference to these plains escapes me.
72. Reading *taqṭîᶜ* or *taftît*, found in other sources, instead of the unintelligible *tabyîḍ*.
73. The verse, not wholly clear, seems to refer to the *Sanctus*, based on Isa. 6:3.

I swear by the original old churches *(kanîsât)*
And by the bless'd Apostle,[75] for his works;

46. By incense *(bayram)*[76] and the bonnet of a novice *(usqûfiyâ),*[77]
And by the contents of the coif (?) of Mary;[78]
I swear by the most solemn and great Fast
And by all blessings[79] and all holy things;

---

74. Dâwûd al-Anṭâkî (*Tazyîn*, ii, 77) identifies the worshipper on the mountain as "the monk Nicholas *(al-râhib Niqûlâ)* who lived in Antioch in the church of al-Brtzfâ (?), and who was sent by Luke as a warner to the people of the dam (? *ahl al-sadd*). He was imprisoned on the mountain of the cloud *(jabal al-ghamâm)* by Isaiah (Shaᶜyâ') the Jew, who had him beaten to make him relinquish Christianity; but he refused. He died of hunger with the Armenians." Apparently he is Nicholas, the proselyte of Antioch mentioned in *Acts* 6:5. Mâr Qûlâ is identified by al-Anṭâkî as "the first patriarch after Luke; the one who divided the churches between the Armenians and the Greeks *(al-Rûm)*."
75. Reading, with T and A *salîḥ* instead of *salîm*. That Christ is meant is supported by the reading *masîḥ*, found in IḤ, Ḥ and YU; but possibly Christianity's missionary *par excellence*, St. Paul, is meant. Al-Anṭâkî, on the other hand, identifies the *salîḥ* as "a man appointed by Mâr Qûlâ in the Greek Church" (*Tazyîn*, ii, 77).
76. Dâwûd al-Anṭâkî (*Tazyîn*, ii, 77) explains it as "the attendant *(farrâsh)* of the monastery". According to al-Bustânî, *Muḥîṭ al-Muḥîṭ* s.v. *BYRM*: *bayram, bayramûn* or *bârâmûn*: a fast-day kept by some Christians on the eve of feast days such as Easter, Christmas, Epiphany; from the Greek *paramonê*? (cf. also Barthélemy, *Dictionnaire Arabe-Français*, p. 73, Graf, *Verzeichnis*, pp. 19, 28). But *bayram* is held in the hand of a worshipper, says a line by Abû Nuwâs (see Wagner, *Abū Nuwās*, p. 195), and a more likely solution seems "censer, incense", from Greek *púrôma*, found in Syriac, cf. Payne Smith, *Syriac-English Dictionary* s.v. *"pîromô"*, A. Schall, *Studien über griechischen Fremdwörter im Syrischen*, Darmstadt, 1960, pp. 88, 220. Graf lists it as *fayram* (*Verzeichnis*, p. 85) or *f.rym* (p. 84) in Arabic.
77. Thus according to the editor's note in T *(ṭâqat al-mubtadi')*; cf. Dozy, *Supplément*: "Bonnet de nuit". It would seem that the word, obviously non-Arabic, is related to *usquf*, "bishop", Greek *episkopos*, yet I have not been able to trace the connection or any other origin. To al-Anṭâkî it is merely a variant of *usquf*. Another derivation could be from Syriac *esqpâ*, from Greek *skúphos*, "beaker, lamp-bowl" [GJR].
78. *mighfar ra's Maryam*: the meaning is unclear; a variant has *mafriq* "parting". Al-Anṭâkî "explains" that Paul sacrificed one thousand heads [of sheep] for Mary's sake on the day she appeared in the Church of the Resurrection *(al-Qumâma*, the Muslim dysphemism for *al-Qiyâma)*, and prescribed a fast of fifteen days from the 15th of September.
79. Again reading *barka* as a variant of *baraka*. But al-Anṭâkî (*Tazyîn*, ii, 78) reads *birka* (lit. "pond, pool") and interprets it as the baptismal font, a meaning I have not found elsewhere.

47. And by the bright day of Epiphany *(al-dinḥ)*,[80]
By Christmas Eve *(laylat al-mîlâd)*, and by Ascension Day *(al-sullâq)*,
And by the sacrilege-removing gold (?),[81]
And Easter: you whose manners are refined

48. By going to one Mass *(quddâs)* after the other,
Which were by priest *(qass)* and deacon *(shammâs)* celebrated,
While handing out the Host on Maundy Thursday *(yawm al-khamîs al-nâsî)*,
And proffering the chalice to each drinker:

49. You shall[82] consent to please a well-bred man
Whose love has kept him far from his beloved,
Who melts from love for him who melts him down,
Whose utmost wish is but the least communion *(taqrîb)*.

50. Please mind me, my commander, mend my state,
And you may count upon a rich reward
From me, and earn my fitting gratitude
Expressed in prose, or else composed in verse.

---

80. Reading, with T, *dinḥ*, all other sources having *dhabḥ* "sacrifice".
81. *wa-'l-dhahabi al-mudhhibi li-'l-nifâqi*: the meaning is not wholly clear. For *nifâq*, see Graf, *Verzeichnis*, p. 113. The context of feasts suggests a connection with the feast of "Golden Friday" *(ᶜarûbtâ d-dahbâ)*, the first Friday after Whitsun [GJR].
82. Here, after the long series of introductory oath phrases ("[I swear] by"), begins their substance, itself introduced by the particle *illâ* (wrongly vowelled *alâ* in IS and Ḥ), like the poem by Abû Nuwâs (see above).

MANIFESTATIONS OF THE DIVINE AS REPRESENTED IN POEMS BY IBN AL-ᶜARABÎ

BY

PETER BACHMANN
Göttingen

I

According to Ibn al-ᶜArabî (1165-1240), whom Dr. Abû al-ᶜAlâ al-ᶜAfîfî appropriately qualified as the teacher of a "mystical philosophy"[1], there is in all created beings some aspiration, different in degree, for reunion with the creator. This aspiration, this craving is nourished by God Himself, He being the only one who really is active. In most men's minds, this aspiration is only a vague one. But, by an act of God's grace, some men - for example, *ṣûfî*s who have discipled their souls while proceeding on the rough mystical way -, are enabled to activate psychic energies inherent in them, to extend the effective range of their consciousness and to give it a definite direction. In brief, they turn towards God, they even encounter - not God, but divine manifestations[2].

This last statement sounds rather simple. But it needs commentaries, because "turning towards God" is - as we learn by some of those who experience it - far from being a simple procedure. On the other hand, for a *ṣûfî*, to encounter a manifestation of the divine, is the consummation devoutly to be wished, even though it is, as we shall see, somehow combined with death.

Now, Ibn al-ᶜArabî, himself a *ṣûfî*, styling himself - proudly and devoutly - as the Prophet Muḥammad's heir, feels impelled to make those who are not yet adepts of the *ṣûfî* art of life comprehend the perils as well as the glories waiting for those who turn (or, are made to turn) towards God. And since Ibn al-ᶜArabî is endowed with a fine sense of the beauty of the Arabic language, and is thoroughly versed in the Arabic poetic tradition, he makes use

---

1. A. E. Affifi, The Mystical Philosophy of Muhyid Din-Ibnul Arabi, Cambridge University Press 1939.
2. An excellent short introduction to Ibn al-ᶜArabî's doctrines is: Rom Landau, The Philosophy of Ibn ᶜArabî, London 1959 (Ethical and Religious Classics of East and West, 22).

of classical and post-classical forms of Arabic poetry when speaking about divine manifestations and *ṣûfî*s witnessing them. In doing so, he is evidently quite sure of the fact that, apart from the language of the Koran, it is the sound of poetic language which moves Arab listeners' feelings most deeply.

II

To give us an idea of how man may experience a divine manifestation, how man may get aware of encountering God, his beloved and loving Lord, Ibn al-ᶜArabî makes use of the preeminent classical form of Arabic poetry, the *qaṣîda* with its three connected parts, the *nasîb* (the hero halting at the effaced encampment where he once met his beloved), the *raḥîl* (the hero's prowess in traversing dangerous steppes or deserts on his way to his patron) and the *madîḥ* (the hero's eulogizing of his patron). Ibn al-ᶜArabî was not at all the first Arabic poet to find out the astonishing aptness of the *qaṣîda* form for conveying an idea of a (the) mystical experience. Remembrance of the beloved, setting out for a patron who only will be met after overcoming many dangers, finally the eulogy of that patron: all three parts of the classical *qaṣîda* could be taken advantage of to illustrate the mystical way to God, the external journey being changed into an internal one. Let us see, how Ibn al-ᶜArabî manages to convert the secular adventures of the classical *qaṣîda*'s hero into spiritual experiences witnessed by those keen on meeting a patron more than secular. He says[3]:

> Verily, the effaced traces of the encampment are the places haunted by the lovers:
> *inna ṭ-ṭulûla d-dârisâti maᶜâhidu al-aḥbâbî.*

The mention of the effaced traces of the encampment haunted by the lovers is an outset strongly reminiscent of the beginnings of many secular *qaṣîda*s. But contrary to our expectations, there is here no lover speaking of his beloved, no poetic Ego speaking of his love, but instead of it a - as it were - detached poet speaking of the lovers in a general way, a manner of communication colouring these lines, as we shall see, with a didactic hue.

3. Arabic text in manuscript no. 7747 (Pet. 281), fol. 3 r., of W. Ahlwardt's Catalogue (Die Handschriften-Verzeichnisse der Königlichen Bibliothek zu Berlin. Neunzehnter Band. Verzeichniss der arabischen Handschriften ... Siebenter Band, Berlin 1895).

No one shall weep at the material marks of the traces except those who are people of insight:
lâ yabkianna bi-rasmihâ illâ dhawî al-albâbî.

By what Ibn al-ᶜArabî tells us about them in the following lines we learn that people of insight are those who are able to discern that the deserted encampment is a material sign, a symbol of the transitoriness of this world in general, and that, consequently, men are in utmost need of a (the) generous patron, *al-wahhâb*, the One who can grant stability, durability:

They set out because they wanted (to reach) the stable position in the (divine) presence of the Donor:
raḥalû yurîdûna al-muqâma bi-ḥaḍrati al-wahhâbî.

This *raḥîl* part differs from corresponding parts of the secular *qaṣîda*s in that the dangers which the heroes have to overcome en route are to be found not far away from the patron but, on the contrary, in the patron's close proximity, even in the patron's very presence. So, the *raḥîl* part, as will be seen, merges in a peculiar kind of *madîḥ*.

The heroes of this *qaṣîda* want to reach *al-muqâm*, the stable position in the divine presence (*ḥaḍra*, a *ṣûfî* term) of the Donor (*al-wahhâb*, being a koranic qualification of God). But what they aspire is not easily gained:

They clang to His door full with longing, (showing) fine specimens
of (all kinds of) refined (*ṣûfî*) culture:
lazimû 'shtiyâqan bâbahû bi-maḥâsini al-âdâbî.

They are rewarded by the signs of His grace:
So, His signs appeared to them from behind that door:
fa-badat lahum aᶜlâmuhû min khalfi dhâka al-bâbî[4].

"From behind that door": like lovers in secular poetry, besieging the beloved's door, the *ṣûfî*s cling to God's entrance, God being their patron and their beloved. The closed door, a sign of separation, begins to prove perme-

4. The manuscript has *aᶜlâmuhum*, which is to be changed, here, into *aᶜlâmuhu*, as it is written in the Berlin manuscript Spr. 1108 (Ahlwardt's Catalogue, no. 7746), fol. 13 r.

able, for His signs (*a^c^lâmuhû*) from behind that door are seen outside of it. Still, there remains that door between Him and them, between *al-ḥaqq* and *al-khalq*. - But the appearance of His signs is a prelude to a far more momentuous experience:

> And He appeared to them without curtains and curtain-keepers:
> *fa-badâ lahum min ghayri mâ ḥujubin wa-lâ ḥujjâbî.*

Now, the *ṣûfî*s are in a situation of utter precariousness. Do they experience God Himself? We have got, here, to the crucial point of the poem, its very heart. What appears, here, is God manifest, but not God essential. When he appears (*badâ*), it is only (pardon for that "only"!) an aspect of Him which can be "seen" directly. The consequences of the sight of this aspect of Him are serious enough:

> Hence, (God's) Majesty seized the perception of their material components by force, without return:
> *fa-maḍâ al-jalâlu bi-rasmihim ^c^izzan bi-ghayri iyâbî.*

A certain aspect of God, His lordly majesty, seizes - what? The exact meaning of *rasm*, here and in the next verse, is difficult to define. *Rasm*, here, is related to *rasm* in verse 2 as meaning something material. But, since the journey (the *riḥla*) which Ibn al-^c^Arabî sketches in his lines is a series of experiences witnessed by the travellers' minds, their *rasm* cannot mean simply their material, physical components, but *rasm* could hint, here, at their awareness of, their perception of those material components. Taking *rasm* in this sense, we could understand this verse as a statement of the overwhelming force of God's majesty conveying the experience of being - momentarily, as we shall see - "out of the body". And what is *bi-ghayri iyâbî*, without return? Since they, indeed, regain the perception of their material components, as Ibn al-^c^Arabî states in his next verse, he can only mean, here, by "without return"- "without return from God in His aspect as the Majestic One", or, in other words: without regaining perception of their material being as long as they are exposed to the effect of encountering God as the Majestic One. The duration of that experience may be, in their eyes, very long, in the eyes of the children of this world, an instant only. We might better say, since they experience a being out of the body, they should, at the same instant, experience a being out of time. Hence their impression that the perception of their bodily being is gone without return, for good.

But Ibn al-[c]Arabî's quite koranic God is conceived of (by men) as being made up of apparently incompatible, but in Him complementary aspects. So, His overwhelming majesty (*jalâl*) is counterbalanced by His gentle beauty (*jamâl*):

> (But His) beauty gave back to them the perception of their material components, so that they could see Him (or, His beauty) behind a curtain:
> *radda al-jamâlu rusûmahum, fa-ra'awhu khalfa ḥijâbî.*

Beauty, *jamâl*, is a divine aspect opposite to the aspect of majesty, *jalâl*, in that respect, too, that, to behold beauty, presupposes to be provided with the sense of perception of something perceived as bodily ("behind a curtain": in a way, indirectly, conveyed materially). God's beauty (related, as it were, to His compassion, *raḥma*) saves them (as bodily beings) from the overriding force of God's majesty (related, as it were, to His being the Lord, *ar-rabb*). Directly encountering the majesty of the Lord ("without curtains") is, as an experience of being out of the body and out of time, an annihilation of - at least of the consciousness of the individual himself.

> And it was as if that which annihilated them had been a lightning
> and the flash of a mirage:
> *fa-ka'anna mâ afnâhumû barqun wa-lam[c]u sarâbî.*

Only after having witnessed the crucial moment of an experience of physical non-being (*al-fanâ'*), the *ṣûfî* will be blessed by meeting his beautiful and compassionate lord in some bodily manner, experiencing aspects of his God, not God Himself, who remains "behind the curtain".The same *ṣûfî*s are blessed, too, by hearing God addressing them as his dear guests:

> He called for them in His (manner of) speaking with "Be welcome, feel at home!":
> *nâdâhumû bi-kalâmihî bi-'l-ahli wa-'l-tarḥâbî.*

Hearing God speaking to them "in His manner of speaking" after having seen Him in his beauty means a doubled bliss, further enhanced by the friendliness of God's address. Therefore:

> They were in ecstasies over what they (had) heard, for they had got drunk without wine:
> *ṭaribû bi-mâ sami[c]û, fa-hum sakrâ bi-ghayri sharâbî.*

They were in ecstasies. Yet they were still they, and God God, whatsoever had been the exact nature of what had happened to them.

By the poet's insisting on the extreme danger inherent in their decisive experience (*maḍâ al-jâlâlu bi-rasmihim ᶜizzan bi-ghayri iyâbî*, and: *mâ afnâhumû*) a - at first sight - rather straightforward sketch of the mystical experience is rendered enigmatic: we cannot forget God as *dhû al-jalâl wa-'l-ᶜizz*, the rex tremendae maiestatis, when finally listening to the friendly welcome of God receiving His dear guests like a benevolent father of a family.

III

Having listened to a single melody, we now turn to counterpoint. To describe the erotic relationship of the creatures to their creator, Ibn al-ᶜArabî, like *ṣûfî* poets before him, draws on the specific procedures of Arabic erotic poetry, not only in its classical forms, but making use of the tuneful strophic forms of the *muwashshaḥ*, too. I am going to quote the text of one *muwashshaḥ* in its entirety[5], trying to translate its lines, which abound in motives of secular poetry, interwoven with spiritual *ṣûfî* terms:

sarâ'iru al-aᶜyân lâḥat ᶜalâ al-akwân li-'l-nâẓirîn,
wa-'l-ᶜâshiqu al-ghayrân min dhâka fî buḥrân yubdî al-anîn:

The thrones (or: mysteries) of the stable beings appeared over the ephemeral things for those who are endowed with the gift of perception (namely, perceiving that the world of the stable - incorruptible - ideas is higher than, but in continuous contact with, the world of growing and decay), and the jealous lover is, because of that, in a crisis, moaning (jealous, because aspiring to the vision of his God, his beloved, but discovering that the world of divine ideas, his well-guarded spiritual property, is combined in an inseparable manner with transient things open to the public):

yaqûlu, wa-'l-wajdu aḍnâhu, wa-'l-buᶜdu qad ḥayyarah:
lammâ danâ al-buᶜdu, lam adri min baᶜdu man ghayyarah, -

5. Dîwân Ibn ᶜArabî, printed at Bûlâq, 1271/1855, p. 85. - I relied upon the text as given in volume 2 of al-Maqqarî's Nafḥ aṭ-ṭîb, ed. Iḥsân ᶜAbbâs, Beirut 1388/1968, p. 181.

he says, and love's ecstasy had emaciated him, and the remoteness (of the object of his desire) had confused him (because he had previously thought of his God as a remote lord, out of reach):
After remoteness has drawn near (become proximity - hinting at his (ecstatic) experience during which he witnessed eternal ideas being united with transient beings), I did not know after that who changed it (he was not sure whether it was by his efforts, or by means of an external agent, that he witnessed the remote divine world to be so near as to be felt even in combination with perishable things);
wa-huyyima al-ᶜabdu, wa-'l-wâḥidu al-fardu qad khayyarah
fî-'l-bawḥi wa-'l-kitmân was-sirri wa-'l-iᶜlân fî-'l-ᶜâlamîn:
"Anâ huwa al-dayyân, yâ ᶜâbida al-awthân, anta al-ḍanîn":
And the servant was misled (because he thought that his lord, being his beloved, was quite near to him), after the Unique One, the Incomparable (God in his essential remoteness again) had let him choose between announcement and secrecy, between hiding and promulgation among the inhabitants of this world (making them, or not making them his confidants as to his experience that fleeting things are connected with stable ones, the latter being more evident manifestations of the divine; but God cautions his loving creature(s) against drawing premature conclusions concerning God's immanence in his creatures, saying:) 'I am the Judge! O admirer of idols, you are the avaricious one.' (That is, I am peerless , weal and woe depends on Me, dont't believe that by admiring material beauty (created beings) you could revere Me. Don't be niggardly in clinging to physical beauty only, but open your soul in a generous way to a divine influence which is beyond material beauty, although united with it.)

In the second strophe of his muwashshaḥ, Ibn al-ᶜArabî, still playing the part of the wise shaikh, expounds how difficult it is to accept that a curtain (material being) separates us from our divine love, and that loving beautiful material beings is not a shortened way leading smoothly into God's proximity. So, the beloved keeping away, God-loving man is left alone with his lamentations:

kullu al-hawâ ṣaᶜbu ᶜalâ 'lladhî yashkû dhulla al-ḥijâb:
All love is difficult for those who complain of the humiliation by the curtain (material being);
yâ man lahû qalbu, law annahû yadhkû ᶜinda al-shabâb,
qarrabahû al-rabbu! Lakinnahû ifku, fa-nwi al-matâb:
O he who has got a (feeling) heart, if it would flare up in the presence of young people, then, the Lord would draw him near to Himself.-

But that is a lie, so make up your mind to repent;
wa-nâdi: yâ raḥmân, yâ barru, yâ mannân, innî ḥazîn,
*aḍnâniya al-hijrân wa-lâ ḥabîbun dân wa-lâ mu*ᶜ*în:*
and exclaim: O Merciful, o Righteous, o Gracious, verily, I am distressed, the (that is, your) keeping away emaciated me, and there is no beloved one near to me, and no one who might help me.

In the next strophe, Ibn al-ᶜArabî, apparently, is speaking about an experience of his own. He threw all his emphasis on transcending the borders of materiality in order to witness a merging in God - but in vain:

fanîtu bi-'llâhi ᶜ*ammâ tarâhu al-*ᶜ*ayn min kawnihî*:
I was annihilated by (the force of) God (he says: *fanîtu bi-'llâhi*, not: *fî-'llâhi*, which is the usual expression), separated from (all) that the eye beholds of His (God's created) perishable beings;
fî mawqifi al-jâhi, wa-ṣiḥtu: ayna al-ayn min baynihî?
(and that happened to me) at the halting-place of dignity (he felt dignified with the quality of being united with God), and (so) I cried out: 'Where is the exhaustion (*al-ain*) resulting from being separated from Him?' (Or: 'Where is the Where, i. e. the intermediate space, separating me from Him'? -

I do not doubt that Ibn al-ᶜArabî makes use, here, of the double meaning of *al-ayn*. Furthermore, if we take the question "Where is the *ayn* of *baynihi*?" quite literally, subtracting *ayn* from *baynihi*, we get bihî: thus, Ibn al-ᶜArabî may hint at the speaker's conviction that there is no longer any interstice separating him from God, but that he is *bihî*, directly connected with God, in Him.)

fa-qâla: yâ sâhî, ᶜ*âyanta qaṭṭu* ᶜ*ayn bi-*ᶜ*aynihî?*
But He (God, or he, the Interstice, with lisân al-ḥâl?) said (to me): 'O you inattentive man, did you ever behold an idea with His eye?' (Or: 'Did you ever behold an eye [of a beloved person] with His eye?';

that is, you remain dependent upon conditions proper to creatures partaking of the gross material share of existence which hinder them from totally, wholeheartedly concentrating their attention on the person they love. Notwithstanding their personal belief to be wholly attracted by their beloved, they remain "inattentive" since they cannot completely transcend their personality, and that means: their egotism. Therefore Ibn al-[c]Arabî goes on in a somehow didactic manner:)

a-mâ tarâ Ghaylân wa-Qaysa, aw man kân fî-'l-ghâbirîn:
Don't you see Ghaylân (that is, the poet Dû r-Rumma, lover of Mayya) and Qays (presumably Ibn al-Mulawwaḥ, the poet who loved Laylâ) or whoever was among the (loving poets) of bygone times;
qâlû: al-hawâ sulṭân, in ḥalla bi-'l-insân afnâhu dîn:
They said: Love is an absolute ruler: if he settles down in a person, that person shall be annihilated by a *dîn* (meaning: a religion, something like a cult of Love, or: an illness):

according to what those poets stated, love, in this world, culminates in *al-fanâ'*, manifesting itself in the lover's body like an illness, dealing with it like a grandseigneur (*sulṭân*). Yet, that *fanâ'* is evidently not what Ibn al-[c]Arabî set his mind on, for he continues:

kam marratin qâlâ: anâ 'lladhî ahwâ! man hû anâ?
How often did he (the love-poet) say: 'I am the one who is in love'. But who is "I"?

Putting forward this all-decisive question, Ibn al-[c]Arabî shows that even those singers of ardent love are not entitled to speak about *al-fanâ'*, since they said - and said more than once: "I am the one who is in love". But who is "I", or: who is authorized to speak of himself as "I"? On the one hand, the individual person who, far from transcending the borders of his individuality, is confined to his consciousness of his being himself. On the other hand, he who may speak of "I" on his own authority is God Almighty. *Al-fanâ'*, when taken in the full depth of its meaning, the effect of a divine manifestation on the mystic who is witnessing it, is a throughout ambiguous experience, bringing about a kind of life which is, however we may understand that, more than life as we know it, but connected with a kind of reduced personal existence akin to death (*mors mystica*). It is because of this ambiguity that the *ṣûfî*, longing for God's manifestation, craves for *al-fanâ'* and fears it:

fa-lâ arâ ḥâlâ, wa-lâ arâ shakwâ illâ al-fanâ:
For, in my opinion, there is no ecstasy and no complaint except (because of) annihilation.

Lastu ka-man mâlâ ᶜani 'lladhî yahwâ baᶜda al-janâ
wa-dâna bi-'l-sulwân. hâdhâ huwa al-buhtân li-'l-ᶜârifîn:
salûhumû mâ kân ᶜan ḥaḍrati al-raḥmân wa-'l-âfikîn:

I am not like the man who turned away from the person he loves after he picked the fruits, and (then) sought comfort in oblivion (*dâna bi-'l-sulwân*, instead of *dâna bi-'l-shukr*, "owed him thanks"!). That means slandering those who have knowledge (of God, those who, like the speaker, have witnessed the manifestation of their Beloved, and remain grateful as long as they live). Ask them what happened resulting from the presence of the Merciful and the liars (apparently, the Merciful changed into the Revengeful?).

In the concluding strophe of his *muwashshaḥ*, Ibn al-ᶜArabî, speaking of himself, gives the outlines of his experience of a divine manifestation, stressing the fact that he felt admitted - not to God, but into the park of intimacy, obviously near to God, a park the splendours of which he enjoys with all his senses, retaining the perception of his body, and thus being separated from the supramundane sphere the perfume of which he is allowed to smell:

dakhaltu fî bustân al-unsi wa-'l-qurbi ka-maknisih:
I entered the park of intimacy and proximity, as if it were His hiding-place;
fa-qâma lî al-rayḥân yakhtâlu bi-'l-ᶜujbi fî sundusih:
there, the sweet basil rose in honour of me, strutting about in his conceit, clad in his silk brocade (, and he said):
anâ hû, yâ insân, muṭayyibu al-ṣabbî fî majlisih:
I am the one, o you human being, who perfumes the ardent lover in His session room.

The next two lines are obviously spoken by the person who entered the park of intimacy and is satisfied when staying there, quasi in the antechamber. He says:

Jannânu, yâ jannân, ijni mina al-bustân al-yâsamîn,
wa-ḥallili r-rayḥân, bi-ḥurmati raḥmân, li-'l-ᶜâshiqîn!:
Gardener, o gardener, gather from the park the jasmine,
and, respecting the sacrosanctity of the Merciful, let be allowed the sweet basil (as a gift) for the lovers!

The sweet basil shall be made *ḥalâl*, allowed in the sense of the religious law, whereas the Merciful Himself, and even in His aspect of the Merciful, not the Lord of the Majesty, shall be respected in His *ḥurma*, that is, he shall remain inaccessible (*ḥarâm*) even for those who love none but Him.

IV

None but Him: In one of the longer *qaṣîda*s collected in Ibn al-ᶜArabî's "*Dîwân*"[6], a God-seeking man, yearning for being united with God, is made to exclaim:

> I do not want anything except my God ... I do not want to be united with anyone except God
> (*wa-anâ mâ urîdu illâ ilâhî ... lâ urîdu 'ttiṣâlâ bi-siwâ 'llâhi ...*).

The double employment of the verb *urîdu* reminds us of the God-seeking *ṣûfî*s described in the first poem which I commented on, where Ibn al-ᶜArabî said of them:

> *raḥalû yurîdûna al-muqâma bi-ḥaḍrati al-wahhâbî,*
> and the stress laid on the "I" in "*wa-anâ mâ urîdu illâ ilâhî*" recalls to our minds the crucial question of Ibn al-ᶜArabî's *muwashshaḥ: man hû anâ*?

In that *qaṣîda* from which I quoted the God-seeker's exclamation, Ibn al-ᶜArabî makes demands on his listeners' discursive faculties when qualifying human volition generally as an inappropriate means to reach God's proximity. For those endowed with the gift of vision, this created world abounds in divine manifestations, God Himself wisely hiding behind them, - let us remember Ibn al-ᶜArabî's hint of the ghastly experience of momentary death resulting from witnessing directly God's majesty.

Even unsuspecting men may lose their lives in too direct an encounter with God. In Sûrat an-Nûr, soon after that famous verse qualifying God as the light of the heavens and the earth, we hear (v. 39) of a mirage in a plain in the desert, and of a thirsty man who supposes that the mirage is real water, till, having come near to it,

---

6. Dîwân Ibn ᶜArabî, p. 474.

he found that it was nothing. But he found God at (the mirage), and (God) presented to him his complete account:
ka-sarâbin bi-qîᶜatin yaḥsabuhu al-ẓam'ânu mâ'an ḥattâ idhâ jâ'ahu lam yajidhu shay'an wa-wajada 'llâha ᶜindahu fa-waffâhu ḥisâbahu.

Ibn al-ᶜArabî makes use of this koranic example (the Koran, as we may expect, being the background-text of his poetry) in a *qaṣîda* of his "*Dîwân*"[7]. He says:

A person becoming immersed in the mirage, said: (Here I have) cold water! - Then, after he came to it (the apparent water), he found only a nothingness resulting, but it was indeed a mirage. Ignorance is proven to be first here, then there (that is, the thirsty man proved to be ignorant when assuming the mirage to be water, and he proved to be ignorant, too, when believing that the mirage was just nothing), and the ignorant man gained evil consequences. He found God at it, so God sufficed him", - sufficed him, but how?

We learn from the 328th chapter of Ibn al-ᶜArabî's "*Futûḥât*" (Bûlâq edition, vol. 3, p. 105) that he takes the koranic "*wa-wajada 'llâha ᶜindahu*" as dependent on the expression "*lam yajidhu shay'an*", hence he is of the opinion that the thirsty man found God at a nothingness (*ᶜinda lâ shay'in*) for, as he states, no thing is like Him. So, God suffices him (Ibn al-ᶜArabî replaces the koranic "*waffâhu ḥisâbahu*" by "*kafâhu*") when teaching him that God is not just nothingness, but - we have to bear in mind every shade of Ibn al-ᶜArabî's careful wording - a nothingness resulting, "*ᶜadam ḥâṣil*", an experienced nothingness, or nothingness experienced as resulting from something, hence being in itself something, if but a mirage. - The verses under discussion run thus in the original:

...fa-qâla shakhîṣun ghâṭisun fî-'l-sarâbî : mâ'an zulâlâ!
thumma, lammâ atâhu, lam yulfi illâ ᶜadaman ḥâṣilan, wa-qad kâna âlâ.
yathbutu al-jahlu hâhunâ, thumma ayḍan hâhunâ, wa-'l jahûlu nâla al-wabâlâ:
wajada 'llâha ᶜindahû, fa-kafâhu ...

Fa-kafâhu, "so God sufficed him". Ibn al-ᶜArabî states that almost bluntly, altering, in what he must have thought an expedient manner, the wording and meaning of his koranic prototype. Thus, he can show his God teaching

7. Dîwân Ibn ᶜArabî, p. 473.

a severe lesson: instead of the water which the thirsty man was looking for and which could have saved his life, he finds a nothingness resulting from the evading image of water, and at that nothingness which underlies imagined (supposed) being, namely water, at that nothingness which will take his life he finds God.

We scarcely can speak of a divine manifestation here, at least not in the proper sense of the word. The experience of God's "resulting nothingness" is complementary of the experience of God's abundant plenty of being as witnessed in the overwhelming manifestation of His divine majesty: both experiences can be, as Ibn al-ᶜArabî points out, perilous, for, to conclude with God's own words (Sûra 4, verse 28): *khuliqa al-insânu ḍaᶜîfan*, notwithstanding all his faculties, among them his ability to experience and describe divine manifestations, man was created as a frail being, but: *khuliqa*, was created by God.

THE EXPERIENCE OF THE DIVINE IN THE POETRY OF THE EGYPTIAN SUFI POET ᶜUMAR IBN AL-FÂRIḌ (576/1181-632/1235)

BY

GIUSEPPE SCATTOLIN
PISAI-Roma

Introduction

1. The Poet and His Mystery

"Pass by the cemetery at the foot of al-ᶜÂriḍ,
Say: Peace upon you, Ibn al-Fâriḍ!
You have shown in your 'Order of the Way' marvels
and revealed a deep, well-guarded mystery.
You have drunk from the cup of love and friendship,
and quaffed from a bounteous, unlimited Ocean".[1]

These verses were written for the shrine (*ḍarîḥ*) of ᶜUmar Ibn al-Fâriḍ, the well-known Egyptian Sufi poet (576/1181-632/1235), by his grandson ᶜAlî *sibṭ* Ibn al-Fâriḍ (d. 735/1335), a century after the poet's death. Ibn al-Fâriḍ's shrine is located in a pleasant site at the foot of al-Muqaṭṭam, a mountain chain East of Cairo, and remains, up to the present day, a favourite center for the poet's devotees, particularly on his feast day (*mawlid*). ᶜUmar Ibn al-Fâriḍ, known in Arabic literature by the exalted title of "the Prince of lovers" (*sulṭân al-ᶜâshiqîn*), has always enjoyed large popularity in Sufi circles and outside them. Ibn al-Fâriḍ's grandson through his daughter (in Arabic *sibṭ*, therefore called in the sources ᶜAlî, *sibṭ* Ibn al-Fâriḍ), hints in his verses at 'a deep, well-guarded mystery' that surrounded the poet's life and still lingers on in his beautiful Sufi poems.

Perhaps attracted by such fascinating charm, many ancient commentators as well as modern scholars have tried to unravel and decipher the mystery of Ibn al-Fâriḍ's mystical experience. Among the most famous ancient commentators are: Saᶜîd al-Dîn al-Farghânî (d. 699/1300), ᶜAbd al-

1. ᶜAbd al-Khâliq Maḥmûd ᶜAbd al-Khâliq, *Dîwân Ibn al-Fâriḍ* (Cairo: Dâr al-Maᶜârif, 1984) p. 25. The verses are quoted from this edition.

Razzâq al-Kâshânî (d. 730/1330), Badr al-Dîn al-Bûrînî (d. 1024/1615) and ᶜAbd al-Ghanî al-Nâbulusî (d. 1143/1731). While among the modern scholars are: Ignazio Di Matteo (d. 1948) and Carlo Alfonso Nallino (d. 1938) in Italy; Reynold Alleyne Nicholson (d. 1945) and Arthur John Arberry (d. 1973) in Britain; Emile Demerghem and Louis Gardet (d. 1986) in France; Issa J. Boullata and Thomas Emil Homerin in the United States, and Muḥammad Muṣṭafâ Ḥilmî, ᶜÂṭif Naṣr Jawdat and ᶜAbd al-Khâliq Maḥmûd ᶜAbd al-Khâliq in Egypt.[2]

Research on Ibn al-Fâriḍ, however, has proved to be a complicated problem for a number of reasons. Firstly, there is very little trustworthy data about his life in the biographical sources. Secondly, apart from his collection of poems *(dîwân)*, no other work of the poet has come down to us and very little is known concerning his teachers and Sufi acquaintances. Thirdly, Ibn al-Fâriḍ's poetical language is a challenging test for any reader, so highly enigmatic that Nallino confessed that it was "a continuous puzzle" for him, Nicholson that "it intended to put to test the cleverness of any reader", and Arberry found it to be "a particularly stubborn problem" [3]

2. The Poet and His Work: a New Picture.

The traditional picture of Ibn al-Fâriḍ has been drawn from information found in early biographical sources.[4] From these sources we know that Ibn al-Fâriḍ was born in Cairo on the 4th of Dhû al-Qaᶜda 576/22nd March 1181, and that he passed in Cairo most of his life, except for a period, probably between 613/1216-628/1231, during which he stayed in Mecca, following an accepted Sufi custom. After his return to Cairo, Ibn al-Fâriḍ lived near al-Azhar mosque, away from public attention, until he passed

---

2. For a complete bibliography on Ibn al-Fâriḍ see Thomas Emil Homerin, *From Arab Poet to Muslim Saint: Ibn al-Fâriḍ, His Verse and His Shrine*, (Columbia, USA: University of South Carolina Press, 1994); Giuseppe Scattolin, "*More on Ibn al-Fâriḍ's Biography*" in *MIDEO* 22 (1994) pp. 202-245.
3. Carlo Alfonso Nallino, "*Il poema mistico di Ibn al-Fâriḍ in una recente traduzione italiana*", in *Raccolta di scritti editi ed inediti* (Rome: Istituto per l'Oriente, 1940) vol. II p 193; Reynold Alleyne Nicholson, "*The Odes of Ibnu'l-Fariḍ*", in *Studies in Islamic Mysticism* (Cambridge: University Press, 1921, repr. 1989) p. 166; ARTHUR JOHN ARBERRY, *The Poem of the Way*, in *Chester Beatty Monographs No. 5* (London: Emery Walker, 1952) p. 7.
4. For more information on Ibn al-Fâriḍ's life, see Homerin, *From Arab Poet to Muslim Saint* pp. 13-54; Scattolin, "*More*" pp. 220-230.

away on the 2nd of Jumâdâ al-Ûlâ 632/23th January 1235, according to the most reliable reports.

It was during his last years that the poet completed and dictated his collection of poems, his *dîwân*. This *dîwân* was edited a century later (around 733/1333) by his grandson, ᶜAlî *sibṭ* Ibn al-Fâriḍ, who, in line with an Arabic literary tradition, wrote a biographical introduction, called *dîbâja*, which literary means 'silk embroidery or ornament'.[5] ᶜAlî's biographical account is so full of supernatural events that the poet's life seems to have been nothing but an uninterrupted series of miracles, visions and ecstasies. Up to now, this has been the most popular and accepted picture of the poet in Sufi and literary circles.

Now, however, new insight of the poet's life has been offered by some Western scholars, particularly by Issa J. Boullata, Th. E. Homerin and G. Scattolin, who have adopted a more critical approach to those biographical sources.[6] These studies have put into question the picture given by the poet's grandson and have focused on Ibn al-Fâriḍ's changing image in time. Earliest sources show that Ibn al-Fâriḍ was perceived first of all as an outstanding poet. It was his grandson that, a century later, magnified and idealized his grandfather's image turning him into a saint (*walî*) endowed with extraordinary powers. In following centuries, Ibn al-Fâriḍ continued to be highly venerated as a powerful local saint and his shrine played an important role in Egyptian history, especially during the Mamluk and Ottoman periods. Nevertheless, after Ibn Taymîya's (d. 728/1328) attacks on Sufis such as Ibn ᶜArabî (d. 638/1240), Ibn al-Fâriḍ became the target of heated disputes concerning his orthodoxy. In modern times there has been a sharp decline in the cult around him, even as his poems have continued to be a source of inspiration for Sufis as well as for some modern writers, e.g. Naguib Maḥfûẓ.

Our knowledge of Ibn al-Fâriḍ's *dîwân*, the only sure written document we have from the poet, has also greatly improved in recent time through newly found manuscripts. Three are the main recensions of Ibn al-Fâriḍ's *dîwân*'s.

---

5. Little is known about ᶜAlî *sibṭ* Ibn al-Fâriḍ (d. ca. 735/1335) except for what he says of himself in his *dîbâja*, namely that he was a *shaykh* of a mosque in Cairo. His *dîbâja* is often found at the beginning of the editions of the *dîwân*: see *Dîwân* (ed. ᶜAbd al-Khâliq) pp. 19-44.
6. Issa J. Boullata, "*Toward a Biography of Ibn al-Fâriḍ (576-632 AH/1181-1235 AD)*" in *Arabica* 28/1 (1981) pp. 38-56; Homerin, *From Arab Poet* pp. 13-54; Scattolin, "*More*" pp. 197-220.

a. The *textus receptus*. This is the recension worked out by the poet's grandson, ᶜAlî *sibṭ* Ibn al-Fâriḍ, around 733/1333, according to his own account.[7] With some variations and additions, this has been the commonly accepted, copied and printed text of Ibn al-Fâriḍ's *dîwân* up to the present day.[8] It consists of twenty seven odes (*qaṣîda*), thirty couplets (*dûbayt*), nineteen riddles (*alghâz*) and a number of isolated verses, in all around 1785 verses.

b. The Chester Beatty manuscript. In the fifties Arthur J. Arberry, published a manuscript he found in the Chester Beatty Collection in Dublin. Due to its 'exceptional importance', as he says, Arberry had it published *in toto*, as it stood, including mistakes, then translated it into English.[9] From the colophon we know that the manuscript was copied in Malaṭiyâ, an important town in eastern Anatolia, in 691/1292, i. e. about forty years before ᶜAlî's recension. The copyist states to have been quite accurate in his work and that he could have access to some copies of Ibn al-Fâriḍ's *dîwân* of "unparalleled accuracy", as he says. Arberry pointed to the striking difference that exists between ᶜAlî's recension and Chester Beatty manuscript: this last lists only fifteen odes, arranged in alphabetical order according to their rhymes, instead of the twenty seven odes of ᶜAlî's recension. From such evidence Arberry could conclude: "We are left with these fourteen [fifteen, with the *Tâ'îya kubrâ*, n.r.] odes, as constituting the genuine and indisputable core of the corpus......future researchers will be well advised to consider attentively the evidence furnished by the Chester Beatty manuscript as to the state of the text towards the end of the thirteen century".[10] Arberry's advice, however, has not been taken into account in the later editions of the *dîwân*.

---

7. *Dîwân* (ed. ᶜabd al-Khâliq), pp. 21.225.
8. Also the last edition of Ibn al-Fâriḍ's *dîwân* worked out by ᶜAbd al-Khâliq Maḥmûd ᶜAbd al-Khâliq (Cairo, 1984) is based on a number of manuscripts, all depending on ᶜAlî's recension.
9. A. J. Arberry, *The Mystical Poems of Ibn al-Fâriḍ,* edited in transcription from the oldest extant manuscript in the Chester Beatty Collection *Chester Beatty Monographs No. 4* (London: E. Walker, 1952); id., *The Poem of the Way*, translated into English verse, in *Chester Beatty Monographs No. 5* (London: Emery Walker, 1952); id., *The Mystical Poems of Ibn al-Fâriḍ,* translated and annotated, in *Chester Beatty Monographs No. 6* (Dublin: Emery Walker, 1956), see especially Arberry's introductions.
10. Arberry, *The Mystical Poems* (1956) p. 6.

c. New manuscript evidence. Arberry's hypothesis has been recently confirmed by another manuscript I happened to found, almost by chance, in Konya (Turkey). A detailed account of it will be provided in future. This manuscript seems to be even older than that of Chester Beatty Collection, since it was probably copied, as far as I can conjecture, in Ṣadr al-Dîn al-Qûnawî's Sufi circles of Konya between 640/1242 and 651/1253, i. e. forty years before that Chester Beatty Collection. So, all the more interesting is the fact that this very old manuscript agrees with that of Chester Beatty Collection in listing the same number of odes, i.e. fifteen, though not in alphabetical order as this latter. However, it confirms Arberry's hypothesis that these fifteen odes constituted "the genuine and indisputable core of the corpus" of Ibn al-Fâriḍ's *dîwân*. This new evidence also proves that, contrary to what people thought in the past, Ibn al-Fâriḍ's *dîwân* had already spread in the Islamic world well before ᶜAlî *sibṭ* Ibn al-Fâriḍ's recension. On the whole, it seems that the question of Ibn al-Fâriḍ's *dîwân* has not yet been completely settled and new evidence may still lay ahead.

3. A Semantic Analysis of al-Tâ'îyat al-Kubrâ.

Interpreting Ibn al-Fâriḍ's mystical experience has always been an intricate problem. Ancient commentators, followed in this by many modern scholars, have often interpreted Ibn al-Fâriḍ's verses in light of Ibn ᶜArabî's philosophical Sufism, i. e. in a monistic vision of being, called in Arabic *waḥdat al-wujûd* (oneness of existence). Such monistic interpretation has also often drawn upon Ibn al-Fâriḍ the condemnation of orthodox Islamic authorities.

I thought, however, that a better approach to a difficult text such as that of Ibn al-Fâriḍ's poem would be to try to understand the meaning of its terms in their poetical context, or, in other words, to explain, as far as possible, 'the text through the text itself', before resorting to any 'foreign' interpretation or explanation. To this purpose a semantic approach to the text seemed to me to be the most suitable, as it help a great deal in grasping the meaning terms have in their context. On this basis, I carried out a semantic analysis of Ibn al-Fâriḍ's great poem, *Naẓm al-sulûk* (i.e. *The Order of the Way*), commonly known as *al-Tâ'îyat al-kubrâ* (*The Great Tâ'îya*) because of its rhyme in *tâ'*. With its 761 verses, this poem occupies a substantial part of the *dîwân* and has always been considered the most complete expression of Ibn al-Fâriḍ mystical vision, therefore one can say that it is the core of his *dîwân*.[11]

In the present article, I will put forward some results of my research hoping that they may shed some light on a better understanding of Ibn al-Fâriḍ's mystical experience. I will also offer a translation of some of the most important verses of the poem, introducing them with short explanations and keeping them in their textual order. The semantic approach has helped in finding the structure of the poem which can be divided into ten main sections. Such a division has proved to be more consistent than those proposed by other scholars. In this way, a direct introduction into the terms and concepts of the poem is offered. After that, I will expose my personal understanding of the poet's mystical experience.

Before entering into the text of the poem, it may be useful to highlight three important key-terms used by the poet himself and by which the three main stages of his mystical experience are defined. These terms are:

- ***al-farq*** (difference, division), i. e. the stage of 'division': in it the poet lives in separation from his Beloved expressed by him in a dialogue with his Beloved. Here the language of love with the full extent of its terminology and expression is used.
- ***al-ittiḥâd*** (unity, identification), i. e. the stage of 'absolute unity': in it the poet experiences complete unity or better identification with his Beloved, expressed by him in formulas such as "I am She" and "She is I, My-self", ending in absolute self-identity with "I am I, My-self".

11. My researches on Ibn al-Fâriḍ, G. Scattolin, *L'esperienza mistica di Ibn al-Fâriḍ attraverso il suo poema al-Tâ'îyat al-Kubrâ - Un'analisi semantica del poema* (Roma: PISAI, 1987) 3 vols.; id., *L'esperienza mistica di Ibn al-Fâriḍ attraverso il suo poema al-Tâ'îyat al-Kubrâ* (Roma: Pisai, 1988); id., "*L'expérience mystique de Ibn al-Fâriḍ à travers son poème al-Tâ'îyat al-Kubrâ"*, in Mideo 19 (1989) pp. 203-223; id., "*The Mystical Experience of ʿUmar Ibn al-Fâriḍ or the Realization of Self (Anâ, I)*, in *The Muslim World*, LXXXII/3-4 (July-October, 1992) pp. 274-286; id., "*Al-Farghânî's Commentary on Ibn al-Fâriḍ's Mystical Poem al- Tâ'îyat al-Kubrâ*" in *Mideo* 21 (1993) pp. 331-383; id., "*'Umar Ibn al-Fâriḍ wa-ḥayâtuhu al-ṣûfîya min khilâl qaṣîdatihi al-Tâ'îyat al-Kubrâ*", in *Maḥmûd Qâsim, al-insân wa-al-faylusûf*, ed. by Ḥâmid Ṭâhir (Cairo: Maktabat al-Anjlû-Miṣrîya, 1992) pp. 405-437, in *Al-Machriq* (Beirut) 67 (1993) pp. 369-400; id., "*Realization of 'Self' (anâ) in Islamic Mysticisim: ʿUmar Ibn al-Fâriḍ* (576/1181-632/1235)" in *Annali* 56 (1996), Napoli, Istituto Universitario Orientale, 14-32; id., "*New Researches on the Egyptian Sufi Poet ʿUmar Ibn al-Fâriḍ* (576-632/1181-1235), in *Philosophy and Arts in the Islamic World*, Proceedings of the Eighteenth Congress of the Union Européenne des Arabisants et Islamisants (UEAI), in *Orientalia Lovaniensia Analecta*, Leuven, U. Peters, 1998, pp. 27-40.

- ***al-jam*ᶜ** (union, universal union), i. e. the stage of 'universal union': in it the poet experiences the unity and synthesis of the One and the Many,the merging of his own Self (*anâ*) into the Whole.

These three stages follow each other or better they are interwoven with each other in the sequence of the verses, as if in a progressive movement towards the apex of universal union. This structure represents the poet's journey in the discoverying of the dimensions and the identity of his own Self (*anâ*) at its fullest and truest extent.

4. Notes on the Translation.

a. The text of the *dîwân* here translated has been on the basis of the Konya manuscript, collated with other editions, particularly that of Arberry.

b. The translation, done into free prose, intends to be as faithful as possible to the Arabic text. To this purpose verses have been divided, as far as possible, into four emystiches that reproduce the structure of the Arabic sentence, but without attempting to reproduce the poems' meter. In this way, sentences become more understandable. Some times explicative words into brackets [] and some Sufi techincal terms are put into brackets (). The valuable translations of Nicholson and Arberry have, of course, been taken into account but changed according to my own personal understanding of the text. The present translation has been kindly revised by prof. Tony Calderbank, professor of English literature at the American University (Cairo), to whom goes my heartly thank.

Excerpta from Ibn al-Fâriḍ's poem: *al-Tâ'îyat al-Kubrâ.*

1. The love prelude (taghazzul) (vv. 1-116).

Resorting to the traditional language of erotic Arabic literature, long since adopted by Sufis to express their spiritual experience of Divine love, the poet proclaims his ardent love for his Beloved. Imitating the stock vocabulary of love poets he describes the pains of his passion: this is burning inside him, wasting him away, moreover, the poet swears to be well prepared to die and be utterly annihilated for his Beloved's sake. But, the Beloved, resorting likewise to the traditional vocabulary of erotic poetry, rebukes the poet, showing that his words are not sincere and that he is still far away from the true self-annihilation (*fanâ'*) in love. In this erotic prelude Ibn al-Fâriḍ makes use of images and expressions that are commonly found in his minor poems to the point that this erotic prelude can be considered a summary of them.

1. The hand of my eye gave me to drink
   the ardent wine of love,
   while my cup was the face of her
   that transcends [any visible] beauty.
2. Through my inebriated glance
   I made my friends fancy
   that it was by quaffing their wine
   that my inner soul had been filled with joy.
3. Through [the glance of] my eye
   I could dispense with the cup:
   her qualities not my wine
   were [the source] of my inebriation.
4. So, in the tavern of my drunkenness,
   time grew ripe for me to render thanks to lads,
   through whom I could together
   conceal and reveal my passion.
5. When my sobriety came to an end,
   I sought union with her,
   no restraint of fear overwhelmed me
   in my expansion [in love] towards her.
6. I disclosed to her the burden of my heart,
   no trace of self-regard was present
   to spy the intimacy
   of my [bridal] unveiling [of my feelings].
7. I said - my state bearing witness to my ardent passion,
   my passion for her obliterating me,
   my need for her
   confirming my existence -
8. "Bestow on me, before love annuls
   what remains of me
   wherewith to look at you,
   your last fleeting glance.

9. And if you forbid me that I see you, grant my hearing
[from you]:'*Thou shalt not* (*see me*)!' (K. 7, 139),
[words] that have sounded sweet
to another before me [= Moses]
10. For, because of my drunkenness, I feel
a need for sobriety [i. e. your vision],
thanks to it my heart - were not for the [burning] passion -
had not be broken [into pieces].

....

83. I never was bewildered until I chose
my love for you as my religion:
ah, how great would my bewilderment have been,
had not my bewilderment been in you!"
84. She replied: "Another's love than mine you sought,
elsewhere your purpose lay,
forsaking in your blindness
my straight path.
85. The disguise of a soul full of vain desires
has beguiled you, whereas you said what you said,
putting on thereby
the infamy of falsehood

....

97. Now, it is time for me to reveal
what your passion really is,
and whose love has consumed you,
denying your pretension of loving me.
98. Surely, you have sworn love,
but to yourself,
and your keeping in existence an attribute of yours
is one of my proofs.
99. You will never love me
as long as you have not been annihilated in me,
and you will never be annihilated
so long as my image is not be made manifest in you.

....

102. Such is love: if you do not die,
you will never win any desire of your Beloved;
so, choose this [to die for love)]
or leave my friendship".

103. I answered to her: "My spirit belongs to you,
it is yours to take it [= make me die]:
what matters it to me
that it should be in my hands?
104. I am not one who loathes
to die for passion:
to be faithful [unto death] is the way I am,
anything else my nature refuses.
....
116. I have come to hope
what others fear:
help with it a dead man 's soul,
for [everlasting] life prepared".

2. A first description of union (vv. 117-196).

In a crescendo of images, the poet discloses the feelings stirred in him by the Beloved's presence in his inmost self. Finally, it is in prayer that his secret comes to light; since in prayer he discovers and becomes fully aware of his radical identity with his Beloved: lover and Beloved are one and the same in prayer, each of them is prostrated to their one reality. Moreover, such a reality of their union has been the same since eternity. In fact, the poet becomes aware now that since eternity he has been always in love with his Beloved and since eternity both, lover and Beloved, were one and the same. After such a sublime revelation, the poet concludes this part explaining to his disciple the way he must follow to reach such a lofty state.

148. In reality, I stood before my *imâm* [who leads the prayer]
and all mankind stood behind me;
there she was,
wherever I turned my face (to pray).
149. In prayer, my eye beholds her
in front of me,
whilst my heart beholds me
that I am *îmâm* of [all] my *îmâms*.
150. No wonder that the *îmâm*
directs his prayer towards me;
for she is dwelling in my heart,
she, the *qibla* of my *qibla* [the direction of prayer].

151. All the six directions [of the Ka^{c}ba and the universe]
have turned towards me ,
with all the acts of piety,
greater and lesser pilgrimage.
152. For her I perform my prayers
at Abraham's station (*maqâm*),
and in them [my prayers] I behold
that to me she addresses her prayers.
153. We two are one in prayer,
prostrating, in [the state of] union (*jam^{c}*),
to his own reality,
each time we prostrate ourselves in worshipping.
154. None has addressed his prayer to me but myself,
neither have I addressed my prayer
to any one but myself,
every time I bow down in prayer.
....
156. Her friendship was granted to me
on the day without day [= without time],
before she appeared [in the visible world],
at the taking of the covenant, in my primal state.
157. And [then] I obtained her love,
neither by hearing nor sight,
nor by merit [acquired],
nor by attraction of nature.
158. I fell passionately in love for her
in the world of the [divine] command,
no [visible] manifestation there;
my intoxication [for her]
came before I came to be in this world.
159. Love caused the attributes dividing us
that were not existing there [in the world of command],
to pass away here [in the visible world],
and they disappeared.
....
162. I am she whom I loved, there is no doubt,
and my soul addressing her [in love]
was addressing myself to myself.
163. My soul is distraught with passion for her,

without from where [that passion came],
but in my vision (*shuhûd*)
it (my soul) was not ignorant of the truth of the matter.

3. A second description of union and further explication (vv. 197-285).

After the teaching imparted to his disciple, the poet comes back to describe again how he has reached the stage of union with his Beloved. He explains that it was after a long ascetic journey that he reached the state of true vision (*shuhûd*) where all visible perceptions (*wujûd*) are canceled: in that state of union he has become aware of his deep reality in which, as he says: "My essence became endued with my essence (*dhât*) (v. 212)Ţhis stage of union is called here *ittiḥâd* which means 'union of identity', because in it the poet discovers his identity with his Beloved: the two are one essence. This stage of 'union of identity' (*ittiḥâd*) follows that of separation (*farq*), described in the first section of the poem.

Then (vv. 219-240), through some examples taken from common experience, the poet tries to explain to his disciple how it is possible that the two be one, a statement that appears to be contradictory to a rational mind. Having proved this point, the poet takes his disciple in a fantastic flight through the history of the well known lovers of Arabic literature to come to the astounding statement that all those lovers were but manifestations of a unique love, i. e. the love between himself and his Beloved, in the end the love of his own essence for itself. This section can be entitled 'the proclamation of the unity of love' in all its manifestations. The poet concludes proving that his statements are in accordance with the religious tradition (vv. 277-285).

204. Until then, I have been an impassioned lover of her,
but when I renounced my own desire,
she did desire me for herself
and love me .
205. Then, I became a beloved,
nay, one in love with one's own self,
and not, as I said before,
that my soul was my Beloved.

....

209. When she appeared,
I made to contemplate my hidden being,

and in the unveiling of my intimacy
I found that I was she.

210. Then, my [perceptible] existence (*wujûdî*)
was effaced in my vision (*shuhûdî*),
and I became severed even from the perception (*wujûd*) of my own vision (*shuhûdî*),
effacing [all perception] not upholding it.

211. Because of the sobriety that followed my intoxication,
I embraced what I beheld,
as a perceiver obliterated in that
which was perceived.

212. So that in the sobriety that followed the obliteration
[of all perception], I was none other that she:
nay, my essence when it became manifest
became one [lit. enwrapped] with my own essence.

213. Here, I will make manifest the beginning of my oneness (*ittiḥâd*).
and I will reach my utmost station,
making my exaltation bend low in humility.

214. When she revealed herself,
she made the whole world manifest to my sight,
so that with my sight
I saw her in every visible thing.

....

259. In them [the lovers] I made myself manifest outwardly,
while by them I veiled myself inwardly:
marvel, at such unveiling in the very act of veiling.

260. Those [beloved women] and those [their lovers]
- no flimsy fancy there -
were our self-manifestations,
in which we [my Beloved and I] appeared
in all [forms] of love and beauty.

261. Every lover, I was he,
and she was every lover's beloved,
and all [lovers and beloved] were but names
of [our] raiment.

262. Those were only names,
whereby in truth I was the designated one:
I was manifesting myself to myself
by means of a soul hidden [in those lovers].

263. I never ceased to be her (*iyyâhâ*),
and she never ceased to be me (*iyyâya*),
without distinction:
nay, it was my essence loving my essence (*dhât*).
264. In the [created] world [*mulk*],
there never existed beside me other than myself,
and the thought of 'being-with' (*ma^cîya*)
never entered my mind.

4. The sublimity the poet's mystical state.(vv. 286-333).

The poet begins describing now the sublimity of the mystical state he has reached, declaring that such a state has taken him beyond all the qualifications of love. He has gone above the state of unity-identity of 'I am She' (*anâ iyyâhâ*) and "I am I, My-self" (*anâ iyyâya*): his journey goes towards the seas of the universal and all-comprehensive union (*jam^c*). He has reached what in Sufi technical terminology is called 'the sobriety of union' (*ṣaḥw al-jam^c*) or 'the second separation' (*al-farq al-thânî*) which is the loftiest mystical state. In it the poet possesses all the privileges of the prophets, he becomes also aware that all qualities and actions of the universe are the profusion (*fayḍ*) of his own qualities. He concludes stating that no Sufi qualification is now suitable to him, for he is now beyond all designation. From this section on, the rest of the poem can be read as a long description of the sublimity of such a state of universal and all-comprehensive union (*jam^c*), seen under different viewpoints.

292. For the valley of her friendship,
my friend of sober heart,
is in the province of my command
and falls under my rule
293. The realm of the high degrees of love
is my possession,
their realities are my army
and all lovers are my subjects.
294. Love has passed away!
I am become far away from it
as one who deems it a veil:
passion is under my degree.
295. I have crossed beyond the boundary of passion (*hawâ*),

for love (*ḥubb*) is now [to me] even as hate,
from the peak of my ascension to unity (*ittiḥâd*).
my journey begins.

....

311. All humans are sons of Adam,
but I alone above my brethren
have attained the sobriety of union (*ṣaḥw al-jam*ᶜ).
312. For this reason, my hearing is like that of Moses (called *kalîm Allâh*),
and my heart has received the [prophetic] knowledge
through the most glorious vision
of an eye like that of Aḥmad (= Muḥammad).
313. My spirit is the spirit of all spirits
and whatsoever you see
to be beautiful in the universe
flows from the bounty of my nature [lit. clay].
314. Leave, then, that which I alone knew
before my manifestation [in the physical world],
and my companions [prophets and saints] did know
aught of me in the in the beginning [lit. seed, i. e. before manifestation].

....

326. From [the stage] 'I am she' (*anâ iyyâhâ*)
I mounted to where is no 'to'
and, in my returning,
I spread my perfume over all [visible] existence.
327. And from [the stage] 'I am I' (*anâ iyyâ-ya*)
[I returned] for the sake of an esoteric wisdom
and external laws
I have established for as a calling to myself.

5. The mysteries of union: the synthesis of the contraries (vv. 334-440).

With this section the poet begins to expose what can be called 'the mysteries of union'. He opens it with a new 'love prelude (*taghazzul*)' (vv. 334-387) which corresponds to the one at the beginning of the poem (vv. 1-116). By now, the meaning of the love symbols has become clear: the two, lover and Beloved, are one and the same essence that reveals itself to itself and loves itself through itself.

Then, the poet continues describing the first marvel of union: the contraries come together and are reconciled in a astonishing synthesis. Here, the poet means the reconciliation between the domain of sensible qualities or visible phenomena (symbolized by the character of the 'railer' of love stories) which is usually opposed to that of spiritual qualities or interior meanings (symbolized by the character of the 'slanderer' of love stories). On the contrary, the poet shows that between the two worlds, visible and invisible, exists a profound correspondence and harmony, clearly shown in the 'Sufi musical sessions' (*samâ*ᶜ), in which the two worlds are experienced to be in tune. The poet ends this section with a passionate defence of this Sufi practice which has been often and bitterly opposed by a number of strict Sunni scholars, such as Ibn Taymîya (d. 728/1328). Thus, continues:

387. Were she to dissolve my body,
she would see that in every atom of it
there is every heart
in which there is every love.
388. And the most marvelous thing I found in her
and what the interior disclosure (*fatḥ*)
has abundantly bestowed on me
through a revelation (*kashf*) that dispelled all doubt,
389. [Was] the vision through which I behold now,
in the essence [or eye] of union (*ᶜayn al-jam*ᶜ),
every adversary as my ally,
and his refusal even as affection.

....

397. By allusion, the one who has the taste (*dhawq*) of it,
understands what I mean;
he can dispense with the clear explanations
[required] by a fastidious inquirer.

....

398. Those two [the railer and the slanderer] are one with us [the Beloved and I]
in inward union (*bâṭin al-jam*ᶜ),
though [we and they] are counted four
in outward separation (*ẓâhir al-farq*).
399. For truly she and I are one essence (*dhât*),
while the one who tells tales [= the slanderer] of her
and the one who turns me away from her [= the railer]
are attributes that appear [from us].
400. That one [the slanderer] is a manifestation of the spirit,
guiding it to its regions

in a vision [of spiritual realities] (*shuhûd*)
that takes place in spiritual form.
401. This one [the railer] helps the soul
driving it to its companions
in a perception [of visible phenomena] (*wujûd*)
that takes place in visible image.
402. But the one who knows, as I do, [the true nature of] those figures,
is unsullied by the *shirk* [associating other realities with God]
of his own fancy
removing the perplexity of suspicion [of *shirk*].

....

405. By the soul (*nafs*) the forms of the [visible] existence
(*wujûd*) were rejoiced,
by the spirit (*rûḥ*) the spirits of [spiritual] contemplation (*shuhûd*) were refreshed.

6. The mysteries of union: he is the supreme Pole (quṭb) of existence (vv. 441-503).

In this section the poet widens his horizon till he reaches full awareness of being the centre of the whole universe: it is around him that the spheres of worlds turn, since he is the supreme Pole (*quṭb*) of existence. The poet resorts here to well known Sufi terminology, without bothering to explain it, taking for granted that it was well understood by his audience. Since he is the Pole of existence, towards him all religious cults are addressed, from him the whole creation receives its movement and by him all spiritual degrees are bestowed in the history of prophets and saints. The source of his sublime state is referred by the poet to the 'covenant of friendship' (*mîthâq al-walâ'*) mentioned in the Koran (K 7, 172). This covenant, which means the first and original witness to God's supreme Lordship, has been one of the main topics of Sufi reflection since the time of al-Junayd (d. 298/910). The poet declares that he was present at that time, when God in pre-eternity asked human souls: "Am I not (*a lastu*) your Lord?", and they answered: "Yes, indeed (*balâ*)!" (K 7, 172). Moreover, he is aware that he was at the same time the one who asked the question and the one who answered: at that time no duality or 'to be-with' (*maᶜîya*) existed, but only absolute unity. Such a mystery (*sirr*), in fact, can be revealed only in the state of union (*jamᶜ*).

494. I have indicated by means
of what the expression can yield,
and that which remains hidden
I have made clear by a subtle allegory.
495. The 'Am I not' (*a lastu*) of yesterday [pre-eternity] is not other
[than what will be manifest] to him who enters on tomorrow [the day of resurrection],
since my darkness has become my dawn
and my day my night.
496. And the secret of 'Yes, indeed!' (*balâ*):
to God belongs the mirror of its revelation;
and to affirm the reality of union (*jam*ᶜ)
is to deny any kind of 'being-with' (*ma*ᶜ*îya*).
497. There is no darkness that covers (my light)
and there is no wrong to be feared (from me),
since the mercy of my light
has quenched the fire of my revenge.

....

500. Therefore, it is upon me that the heavens turn:
marvel at their Pole (*quṭb*) which encompasses them,
though the pole [in the visible world]
is only a central point.
501. No Pole was there before me unto whom I succeeded,
after having passed the three degrees [of Sufi hierarchy],
since, usually, the Pegs (*awtâd*) rise to the rank of Pole (*quṭb*)
[coming] from the rank of Substitutes (*abdâl*).
502. Do not overstep my straight line,
for in the angles there are hidden realities:
seize the best opportunity [of my guidance].
503. From me and in me the [divine] friendship
appeared in the [world of] seed [the beginning in eternity],
from me and unto me the milk [of knowledge] was poured abundantly
from the breasts of union.

7. The mysteries of union: essence (dhât), attributes (ṣifât), names (asmâ') and acts (afᶜâl) are in him but one reality (vv. 504-588).

This section, too, opens with love verses (*taghazzul*) in which the poet sings his love for his Beloved, but now in the complete intoxication (*sukr*) of union. Here, all pronouns are turned into the first person, creating strange but enchanting melodies of sounds and images. Then, taking a more theological tone, the poet declares that his state of union is far above all the distinctions known in classical theology, i. e. the distinction between essence (*dhât*), attributes (*ṣifât*), names (*asmâ'*) and acts (*afʿâl*) in God. The poet affirms that all these terms designate in him but one reality. Besides, in such a state of union each one of his faculties is qualified by the qualities of all the other faculties so that a complete 'inter-change' of operations takes place in him: another marvel of his sublime state of union.

511. I ask her of myself,
whenever I encounter her,
and inasmuch as she bestows on me [true] guidance, she misleads [me in my quest].
512. I seek her from myself,
though she was ever beside me:
I marveled at the way
she was hidden from me by myself.
....
515. I quest myself from myself
that I might guide myself by my own tongue
to the one who is asking guidance from me
in my ceaselessly seeking for myself.
516. I ask myself that I lift the veil
and uncover my face,
my [only] means to reach myself
was through me.
517. I look into the mirror of my own beauty
that I might behold
the loveliness of my [visible] existence
in my contemplation of my countenance.
....
528. I made myself behold myself,
inasmuch as in my beholding
there existed none other than myself
who might decree intrusion [of duality].
....
578. [In the end] I realized that we [the Beloved and I] are in reality one,
and the sobriety of union (*ṣaḥw al-jamʿ*)

confirmed the blotting out of multiplicity [of scattering qualities].

579. So, the whole of me was tongue and eye,
ear and hand:
to speak and behold,
to hear and seize.

580. My eye speaks,
while my tongue contemplates,
my ear utters words,
while my hand listens.

....

586. There is no organ in me
that has been specialized for a particular function
to the exclusion of the rest [of organs)],
as the eye for seeing.

587. In me every atom,
notwithstanding its own singularity,
comprises the sum of all acts
of all the members:

588. It speaks, it listens,
beholding one who can dispose,
by virtue of an all-powerful hand,
of his whole totality in one instant.

8. The mysteries of union: his action extends through time and space, beyond all limits (vv. 588-650).

In such a state of union, the poet becomes all the more aware that, because he is the supreme Pole (*quṭb*) of the universe, his action reaches beyond all limits of space and time. It was he who performed the miracles (*muᶜjizât*) attributed to the prophets, and the wonders (*karâmât*), attributed to the saints, in every place and time. But, above all, in him the highest Divine qualities are displayed, namely the qualities of majesty (*jalâl*), beauty (*jamâl*) and perfection (*kamâl*) in a reciprocal inclusion. He can perceive and contemplate these qualities in all phenomena which are, in the end, but manifestations of himself to himself. Some of the most astonishing and much controversial verses of the poem are found in this section.

593. I survey all the horizons [of the earth]
in a flash of thought,

and I traverse all the seven layers of heaven
in one step.

....

600. Such is the soul: if she casts off her [lower] passion,
her powers are multiplied,
and it can endow every atom [of existence]
with all her energy.

....

638. But for me, no (visible) existence (*wujûd*) would have come into being,
no vision (of unity) (*shuhûd*) would have existed,
and no covenants (*ᶜuhûd*) would have been sealed in fidelity.
639. There is no living being but his life is from my life,
and every willing soul
is obedient to my will.
640. There is no speaker but tells his tale with my words,
nor any seer
but sees with the sight of my eye.
641. There is no listener but hears with my hearing,
and none that grasps
but with my strength and might.
642. And from among the whole of creation
there is none save me,
that speaks or sees or hears.
643. In the world of composition [the visible world]
I made myself manifest in every visible form
by means of a [spiritual] reality
which has been adorned with a sensible perception.
644. And in every [spiritual] reality,
not revealed by my [visible] manifestations,
I represented myself,
though not in bodily form.
645. And in that which the spirit beholds
by the unveiling clairvoyance
I was hidden by my subtlety
beyond any fatigued thought.
646. In the 'expansion' (*basṭ*) of mercy,
the whole of me is desire,
whereby expand
the hopes of the inhabitants of the globe [earth].

647. And in the 'constriction' (*qabḍ*) of terror,
the whole of me is reverential awe,
and over whatsoever I turn my eye,
it reveres me.
648. But in the union (*jamᶜ*) of both these attributes
the whole of me is nearness:
hasten and draw near
to my excellent qualities!
649. Where 'in' has come to an end,
I did not cease to experience through myself
the majesty (*jalâl*) of contemplating myself
[arising from] the perfection (*kamâl*) of my nature.
650. And where there was no 'in',
I did not cease to contemplate in myself
the beauty (*jamâl*) of my [visible] existence,
though not through the sight of my eye (cf. v. 1).

9. The mysteries of union: examples and explications.(vv. 651-731).

In this section of the poem the poet intends to explain again to his disciple his experience that may sound absurd to a rational mind: how is it possible that unity and multiplicity are found together? How is it possible that he is in everything and everything is in him? This section is parallel to that of vv. 219-285 in which similar explanations are given.

To this purpose, the poet resorts to some examples taken from common experience. Then, in a long passage (vv. 677-706) he introduces a description of the play of the shadow puppets as the most suitable example to illustrate his intent, because in it the unity of the one agent (the showman) and the multiplicity of forms (the shadows on the screen) appears quite clearly. This passage has become very famous in Sufi and non-Sufi literature.

The poet concludes this section extolling again the sublimity of his state of union (*jamᶜ*): he is the light of existence, he is the source of all actions in the universe, every being witnesses to his transcendent unity (*tawḥîd*)..

704. Whatever you have contemplated (in the play)
was the act of only one, alone,
but [enwrapped] in the veils of occultation.

705. And when he removed the curtain,
you beheld none but him,
and no confusion remained
about the forms [of the shadows].
706. You did realize at his unveiling
that by his light you were guided
to [see] his actions in darkness .
707. Like him, I was letting down the curtain
between me and myself,
in which the soul has become obscured,
in the light of darkness,
708. So that I might gradually appear to my senses,
becoming familiar to them [for my final revelation],
in my ever-creating work
time after time.
709. I compared his play [of illusion]
with my earnest work [in reality]
in order to bring near to your understanding
the aims of my far-off purposes.
710. A reciprocal resemblance joins us [showman and I]
as to our forms of manifestation,
though his case
is not comparable to mine.
711. His figures [the puppets] were the forms of his action
manifest upon the screen;
but, when he revealed himself,
they became naught and disappeared.
712. My soul resembled him in action,
while my senses were like the figures [puppets],
and my [bodily] disguise my screen.
713. In fact, when I removed the screen from myself,
as he did (from himself),
so that my soul appeared to me
without veiling,
714. And already the sun of vision had risen
and all [visible] existence was illuminated,
and through me the tethering-ropes [of senses]
were untied.
715. Then, I slew the youth of my soul [= my lower soul],

while setting up the wall of [= establishing] my laws
and staving in my boat [= my bodily individuality].

716. [From that state] I turned to bestow
my abundant grace over the whole world,
according to the actions
[required] at every time.

717. Were I not veiled by my attributes (*ṣifât*),
the manifestations of my essence (*dhât*) [i. e. the created beings]
would have been burnt
by the splendour of my glory.

718. And the tongues of all created beings
- if you could be aware of it -
bear witness to my unity (*tawḥîd*)
in a clear, eloquent way.

10. The mysteries of union: he is the goal of all religions, since these are its own manifestations in human history (vv. 732-761).

The poet now widens still further his horizon to include the whole history of religions throughout the ages. In his mystical state of all-comprehensive union (*jam*ᶜ) he discovers that he has always been the true goal of all religions and of their acts of worshipping, even if the worshippers themselves were not aware of such a reality. This idea, called 'the unity of religions', has been very often the object of Sufi speculation, as in Ibn ᶜArabî's mystical philosophy and that of his school.

More specifically, the poet affirms that he has been manifesting himself throughout the religious history of the prophets, and that of Islam in particular. In fact, he has come to the awareness of having been, before all visible manifestation, the 'Eternal Light', that has existed since all eternity and has been the source of all visible lights.

Concluding his poem, Ibn al-Fâriḍ seems to unveil something of the deep mystery that has been surrounding his verses up to the present point. He affirms quite clearly that he is one and the same with that 'Eternal Light', expression used in Sufi tradition to designate the 'Eternal Light of Muḥammad' (*al-nûr al-muḥammadî*) or the 'Eternal Reality of Muḥammad' (*al-ḥaqîqat al-muḥammadîya*). This concept has had a long history in Sufi thought since the 3rd/9th c. in Sufis such as Sahl al-Tustarî (d. 283/896) and al-Ḥusayn b. Manṣûr al-Ḥallâj (d. 309/922). The same idea has been largely developed in Ibn al-Fâriḍ's time by Muḥyî al-Dîn Ibn ᶜArabî (d. 638/1240), the 'greatest Sufi master', with the idea of the 'Perfect Man' (*al-insân al-kâmil*).[12] Such a concept seems to be a basic clue to understanding the deep mystical experience Ibn al-Fâriḍ intended to convey throughout his poem.

738. In all religions men's eyes
did not go astray,
neither did their thoughts deviate
in every religious belief.
739. Those who heedlessly fell in love with the sun
lost not their way,
since its brightness comes from the light
of the unveiling of my splendour.
740. If the Magi (Zoroastrians) adored the fire,
- which, as tradition tells,
was not quenched for a thousand years -
741. They intended none but me,
although the direction [of their worship] was towards other than me,
and they did not [clearly] manifest
the purpose of their intention [towards me].
742. They once saw the radiance of my light
and deemed it fire,
and so they were led astray from the true guidance
by its rays.
743. But for the veil of the [visible] world,
I would have openly declared [my reality],
only my observance of the laws of manifestations
keeps me silent.

....

751. My [real] kinship has been indicated
by the dispenser of the mystical union (*mufîḍ al-jamᶜ*)
when he greeted me [with the words of revelation] 'or nearer' (K 53, 9)
[which indicate the spiritual state of Muḥammad]
752. From his light the niche [= the inmost part] of my essence (*dhâtî*) has shone on me,
and has illuminated through me
my evening [my existence in the phenomenal world]
as my morning [the day of resurrection].

---

12. For more references, see note No. 14.

753. I was made to behold that I was there [in that Eternal Light],
and [really] I was he,
and I beheld that he was I
and the [Eternal] Light was my splendour.
754. In me the valley [of Sinai K 20, 10-12] was sanctified,
and in it I took off my sandals
[as a boon] to my companions,
and I bestowed my gifts.
755. I beheld my lights,
and I was the guidance towards them;
marvel at a soul (*nafs*),
that shines upon them (its own lights).
756. I firmly founded my Sinais (= human hearts)
and there I was in conversation with myself,
I fulfilled my desires
and my essence (*dhât*) was my interlocutor.
757. My moon did never set,
nor my sun disappear,
by me are guided
all the brilliant stars [= the great Sufi masters].
758. The planets of my celestial spheres
moved in my dominion at my command,
and my angels fell prostrate
before my sovereignty.
759. In the world of recollection
the soul owns its eternal knowledge:
from me my disciples
seek it as their guidance.
760. Hasten, then, to my eternal union (*jamᶜ*):
in which I have found the full-grown elders of the tribe [the Sufi masters],
to be [inexpert] as little babes.
761. In fact, my contemporary fellow men
drink but the dregs of what I left,
and so did those before me:
all virtues are but the left over of my [abundance].

C. Ibn al-Fâriḍ's Mystical Experience: an Insight.[13]

Having gone through some of the most relevant verses of Ibn al-Fâriḍ's *Great Tâ'îya* and having tasted something of his mystical experience, I offer here in short the main results of my semantical analysis of this poem with my understanding of it. This will help entering in a more complete way into Ibn al-Fâriḍ's mystical world. This does not mean that every thing will become now clear. On the contrary, perhaps, the mystery of his mystical experience will increase the more we want to come closer to it. However, one of the most momentous results of a semantic analysis is avoiding to make the poet say want he didn't want to say; this is a must in an objective approach to any author Sufi or not.

1. A Journey from Love to Union.

Ibn al-Fâriḍ has been celebrated in Arabic literature as the 'Prince of Lovers' (*sulṭân al-ᶜâshiqîn*), as if love were the core of his mystical experience. Contrary to such a long tradition, after a careful semantic analysis of the language love in the poem, I have come to the conclusion, that love is not the central theme of the poet's experience. Love, important as it may be in Ibn al-Fâriḍ's poetry, appears to be but a stage in his mystical journey. In fact, one of the results of the semantic analysis was to show that the terms and synonyms of love appear in the first two stages the poet's mystical journey, namely those of division (*farq*) and unity-identity (*ittiḥâd*), but not in the final stage, that of all-comprehensive union (*jamᶜ*). In fact, the poet had explicitly declared (v. 295):

> I have crossed beyond the boundary of passion (*hawâ*),
> for love (*ḥubb*) is now [to me] even as hate,
> from the peak of my ascension to unity (*ittiḥâd*).
> my journey begins.

His mystical journey goes beyond both the stage of division (*farq*), in which the erotic language is predominant, and that of unity-identity (*ittiḥâd*), in which only the term love (*ḥubb*) plays a significant role. The final goal of the poet is, beyond doubt, the stage of universal and all-comprehensive union (*jamᶜ*). On this basis, it seems to me that the traditional designation of

---

13. For more information, see my researches in note No. 11.

Ibn al-Fâriḍ as 'the Prince of Lovers' (*sulṭân al-ᶜâshiqîn*) does not fully express the core of his Sufi experience. In my view, Ibn al-Fâriḍ should be designated rather as the 'Poet of universal and all-comprehensive union (*jamᶜ*)'. This last stage seems to be the utmost stage and the highest realization of his mystical quest.

The poet starts his journey declaring his impassionate love for his Beloved, whom he does not define Then he continues describing the discovery of his unity and self-identity (*ittiḥâd*) with his Beloved, expressed in carefully elaborated formulas such as: *anâ iyyâ-hâ* (I am She), *hiya iyyâya* (She is I, My-self), *anâ iyyâya* (I am I, My-self). The experience of unity-identity (*ittiḥâd*) plunges the poet into a state of spiritual intoxication (*sukr*), in which his individual self and self-awareness are completely obliterated in the identification with his Beloved. But, sublime as such a state of intoxication of love might be, the Sufi poet is quite aware that this is not the peak of his spiritual ascension (*miᶜrâj*).

Far above the heights of unity-identity (*ittiḥâd*) lie the "seas of universal union" (*biḥâr al-jamᶜ*), the true aim of his mystical journey. At this stage, the poet experiences that the opposites come together, the One and the Many merge in a synthesizing and dynamic unity and, finally, his own self and the whole universe become one and the same in a movement of reciprocal merging and inclusion. The poet now becomes aware that his *anâ* (I, My-self) is not only the source of everything, but is in everything, beyond all limits of space and time. Awake to this new vision of reality, the poet can now sing new melodies, strange and provocative, even shocking for shortsighted faithful, yet highly fascinating and enchanting. Plunged into the seas of universal union (*biḥâr al-jamᶜ*), Ibn al-Fâriḍ gives expression to his extraordinary experience in a bewildering variety of terms and images, as if soaring up into a world of complete freedom, not subjected to the laws of our daily, empirical experience.

Notwithstanding a long literary tradition of commentaries and studies, the semantic analysis of Ibn al-Fâriḍ's vocabulary proves that his terms must not necessarily be interpreted according to the philosophical contents they have in Ibn ᶜArabî's Sufism, as many commentators have done. For example, the term *wujûd* in Ibn al-Fâriḍ's verses is always related to the language of duality and multiplicity, i. e. to the stage of imperfection and division (*farq*), a stage that must be overcome in the true and real vision (*shuhûd*) where unity becomes manifest. It is in such vision that the poet discovers first his identity with his Beloved (*ittiḥâd*), and, then, the full reality of the universal union (*jamᶜ*). In fact, the semantic analysis proves that the term *wujûd* means in Ibn al-Fâriḍ's vocabulary 'the visible existence and its perception' and not the general idea of 'being' as it has in philosophy and Ibn ᶜArabî's Sufism. In this sense, it appears impossible to describe Ibn al-Fâriḍ's Sufism in terms of *waḥdat al-wujûd*, meaning 'unity of existence or being'. This would amount to a contradiction in terms, since the term *wujûd* in Ibn al-Fâriḍ's vocabulary is always related to multiplicity. The same remark has proved true also for some other basic terms, which I call 'pivotal terms' of the poem, such as 'soul' (*nafs*), 'spirit' (*rûḥ*) and 'essence' (*dhât*).

On the whole, I think that the semantic analysis of Ibn al-Fâriḍ's poem proves that there is an evident discrepancy between his vocabulary and that of Ibn ᶜArabî: the first is essentially poetic and experiential, the second is rather philosophical and abstract. Therefore, it is wrong in my view to interpret Ibn al-Fâriḍ's language in light of Ibn ᶜArabî's Sufi monism, and to load his poetic vocabulary with the whole set of philosophical ideas and speculations of Ibn ᶜArabî's monism, as many commentators and scholars have done in the past.

Yet, after such a long and detailed semantic analysis of the poem, a fundamental question remains to be answered regarding the poet and his experience: what is in the end, beyond all poetic images and expressions, the very core and source of Ibn al-Fâriḍ's mystical experience?

2. The experience of anâ (I, My-self) as the 'Perfect Man' (al-insân al-kâmil).

The semantic analysis of the *Tâ'îya* has shown, beyond doubt, that the vocabulary of the poem is clearly built and centered on the term *anâ* (I, My-self): this term seems to be the true 'focus-word' of the whole vocabulary of the poem and so the key-word to understand the poet's mystical experience, which appears to be a progressive discovery of his mystical *anâ* (I, My-self). The basic traits of the poet's *anâ* (I, My-self), as described in the *Tâ'îya*, can be summarized as follows:

i.- the poet's *anâ* was present in the pre-eternal covenant of friendship (*mîthâq al-walâ'*), in which there was perfect unity and identity between the one who witnessed and the one who was witnessed, i. e. the one who asked the question: "*a lastu bi-rabbikum*?" (Am I not your Lord?), and those who answered: "*balâ*" (Yes, indeed)! (K 7, 172).

ii.- the poet's *anâ* is the permanent source of effusion (*fayḍ, imdâd*) of all qualities and operations on the whole universe. These are, in reality, its own manifestations in which the poet's *anâ* veils itself and then discovers itself, its own identity (*dhât*), in the act of true vision (*shuhûd*) of his unity-identity (*ittiḥâd*).

iii.- the poet's *anâ* is also the source of inspiration (*rûḥ*) in the history of the prophets and saints (*awliyâ'-anbiya'*), bestowing on them the power to perform miracles and wonders (*muᶜjizât-karâmât*). In them and through them it was the poet's *anâ* that was sending and manifesting itself to itself, revealing itself to itself.

iv.- the poet's *anâ* reaches the full awareness of its reality (*ḥaqîqa*) at the end of its mystical journey, in the stage of universal and all-comprehensive union (*jamᶜ*): there the poet discovers the true dimensions of his *anâ*, finding himself in everything and everything in himself. Such a transcendent experience leads the poet to utterances that may be shocking for orthodox minds, but for the poet they are the only faithful and true phrasing of his mystical state.

Such a lofty reality of the poet's *anâ* is designated as *al-quṭb* (the Pole) in vv. 500-1, and *mufîḍ al-jamᶜ* (the bestower of union) in v. 751. These concepts were already well known in Sufi tradition, and, seemingly, Ibn al-Fâriḍ took it for granted that their contents were familiar to the Sufi circles he was addressing. By these terms, Sufis used to designate the highest realization of humanity, expressed in the idea of the 'Perfect Man' (*al-insân al-kâmil*). The 'Perfect Man' was thought to be the manifestation in human history of the Islamic *Logos*, i. e. the First and Eternal Manifestation of the Divine Essence, called in Sufi tradition the 'Eternal Reality of Muḥammad' (*al-ḥaqîqa al-muḥammadîya*). Because of this, the 'Perfect Man' meant for Sufis the full realization of the Divine qualities in Human form, and so, the 'Perfect Man' is the 'microcosm', the summary of the whole universe.[14]

Here, I think, lies the core of Ibn al-Fâriḍ's mystical experience. From a careful analysis of the poem, it appears that the notion of the 'Perfect Man' (*al-insân al-kâmil*) must have played a special role in shaping Ibn al-Fâriḍ's mystical vision. The qualities of the poet's *anâ* in the stage of *jamᶜ*

---

14. For information and bibliography on this concept, see G. Scattolin, "*Realization of 'Self' (anâ) in Islamic Mysticism*" in *Annali* 56 (1996), (Napoli: Istituto Universitario Orientale) pp. 14-32 id., "*New Researches on the Egyptian Sufi Poet ᶜUmar Ibn al-Fâriḍ* (576-632/1181-1235), in *Orientalia Lovaniensia Analecta*, Leuven, U. Peters, 1998, pp. 27-40.

are quite similar to those of the notion of 'Perfect Man', found in Sufi literature contemporary to Ibn al-Fâriḍ. Such notion must have been the common ground from which both Ibn al-Fâriḍ and Ibn ᶜArabî have drawn their Sufi vision, but each one according to his own character. In this way, one can account in a more logical way for the similarities and dissimilarities existing in the two Sufis, and do justice at the same time to their peculiarities.

To sum up, if I were to indicate the core of Ibn al-Fâriḍ's mystical experience, I would suggest that it must be sought, first of all, in his personal and deep assimilation of the concept of the 'Perfect Man' (*al-insân al-kâmil*). Through such a realization, the poet has reached full awareness of having attained his most profound aspiration, which is the source of all mystical experience, namely, the union with the Absolute. He has found that his empirical 'self' (*anâ*), perceived at the beginning of the path still in the stage of multiplicity and duality (*farq*), has passed away into the pure vision and transparency of the true, unique 'Self' (*anâ*), the absolute One. Now, in the stage of universal and all-comprehensive union (*jamᶜ*), the poet experiences only one absolute 'Self' (*anâ*), the unique center and source of all qualities and movements in the universe. Into such an absolute 'Self' (*anâ*) the poet has completely merged, with no traces left of his previous, empirical 'self' (*anâ*). In a new transparent and transcendent awareness, the Sufi poet realizes that whatever said or done in the universe is operated by that One and Absolute Subject, the unique Center of All, the only One who can say in Reality '*anâ*' (I, My-self).

3. Poetic and Mystical Taste (dhawq).

Completely merged in that union, Ibn al-Fâriḍ tries to convey in poetic form something of his extraordinary experience, drawing from the literary and religious sources of his own tradition. Ibn al-Fâriḍ's poetic language is largely indebted to the classical Arabic literature, especially to the erotic poetry, from which he freely takes all kinds of images and motives to phrase his extraordinary experience.[15] His expressions may sound many a time absurd, even hubristic, to the mind of common faithful, not acquainted with the deep transformation experienced by the poet. Yet, these expres-

15. For the development of Sufi poetry, see Annemarie Schimmel, *As Through a Veil*, (New York: Columbia University Press, 1982); in particular "The Development of Arabic Mystical Poetry", pp. 11-48.

sions are for Ibn al-Fâriḍ the only possible articulation and utterance in human language of that lofty Reality in which he now exists. Conscious that words fall always short of expressing such a transcendent Reality, the poet clearly warns (v. 397):

By allusion, the one who has the taste (*dhawq*) of it,
understands what I mean;
he can dispense with the clear explanations
[required] by a fastidious inquirer.

Such mystical Reality always extends far beyond any rational capacity (*ᶜaql*) of humans and can only be perceived by an interior intuition and taste, expressed in Arabic by one term, *dhawq*, which literally means 'to taste, to have the taste of something'. Taste (*dhawq*) means in Sufi language the inner perception of the most interior and profound aspect of reality with the ability to express it in a suitable linguistic form. This may happen both on poetical and mystical level.

Here, one touches upon an important and much discussed topic, that of the relationship between 'poetic' and 'mystical' language, and the source of both.[16] A lot of questions have been raised in this respect. To what extent are the two experiences, the poetic and the mystical, similar or not? To what extent can human language express what is beyond human rational capacity? Since both the poetic and mystical experiences have to express themselves through symbolic language, to what extent do the two languages correspond?. To what extent do those symbols express only the 'depths' of human spirit (as Jungian archetypes?) or are they able to convey something of a transcend experience, i. e. the 'depths' of Being, in whatever way it might be thought of, as personal or impersonal? Is the aesthetic bliss of the artistic work, the act of producing and of enjoying it, the same as the luminous night of mystics, the source of their ecstasy?

---

16. For an introduction to this topic, Louis Gardet, "*Poésie et expérience du Soi*", in Louis Gardet - Olivier Lacombe, *L'expérience du Soi. Étude de mystique comparée*, (Paris: Desclée de Brouwer, 1981) pp. 249-317; on the symbolism in mystical language, see Evelyn Underhill, "*Mysticism and Symbolism*" in *Mysticism*, (1st ed. 1910; 12th ed. 1930, New York: Image Book, Double Day) pp. 125-148; Germano Pattaro, "*Il linguaggio mistico*", in *La mistica - Fenomenologia e riflessione teologica*, ed. by Ermanno Ancilli - Maurizio Paparozzi (Roma: Citta' Nuova, 1984) vol. I, pp. 483-506; Carl-A. Keller, "*Le rôle de l'imagination*", in *Approche de la mystique*, (Le Mont-sur-Lausanne: Editions Ouverture, 1989) vol. I, pp. 149-212..

Many different answers have been given to such questions which can not be dealt here in detail. It seems, however, quite agreed that, historically, the two languages, the poetic and the mystical, are often associated, as if by an inner connaturality. Poetic taste and mystical intuition, both expressed in Arabic by the same word *dhawq*, prove to be very much interrelated and they are often united in the same person, the mystic-poet. In all world literatures, in Islam as well as outside it, it is out of the field of mystics that some of the most outstanding and finest artists, poets in particular, have emerged: Ibn al-Fârịd in Arabic literature, Jalâl al-Dîn Rûmî (d. 672/1273) in Persian literature, Yûnus Emre (d. 721/1321) in Turkish literature, John of the Cross (d. 1591), in Spanish literature, just to mention some names.

In conclusion, it seems to me that the basic trait of Ibn al-Fârịd's character must have been a remarkable blending of poetic and mystical taste (*dhawq*). Such a profound taste, together mystical and poetic, seems to be the source of inspiration of his verse, in which the sense of poetic beauty along with the dramatic tension of the spiritual quest of his 'Self' (*anâ*) is never lost, even in the most technical explanations of his Sufi path. Compared with Ibn al-Fârịd's poems, Ibn ᶜArabî's verses sound much more artificial. In this latter the thinker prevails on the poet. Ibn al-Fârịd, on the contrary, appears throughout his poems always deeply moved and fascinated by the presence of his Beloved he can perceive, through his profound poetic and mystical insight, in everything. As a gifted poet, he was able to express such an experience in a highly impressive and artistic form that has always excited the enthusiasm of his admirers, especially in Sufi gatherings, as the following verses of his *Tâ'îya* can show (vv. 420-423):

> "At dawn her remembrance to my soul is brought
> by her sweet-scented breeze
> that from the north breathes.
> My ear is filled with joy in the morning light
> through her memory woken by doves,
> cooing on the green boughs.
> My eye is gladden in the evenings by her presence
> brought to its pupil
> by flashes of glowing light.
> My lips are given a taste of her recollection
> by cups of wine
> passed round me at night".

These verses show that Ibn al-Fâriḍ was a fine poet moved by a profound mystical experience and capable of uniting in himself in a charming and beautiful way both the poet and the Sufi.

Ultimately however, after all work done, one has to acknowledge that the poet took the secret of his mystical experience with him, in his return, in the silence of death, to the mysterious sources of his mystical journey: to that "Sea of love and friendship", to that "bounteous and unlimited Ocean", in which he found his true, real 'Self'. His poems have been left to us to be read as traces (*âthâr*) of a path to follow ("The Order of the Way" is the literal translation of the original title of his poem) towards that transcendent Reality.

Finally, my research has not been intended as a 'fastidious explanation' of Ibn al-Fâriḍ's mystical experience. Rather, my intent has been to offer just a elucidation of the poet's language, so that the reader may have access, according to his own intuition and taste (*dhawq*), to the same Reality that has been the ultimate quest of this most outstanding Egyptian Sufi poet, ᶜUmar Ibn al-Fâriḍ.

HUMOROUS APPROACH OF THE DIVINE IN THE POETRY OF AL-ANDALUS

THE CASE OF IBN SAHL

BY

ARIE SCHIPPERS
University of Amsterdam

Quoting two lines with Koranic allusions by Ibn Sahl in his famous book on Hispano-Arabic Poetry, A. R. Nykl says in a note: 'These two allusions do not show great respect for the Qur'ân; they are examples of the typically Isra'îlî mocking sarcasm' (p. 354)[i]. Here is not meant sarcasm in the sense of a bitter or wounding remark, but more a scornful and mocking use of what was considered by the Muslims as God's speech, a disrespect shown by mixing the sacred and the profane. By combining these quotations with his love for a boy called Mûsâ--namesake of the Biblical prophet Moses--he derided Judaism and Islam at the same time. In the following we will examine Ibn Sahl's disrespectful and mocking style in the light of his Mûsâ poems and the many allusions from the Koran and the Bible and early Islamic religion[1].

Ibn Sahl was called in full Abû Isḥâq Ibrâhîm Ibn Sahl al-Isrâ'îlî al-Ishbîlî. The name al-Isrâ'îlî denotes that he was born of a Jewish family, and later officially converted to Islam. He was born in Seville in about 609/1212-3 and spent nearly all his life there, devoting himself entirely to poetry. The editor of his *Dîwân*, Qûbaᶜah, divides his life into three periods: the Sevillian, the Minorcan, and the Ceutan period. He seems to have been most fertile and prolific during the first of these. He frequented *majâlis* (poetic seances) in the parks known as Marj al-Fiḍḍa, Al-ᶜArûs and Fam al-Khalîj. There he also met Ibn Saᶜîd, author of the biographic work *al-Qidḥ*

---

1. I consulted the following works and editions: Muhammed Soualah, *Ibrâhîm ibn Sahl, poète musulman d'Espagne, Son Pays, sa Vie, son Oeuvre et sa Valeur littéraire*, thèse produite à la Faculté des lettres de l' Université d'Alger, Adolphe Jourdan, Alger 1914; *Dîwân Ibn Sahl*, ed. Butrus Bustani, Maktabat Ṣâdir, Beyrouth 1953; *Dîwân Ibn Sahl al-Andalûsi*, Dâr Ṣâdir, ed. Iḥsân ᶜAbbâs, Beyrouth 1967; *Dîwân Ibn Sahl al-Isrâ'îlî*, ed. Muhammad Qubaᶜah, Manshurat al-Jamiᶜat al-Tunisîyah, Tunis 1985 [our edition of reference in this article]; Ben Sahl de Sevilla, *Poemas*, Selección, traducción, e introducción de Teresa Garulo, nueva edición, bilingüe, poesía Hiperión, Madrid 1996.

al-Muᶜallâ. During this first period, he did not become involved in the nasty politics of his time. In 625/1227, at the age of only sixteen, he impressed his contemporaries by inserting a verse by al-Haythami in a poem in praise of Muḥammad b. Yûsuf b. Hûd.

Not much is known about the Minorcan period, but it is thought that Ibn Sahl left Seville for a while. His patron on Minorca was apparently Abû ᶜUthmân ibn Ḥakam, governor and famous *adîb*. At this time, Ibn Sahl engaged himself in political life, although we know almost nothing about this period of his life. According to al-Râᶜî, Ibn Sahl settled in Ceuta after Seville had fallen to Ferdinand III (646/1248). In Ceuta he became one of the secretaries of the governor, Abû ᶜAlî Ibn Khalaṣ. In 649/1251, when the latter decided to despatch his son with a message for Abû ᶜAbd Allâh al-Mustanṣir I, the Ḥafṣid ruler of Ifrîqiya, Ibn Sahl was chosen to accompany him. The travellers set sail on board a galley which was wrecked in a violent storm, and all its occupants perished. According to others, however, he died in 1261.

The *Dîwân* of Ibn Sahl consists almost exclusively of love poems (mostly devoted to a youthful person named Mûsâ), laudatory poems, satirical poetry and *muwashshaḥât*. Mûsâ might be a symbol in connection with Ibn Sahl's original faith. The name of the real, youthful Mûsâ was supposedly Mûsâ ibn ᶜAbd al-Ṣamad, but it may be clear that this original Mûsâ may not have had the eternal youth which his namesake disposes of in Ibn Sahl's poetry. His role is an icon of the beloved one and is comparable with the Lauras and Beatrices in Italian love poetry. Ibn Sahl clearly elaborated his own individual genre of *mûsâwîyat*. Like Ibn Khafâjah, he probably worked upon and reworked his poetry throughout his whole life, although Ibn Sahl lived only half of the more than eighty years that Ibn Khafâjah did. Thus his *mûsâwîyat* may have been his trademark as a poet throughout his career, regardless of the real circumstances of his possible love for a Mûsâ, let alone his supposed love for a certain youth called Muḥammad, which probably derives from a funny, satiric poem by Ibn Sahl in the style of Abû Nuwâs, whom Ibn Sahl mentions two times in his work as his forerunner[2]. Therefore there is no justification for calling his poetry romantic, as Monis did[3]. Ibn Sahl's *mûsâwîyat* are a rhetorical and thematic

2. Cf. *Muwashshaḥ* no. 19: line 3: 'Say to a reproacher who forbids: leave me alone with the religion of Abû Nuwâs' ; *Muwashshaḥ* no. 21: "I followed in this [i.e. drinking the wine of the cheek of the beloved] Abû Nuwâs'.
3. See E.I. (second edition) s.v. Ibn Sahl.

construct of his own, composed in a very satirical and ironic vein. He calls himself ᶜUdhri[4], his love is supposedly unrequited, but his attitude clearly is only playful and dissimilating, combining religious motifs from the Koran and the Bible in a funny way. One should not take his so-called ᶜUdhri love too seriously.

Perhaps his 'serious' poetry consists of his laudatory poems. Here he speaks earnestly about Islam and other religious matters, but more as a superficial symbol for the justification of the patron's power than something deeply religious, and merely in an abstract superficial way. Like many other Arab poets, religion did not seem to play a major role in Ibn Sahl's life. Poets are representatives of the secular world, and are thus the natural counterparts to *faqîh*s, *ṣûfî*s, rabbis and other pious and devote men, representing the opposite pole of society. Therefore one should also look with a secular eye at one of his first long laudatory poems which describes the march of a caravan of pilgrims towards Mecca (See Poem no. 87 [Ṭawîl]).

The question of his Islamic faith has been amply discussed. A Jew who converts to Islam (*Yahûdî 'aslam*) is never taken seriously. But Qûbaᶜah, the editor of his *Dîwân*, accepts the sincerity of his conversion with the following words (pp. 27-28):

> 'All of them who spoke of Ibn Sahl or studied him have immersed themselves in the case of his Islamic faith [we are reminded of the ancient: Ibn Saᶜîd, Abû Ḥayyân from Granada, al-Râᶜî and al-Maqqarî, and of the recent: Muḥammad Sawâliḥ, Iḥsân ᶜAbbâs, Ḥusayn Mu'nis, and many others]. Did the poet really embrace Islam, or did he stick with the religion of his forefathers, and merely profess Islam in external appearance? It seems that the incentive for immersing oneself in this case is the frequent mention of Mûsâ [Moses] in his poetry and his love for him, in addition to his Jewish descent. This was enough to say that Ibn Sahl remained attached to his old belief, expressing this in an indirect manner. But we are inclined to speak about his Islamic faith because most of the biographies, and especially those which were written in Ibn Sahl's time, state that he came to Islam and shower the poet with high praise. As testimony to this, they produce a trustful support which cannot be contested. Thus doubt of his Islamic faith is only doubt of the truthfulness of the intention of the poet and his uprightness. We do not find in his poetry--despite the fact that the majority of it is realistic, love poetry--anything that could be explained or interpreted in such a way that the writer of this poetry remained Jewish. Further

4. See Poem no. 60 [Sarîᶜ]: verse 13.

on his name became ᶜal-Isra'îlî' and not 'al-Yahûdî' [the name other Jewish poets from Muslim Spain and their scholars are given], a clear sign that the poet abandoned the religion of his forefathers and was known between his contemporaries because of his Israeli descent.'

Apparently, for Ibn Sahl himself this was not a problem. According to Ibn Saᶜid's *al-Qidḥ al-Muᶜallâ*[5], Ibn Sahl said to Ibn Saᶜîd: 'The appearances are for men, for God what is hidden.'

To give an impression of the structure of a *mûsâwîyah*, I will translate one of the small poems in its entirety, after which I will give an account of the Koranic allusions, the comparisons of Mûsâ with Moses and the other prophets, the mention of Mosaic attributes such as magic, light, the stick to cleave the waters and to beat the rock, Mount Sinai and others, ending with some general religious notions such as the worship of the beloved and the references to Paradise and Hell.

In poem no. 101 [Ṭawîl] Ibn Sahl said[6]:

1. *Sali al-ka'sa tazhû bayna ṣabghin wa-ishrâqi/ a-dhuwwiba fîhâ al-wardu am wajnatu al-sâqî ?//*
2. *Ku'ûsun tuḥayyîhâ al-nufûsu ka-'annahâ/ ḥadîthu talâqin fî masâmiᶜi ᶜush-shâqi//*
3. *Idhâ qatalûhâ bi-'l-mizâji li-yashrabu/ aᶜâshu munâhum baᶜda mawtin wa-ikhlâqi//*
4. *Tathûru ka-'annahâ al-mâ'a yalsaᶜu ṣirfahâ/ fa-ṣawtu al-mughannî mithlu haynamati al-râqî//*
5. *Bi-Mûsâ idhâ mâ shi'ta sukriya ghanninî /wa-adhiq ku'ûsa al-khamri ayyata idhâqi//*
6. *Wa-in shi'ta iᶜjâzan, ḍarabta bi-dhikrihi / fu'âdî, fa-fajjarta al-ᶜuyûna bi-âmâqî//*
7. *Yuṣâᶜidu anfâsî ḍujan nafasu al-ṣabâ/ wa-taqdaḥu nâru al-barqi nîrâna ashwâqî//*

---

5. Cf. Soualah, p. 186.
6. All references to poems and *muwashshaḥ*s in the text are according to the edition of Muhammad Qubaᶜah, Manshurat al-Jamiᶜat al-Tunisîyah, Tunis 1985, indicating the numbers of the poems, mentioning the metre between square brackets.

8. *idhâ ana ḥammaltu al-balîla ṣabâbatî/ ghadat ka-samûmi al-fatki lafḥata iḥrâqi//*
9. *Ta^c rifu minnî al-rîḥu zafrata ^c âshiqin/ wa-yafhamu minnî al-barqu naẓrata mushtâqi//.*

1. Ask the glass--because it is splendid between colouring and illuminating--whether the roses or the cheek of the pourer has been made fluid in it?

The poet describes how in the glass there is wine as red as roses or as red as the blushing cheeks of the youth who pours the wine. The pourer is the object of the poet's love.

2. They are glasses which greet the souls as if they were the conversation during a love rendezvous with a beloved in the ears of lovers.

3. When they kill the wine by mixing it with water so that they can drink it, they bring back to life their wishes which were nearly dead.

4. The wine gives a bound, when the water bites in his purity; thus the voice of the singer sounds as the whispering of the snake-worshipper.

The water is compared with a snake, which bites the wine, so that it jumps up in pain: the singer functions as snake-worshipper. The jumping up of the water stands for the bubbling of the wine during the mixing.

5. By Mûsâ! If you want my drunkenness, then sing for me and fill the glasses with quite a filling!

The poet invokes Mûsâ, who reminds us of the prophet Moses, whose miracle is alluded to in the next line.

6. If you want a miracle, beat then on my heart by mentioning his name, so that you make wells stream in my eyes.

So the poet says: If you pronounce the name of my beloved Mûsâ, then you make him perform a miracle like that of the prophet Moses, when he smote the rock twice and the water came out abundantly, which reminds us of Numeri 20: 11 and *Sûrat al-Baqara* ['the Cow'; no. 2]: verse 60 ["Strike the

Rock with thy staff"] and *Sûrat al-'Aᶜrâf* ['The Elevated Places'; no. 7]: verse 160.[7]

7. The deep sighing of my breathing, the cool morning wind looks like it, but in the intestines the fires of my longings are kindled.

8. When I would make the moist wind carry my burning longings, then it would break out as a destroying and hot wind

9. The wind knows my sighs as if from a lover, the lightning grasps my glance as if from a longing beloved.

The poet says that the wind is an expert in the field of sighs and the lightning is one in the field of passionate lightning, so they will deeply understand his situation.

In this poem, we see how as well as common love motifs there are those connected with the namesake of the boy Mûsâ, namely the prophet Moses, in this case the beating on the rock which is one of his characteristic deeds, as noted in the Hebrew Bible and the Koran. So we read in Numeri 20:11: "And Moses lifted up his hand, and with his rod he smote the rock twice: and the water came out abundantly, and the congregation drank, and their beasts [also]." And *Sûrat al-'Aᶜrâf* ['The Elevated Places'; no 7]: 160b says: "We suggested to Moses, when his people asked him to give them drink: 'Strike the rock with thy staff'; then there gushed out from it twelve springs."

The name-dropping of *Sûra* names occurs more than twenty times in the poetic works of Ibn Sahl. For example, in poem no. 91 [*Ṭawîl*]: 9. In this line, the *Sûrat al-Aᶜlâ* ['The Most High'; no 87] is called *'Sabbiḥ' Sûra* because the first word of it says: "Praise the name of your Lord". At the end, in verse 19, the first writings--the writings of Abraham and Moses--are spoken of.

---

7. Translations Koranic and Bible texts in this article are according the usual translations (King James and Revised version of the Bible; Richard Bell, *The Qur'ân, translated, with a Critical Re-Arrangement of the Surahs*, Edinburgh, I-II, 1937; and Mawlana Muhammad "Ali, *The Holy Qur'ân*, 4th edition, Ahmadîyah, Lahore, Pakistan, 1951).

Other references are, for instance, poem no. 162 [Sarî^c] which refers to *al-Fatḥ* ['The Victory'; no. 48] and *Yâ Sîn* [no. 36], saying in lines 1-2:

1. *Qad kataba al-ḥusnu ^{c}alâ khaddi-hi:/ innâ fataḥnâ la-ka fatḥan mubîn//*
2. *Yâ qalbu, in milta 'ilâ ghayrihi/ mâ 'anta 'illâ fi ḍalâlin mubîn//*

1. Beauty has written on his cheek: "We have gained a clear victory over you." [*Sûrat al-Fatḥ* no. 48: verse 1]
2. O heart, when you bend yourself towards another than him, you are nothing but in clear error [*Sûrat Yâ Sîn* no. 36: verses 24 and 47].

The satirical trait of the poet may be obvious here.

Poem no. 164 [Kâmil]: line 2 mentions two *Sûra*s:

2. *Wa-agharra tatlû al-Fajra ghurratuhu kamâ/ yatlû li-qalbî Fâtiran bi-jufûnihi*

"And a noble one whose face [forehead] recites the *Sûrat al-Fajr* [='The Daybreak'; no. 89] is as if he recites with his eyelids for my heart the *Sûrat al-Fâtir* ['The Originator'; no. 35]."

Poem no. 41 [Ṭawîl] combines two other *Sûra*s:

1. *La-qad kuntu 'arjû 'an takûna muwâṣilî/ fa-jarra^{c}tanî bi-al-bu^{c}di fâtiḥata al-Ra^{c}di//*
2. *Fa-billâhi barrid mâ bi-qalbî min al-jawâ/ bi-fâtiḥati al-A^{c}râfi min rîqika al-shahadi//*

"1. I had hoped that you were the person who would have had contact with me, but you made swallow me by your distance the opening letters of the *Ra^{c}d* ['Thunder'; no. 13]"

This *sûra* begins with the letters *alif lam mîm râ'* meaning *al-marr*, 'departure, going away'; or *al-murr* 'bitterness'.

"2. By God! Make cold the burning love which is in my heart with the opening letters of the *A^{c}raf* ['the Elevated Places'; no. 7] of your honey like saliva"

Here again, the poet plays with the mysterious beginning letters of the mentioned *Sûra*, namely *alif, lam, mîm, ṣâd= al-maṣṣ* which means 'sucking'.

Finally, I mention poem no. 150 [Khafîf], in which *Sûrat Yâ Sîn* [no. 36] and *Sûrat Yûsuf* [no. 11] are referred to:

> 16. *Kataba al-shaʿru fîhi sînan fa-ʿawadhtu bi-Yâ Sîna ḥusna dhâka al-sîni//*
> 20. *Akbarûhu wa-lam tuqaṭṭaʿ akuffu/ bi-madan, bal qulûbuhum bi-al-jufûni//.*

> "16. The hair wrote on him a *Sîn* and I sought the protection of *Yâ Sîn* [no. 36] against the beauty of this *Sîn*.
> 20. They [mankind] were astonished at him without their hands being cut with long knives, much more, even the hearts were not cut by the eyelids"

Line 20 alludes to the women mentioned in *Sûrat Yûsuf* no 12: verse 31 which goes as follows: 'So when they saw him they were so astonished at him, that they cut their hands'.

Speaking about prophets such as Yûsuf or Joseph, the poet confronts us generally with the theme that Mûsâ is even more beautiful than Joseph, or is at least as beautiful as him. Poem no. 60 [Sarîʿ]:13 says for instance:

> 13. *Yâ yûsufîya al-ḥusni yâ Sâmiriyya-l-hajri ashfiq li-al-hawâ al-ʿudhrî//*
> "13. O Yûsuf-like in beauty, Samaritan-like in separation, have compassion with the ʿUdhrite love."

The Samaritan in *Sûrat Ṭâ Hâ* [no. 20]: verse 97 is someone who apparently had a bad influence on the people of Israel[8], because another verse says in *Muwashshaḥ* 10: 24 (referring to the boy):

> 24. *Afdîhi min Sâmirî/ khitâbuhu bi-"lâ misâs"//*

> 24. I redeem him from a Sâmirî who has to say [during his whole life-time]: 'No contact (*lâ misâs*)'."

---

8. The Samaritan in the Koran is understood as the man who made the golden calf [see Ex. 12: 35].

In his poems, there are also references to the Christian Trinity, because of the tripartite body of the ideal youth[9]. Jesus or ᶜIsâ occurs in many poems because of his wondrous ability to revive the dead. Also Mûsâ is compared with Jesus in poem no. 142 [Wâfir]:

2. *Fa-Mûsâ laḥẓuhu yuḥyî al-rufâta/ ḥakâ ᶜÎsâ bi-iḥyâ'i al-ramîmi//*
2. *Fa-mûsâ laḥẓihi yuḥyî al-rufâta/ ḥakâ ᶜÎsâ bi-iḥyâ'i al-ramîmi//*

"2. Because Mûsâ, when reviving the decayed bones by his glance, looked like ᶜIsa [Jesus] in his reviving the rotten bones."
"2. Because the knife of his glance when reviving the decayed bones, looked like ᶜIsa [Jesus] in his reviving the rotten bones."

In poem 139:11 [Wâfir] there is a parallel of Mûsâ to ᶜIsâ:

11. *La-in wâṣalta, yâ Mûsâ, muḥibban/ la-qad aḥyayta yâ ᶜÎsâ ramîmâ//*
"If you bring yourself in contact, o Mûsâ, with a lover, then you, o ᶜIsâ [Jesus], will bring to life again a decayed body."

In *Muwashshaḥ* 40:11-12 we find a similar expression:

11. *Yâ ṭabîba al-saqâm/ yâ ḥayâta al-anâm//*
12. *Rabbu ᶜÎsâ bni Maryam/ muḥayyî rufâti al-rimâm//*

"O, healer of disease, O life of men,
Lord of Jesus [ᶜIsâ], Maria [Maryam]'s son, the reviver of decayed bones"

I cannot deal at length with the other prophets who crop up in Ibn Sahl's poems (such as Zakarîya[10], Shuᶜayb/Jethro[11], Jacob[12], Abraham[13] and Aaron[14]), but I should mention the prophet Muḥammad. The famous lines of poem 38 [Ṭawîl] go as follows:

---

9. Cf. *Muwashshaḥ* 10: 8-10.
10. Poem no. 169 [Khafîf]: verse 5; this poem as a whole contains many allusions to *sûrat Maryam* ['Mary'; no. 19; verse 7 mentions Zacharias].
11. Poem no. 126 [Ṭawîl]: verse 2.
12. *Muwashshaḥ* no. 41: line 17.
13. Poem no. 133 [Kâmil]: line 2, see note 21 hereafter.
14. Poem no. 72 [Kâmil]; line 13.

1. *Tasallaytu ᶜan Mûsâ bi-ḥubbi Muḥammadi/ law-lâ hudâ al-Raḥmâni mâ kuntu ahtadî//*
2. *Mâ ᶜan qillî fâraqtu dhâka wa-innamâ/ sharîᶜatu Mûsâ ᶜuṭṭilat bi-Muḥammadi//*

"1. I have sought diversion from Mûsâ in the love for Muḥammad; were there not the guidance of the Merciful, I would not have found the right way;
2. Not because of my insufficiency did I separate from the first mentioned person, but it is so that the Law of Moses has been abolished by Muḥammad."

This poem does not necessarily imply the poet's amorous liaison with a boy called Muḥammad. In my view, it is nothing but a coquettish expression used by the poet to frighten his boy Mûsâ, in the same way that Abû Nuwâs teased his boy Hamdân by saying that he had sworn to have relationships only with women in the future[15].

Another group of persons celebrated in Ibn Sahl's poems are famous personalities of early Islam, among whom are also enemies of the prophet Muḥammad: so we find Zubayr ibn al-ᶜAwwâm[16], a prominent companion, Abû Ṭâlib[17], Abû Lahab[18], and Abû Jahl[19], leader of the Meccans and a strong opponent of the prophet. One of the Abû Lahab passages in poem no. 14 [Basîṭ] is full of allusions to the Koran:

1. *A-mâ tarâ damahu fî-al-ṭashṭi ḥîna jarâ/ sulâfata al-râḥi fî ka'sin min al-dhahabi//*
2. *Law lam takun min dami al-ᶜanqûdi rîqatuhu/ la-mâ 'ktasâ khadduhu al-qânî Abâ Lahabi//*
3. *Tabbat yadâ ᶜâdhilayya fîhi wa-wajnatuhu/ ḥammâlatu al-wardi lâ ḥammâlatu al-ḥaṭabi//*[20]

---

15. Ewald Wagner, *Abû Nuwâs: Eine Studie zur arabischen Literatur der frühen Abbasidenzeit*, Wiesbaden, 1965 (Franz Steiner), p. 175; Al-Jurjânî, ᶜAlî ibn ᶜAbdal- ᶜAzîz, *Al-Wasâṭa bayna-l-Mutanabbî wa-khuṣûmihi*, ed. Muh. ibn Faḍl Ibrâhîm e.a., Cairo, 1951, pp. 59-60, lines 1-5.
16. Poem 134 [Kâmil]: line 3.
17. Poem 126 [Ṭawîl]: lines 1,2.
18. Ibidem.
19. Ibidem.
20. See Ewald Wagner, *Abû Nuwâs: Eine Studie zur arabischen Literatur der frühen*

4. *Ḥattâ 'idhâ dakhalat fî kunnihi yaduhu/ ka-'l-shamsi ghâbat ᶜani al-'anẓâri fî al-ḥujubi//*
5. *Irjiᶜ li-mâ qâla fî al-tanzîli khâliqunâ/ ikhfiḍ janâḥaka, yâ Mûsâ, mina al-rahabi//.*

"1. Didn't you see his blood in the basin when the young first wine flowed in a cup of gold
2. Were his saliva not from the blood of the bunch of grapes, then his scarlet cheek would not be covered with Abû Lahab [a fire]
3. May the hands of both my reproachers [of my liaison with him] be cut off because his cheek is a bearer of roses not a bearer of firewood.
4. So that when his hand enters in his sleeve, it is as if it is like a sun hiding herself from the eyes in the veils
5. Come back because of what our Creator said in the Revelation, namely: 'Lower your wing [of humility], O Mûsâ, out of fear'."

How artistically interwoven with the red cheeks bearing fire [Abû Lahab] and the bearer of firewood, the cutting of hands and the lowering of the wing, occurring in *Sûrat al-Lahab* ['The Flame'; no. 111] and *Sûrat al-Isrâ'* ['The Nightly Travel'; no. 17] verse 24!

Another important issue in the description of the boy Mûsâ are the attributes of the prophet Moses given to him: the eyes are magic, although the prophet Moses annihilated the works of the magicians at Pharaoh's court. Poem 133:1 [Kâmil] says:

1. *Wa-mukarririn siḥra al-lawâḥiẓi ahyafa/ qalbî bi-mûsâ nâẓirayhi kalîmu//*
2. *Sakana al-fu'âdu wa-lam yakhaf nîrânahu/ a-yakhâfu ḥarra al-nâri 'Ibrâhîmu//*

"A svelte young boy repeating the magic of his glances, my heart is wounded [*kalîm*] by the sharp knife [*mûsâ*] of his eyes.
My heart is quiet without fearing its fires, would Ibrâhîm fear the heath of a fire?"

Abbasidenzeit, Wiesbaden, 1965 (Franz Steiner), pp. 166, 321 for the same Koranic illusions in the poetry of Abû Nuwâs.

The first line is a pun on the name Mûsâ [Moses] and his title al-Kalîm ['The Interlucutor'], the second line alludes to the prophet Ibrâhîm [Abraham], who, according to the Islamic religion, was the first Muslim, and therefore his people were about to burn him in the fire, but the fire was turned into coolness for Abraham[21]. Ibrâhîm is also the name of Ibn Sahl.

The signs or miracles of Mûsâ appear in *Muwashshaḥ* 24:

14. *Yâ siḥra al-jufûni, ṣaddaqtu/ îmânan bi-'l-siḥri wa-'l-sâḥir//*
15. *Daᶜânî Mûsâ fa-âmantu/ bi-âyâti ḥusnihi al-bâhir//*

"14. O magic of the eyelids, I was sincere in my belief in magic and the magician.
15. Mûsâ called me and I believed in the miracles of his splendid beauty."

In the following fragment from poem 166 [Kâmil], the famous stick with which Moses struck the sea is mentioned, as is Pharaoh's host being drown in the sea, and everything is adapted to the new Mûsâ:

2. *Yahdî ilâ dîni al-ṣibâ wa-li-ḥusnihi/ âyun yuḍillu bihinna man yahdîhi//*
3. *Faᶜalat faᶜâla ᶜaṣâ al-Kalîmi liḥâẓuhu/ bi-muṣaddiqin daᶜwâhu lâ yaᶜṣîhi//*
4. *Tasᶜâ li-qalbi al-ṣabbi min-hâ ḥayyatun/ awdat bihi lasᶜan fa-man yarqîhi*[22]*//*
5. *Wa-'arâ qulûba al-ᶜâshiqîna taḥayyarat/ min tîhihi fî mithli qafri al-tîhi//*
6. *Jadda al-ghalîlu wa-law 'arâda tafajjarat*[23]*/ mithla al-ᶜuyûni lanâ marâshifu fîhi//*
7. *Shaqqat ẓubâ 'alfâẓihi baḥra al-hawâ/ shaqqa al-ᶜaṣâ li-'l- ṣabbi kay turdîhi//*
8. *Ḥattâ idhâ amᶜantu fîhi mugharraran/ aghraqtanî maᶜa jundi ṣabrî fîhi.//*
9. *Fa-daᶜawtuhu: innî bi-ḥubbika mu'minun/ law 'anna îmâna al-shajîyi yunjîhi//.*

21. See *Surat al-Anbiyâ'* ['The prophets'; no. 21] verse 68- 69: 'They [his people] said: "Burn him and help your gods, if you are going to do (anything). We said: "O fire be coolness and peace for Abraham"' . The following lines by Ibn Sahl develop upon the same theme: poem no. 121[Wâfir] line 6; *Muwashshaḥ* 10: line 4.
22. Cf.*Sûrat al-Aᶜrâf* ['The Elevated Places'; no. 7]: verses 103-126.
23. Ibidem, verse 160. See above.

"2. He guides to the religion of love, but by the miracles of his beauty the ones whom he leads, are misled.
3. His glances have the effect of the stick of the Interlocutor [= Moses, al-Kalîm] on a believer of his religion who does not rebel against him.
4. A snake of his glances strives for the heart of an ardent lover, in order to destroy him by biting. Who can use magic against [this snake]?
5. And I see the hearts of the lovers loosing themselves because of his haughtiness in the same sort of desolation of desert [as the Israelites did].
6. And the thirst became heavy, but if he only would want, the lips of his mouth would burst out like fountains.
7. The lances of his glances divided for the lover the sea of love like the stick did, so that these [glances] destroyed him.
8. So that when I am eager for [the sea of your love] as someone who is seduced and misled, you will drown me with the host of my patience [instead of that of the Pharaoh] in it.
9. So that I called him: I am believing in your love, if a grieved one could be saved by his belief."

Here we also see the very frequent theme of the religion of love, instead of God's religion. Other Koranic mosaic themes in Ibn Sahl's poetry are the forbidden nurses[24], Moses put into a chest, cast into the river[25], the Sinai[26], the prophetic tradition[27], Moses' light[28], his falling into a swoon in the neighbourhood of God's presence[29] and again the cleaving of the water[30].
Here are some examples:
- In *Muwashshaḥ* 14: 8-10 occur the motifs: 'cleaving water', alluding to *Sûrat Ṭâ Hâ* (no.20): verse 77 ["Then strike for them a dry path in the sea"] and *Sûrat al-Shuᶜarâ'* ['The Poets'; no 26]: verse 63 ["Strike on the sea with thy staff"] and *Sûrat al-Baqara* ['the Cow']: verse 60 ['Strike the Rock with thy staff"] and *Surat al-Aᶜrâf* ['The Elevated Places; no.7] verse 160:

8. *Qad balaghta, Mûsâ, mina al-hajri/ kulla multamas//*

---

24. Poem no. 152 [Ṭawîl]: verses 6, 12; *Sûrat al-Qaṣaṣ* ['the Narrative'; no. 28]: verse 12.
25. *Muwashshaḥ* no. 36: line 13; *Sûrat Ṭâ Hâ* [no. 20]: verses 37-41; *Sûrat al-Qaṣaṣ* ['the Narrative'; no. 28]: verses 7-13.
26. *Muwashshaḥ* 14: verse 10; Poem no. 142: line 4.
27. Poem no. 142 [Wâfir]: verse 7.
28. Poem no. 122 [Sarîᶜ]: verse 7.
29. See below.
30. See below.

9. *Law shaqaqta dam^cî ^calâ al-l-barri/ lam ya^cud yabas//*
10. *Khalli Ṭûra Sînâ fa-fî ṣadrî/ li-al-hawâ qabas//*

"8. You have reached in separation everything askable;
9. When you cleaved my tears on the dry land, it did not become dry again."

This is can also be an allusion to Ex. 14: 21: "And Moses stretched out his hand over the sea; and the LORD caused the sea to go [back] by a strong east wind all that night, and made the sea dry [land], and the waters were divided." and also to Numeri 20: 11 ["He smote the rock twice and the water flew abundantly"]. Then the poet continues:

"10.Go away from the [Sinai] mountain because in my heart there is a firebrand [*qabas*]."

This alludes to *Sûrat Ṭâ Hâ* (no. 20) : verse 10: "When he saw a fire, he said to his people: Stay, I see a fire; haply I may bring to you therefrom a live coal [*qabas*]." and *Sûrat al-Qaṣaṣ* ['the Narrative'; no. 28]: verse 29: "He perceived a fire on the side of the mountain. He said to his family: 'Wait, I see a fire; may be I will bring to you from it some news or a brand of fire, so that you may warm yourselves.'".

In poem no. 142: 3-7 [Wâfir] Mount Sinai and the prophetic tradition are mentioned with an allusion to *Sûrat al-Qaṣaṣ* ['the Narrative']: 29:

3. *Wa fî kanafi al-khudûdi lahu ^cidhârun/ rawiya al-âyâti ^can ahli al-raqîmi//*
4. *Bi-Ṭûri khudûdihi ânastu nâran/ fa-inna bi-hâ hudâ qalbî al-kalîmi//*
5. *Wa-law fajara al-ḥumayya min lamâhu/ la-'askarati al-ḥumayya bi al-shamîmi//*
6. *Wa-ẓahrin qad ḥakâ fî al-shakli Dâlan/ ^calâ Alifi al-qawâmi al-mustaqîmi//*
7. *Ḥadîthu jufûnihi kam ^camma jafnî/ yusalsiluhu ^cani al-fiqhi al-qadîmi//*

"3. And on the side of his cheeks he has juvenile down which transmitted the Koranic verses from the men of the tablets;
4. On his cheeks which resemble Mount Sinai, I perceived from far a fire; verily there is a guidance for my wounded heart in [that fire].
5. And suppose an anger would burst out from the redness of his cheeks, then the flush of youth would inebriate by its sweet smell.

6. And a back which in form resembles a *Dâl* upon the *Alif* of a straight figure;
7. How much the narrative tradition [*Ḥadîth*] of his eyelids embraced my eyelid, chaining it up, on the authority of the old religious jurisprudence [the Law of Moses]."

In *Muwashshaḥ* 24: 21- 22 the poet mentionens the lightning, the cloud, and the swoon from *Sûrat al-A*ᶜ*raf* ['The Elevated Places'; no. 7] verse 143; cf. 139: "fell down thunderstruck/fell down in a swoon"]:
Muwashshaḥ 24: 21-22:

21. *In abdâ min thaghrihi barqan/ fa-dam*ᶜ*î saḥâbatun tharrah//*
22. *Wa-aḥkî samîyahu ṣa*ᶜ*qan/ in marrat min dhikrihi khaṭarah//*

"21.When he shows of his mouth the lightning so that my tears are a cloud full of water.
22. I am alike to his namesake, falling down in a swoon, when a pompous walk passes which denounces his arrival."

In poem no. 88 [Ṭawîl]: 1-3, the sea, Pharaoh, and the marvels are broached. Here we find an allusion to *Sûrat Ṭâ Hâ* (no. 20): verse 78 ["So the Pharaoh followed them with his armies, and covered them of the sea that which covered them"] and the marvel of the staff turning into a gliding serpent [*Sûrat Ṭâ Hâ*: verse 20; see also verses 55-73 on Moses and the enchanters]:

1. *A-Mûsâ la-qad awradta-nî sharra mawridin/ wa-mâ ana Fir*ᶜ*awnu al-kafûru al-sharâ'i*ᶜ*i//*
2. *Saḥarta fu'âdî ḥîna 'arsalta ḥayyata/ al-*ᶜ*idhâri wa-qad 'aghraqtanî fî madâmi*ᶜ*i//*
3. *Mâ kuntu 'akhshâ an takûna manîyatî/ bi-kaffay-ka, wa-'l-ayyâmu dhâtu badâ'i*ᶜ*i//*

"1. O Mûsâ you have led me to the worst drinking-place, but I am not a Pharaoh who sins against the religious Laws.
2. You bewitched my heart when you sent [me] the serpent of the juvenile down and yet you drowned me in my tears.
3. I was not afraid that my Fate of Death was between your hands, when the Days were full of marvels.

In poem 105 [Ṭawîl]: 1-2 allusions are made to *Sûrat al-Aᶜrâf* ['The Elevated Places'; no. 7] verse 143 ["When his Lord manifested His Glory to the mountain, He made it crumble and Moses fell thunderstruck"]:

1. *Ṣuᶜiqtu wa-qad nâjaytu Mûsâ bi-khâṭiri/ wa-aṣbaḥa Ṭûru al-ṣabri min hajrihi dakkâ//*
2. *Qâlû: 'slu ᶜanhu aw tabaddal bihi hawan/ a-baᶜda al-hudâ arḍâ al-juḥûda awi al-shirka//*

1. I fell thunderstruck when having whispered secrets to Moses as it pleased me, and the Mount [Sinai] of my patience became crumbled.
2. They said: 'Console yourself from him or replace him with someone other in love'. Should I after having followed the right course be pleased with apostasy or polytheism?

From the foregoing we can see how much the Mûsâwîyat love poems by Ibn Sahl are an intellectual exercise, playing with intertextuality by means of Koranic quotations and allusions. In poem no. 105 also the idea of the parallel of love and religion is elaborated. Mûsâ even is sometimes compared with God, e.g. in *Muwashshaḥ* 14:

19. *Mâ kâna ḥubbuka yâ fitnah/ fî al-ḥashâ makîn//*
20. *Lawlâ muḥayyâka lî jannah/ wa-hawâka dîn//*
21. *Aḥyî muhjatan anta mufnîhâ/ mubdi'un muᶜîd//*
22. *Law ruziqat min waṣlika al-ghâlî/ jannatu al-shahîd//*

"19. Your love, o temptation, would not have a place in my heart,
20. Were it not that your face is my paradise and my love for you a religion.
21. Revive my soul [life-blood] which you have wasted, Beginner and Repeater,
22. If only the paradise of a martyr [of love] could be provided with a high priced reunion with you."

The religious theme crops up again and again in the rest of Ibn Sahl's poems, just as there are countless references to Paradise and Hell.

In all probability, Ibn Sahl composed his collection of Mûsâ poems according to a pre-established plan, with the deliberate intention of making his so-called love for a young boy Mûsâ his trademark[31]. As a poet, he did not like the heavy-heartedness of the religious functionaries of his time. He remained young enough to devote his poems to the religion of love, without the earnestness of old age which obliged a poet like Ibn Khafâjah to complain.

31. Salma Jayyusi suggested that Ibn Sahl never really converted to Islam, and that his *musâwîyât* reflect his secret adherence to Judaism

Part II:

Modern Poetry

THE KORAN AS SUBTEXT IN MODERN ARABIC POETRY

BY

STEFAN WILD

I. Elements of the literary background

The Lebanese poet Khalîl Ḥâwî (1919-1982) once said in an interview: "Each language is connected with a creative genius: for the English language it is Shakespeare, for the German language it is Goethe, and for Arabic it is Jahiliyya-poetry, the Koran, and al-Mutanabbi"[1] . Such a statement contains a good deal of truth for any modern Arab poet regardless of his religious affiliation. In a way, every utterance in literary Arabic is tied up with the Koran. The whole language, after all, would not be what it is without the Koran. In this general sense, therefore, the Koran is the subtext of every utterance in Arabic to this very day. Perhaps a negative example illustrates this best: when one of the first translations of the Old and the New Testaments into Arabic came out in the 19th century, the complete absence of any "Koranic style" in this translation was as much intentional as remarkable. "(T)he American edition of the Bible emerged as the first book of real importance in Modern Arabic in which the Koranic style is totally absent"[2]. Not a few Arabic Christians, however, looked and listened with envy to the Koranic texts as read and recited by their fellow Muslims. One might even claim that in Arabic ears the Koran acts as a negative subtext even for the Arabic version of the Bible. One might therefore be led to think that a specific Koranic subtext in modern poetry must be a traditional element used mainly when traditional religious values are evoked. When occurring in a modern context, this Koranic intertextuality would tend to force a religious, classical ring on a verse. While this is not entirely untrue it may be all the more surprising that one of the most rebellious and most modern Arabic poets, Adonis, stated that modernity in Arabic poetry has its roots in the Koranic text. To explain this,

---

1. *Muḥyiddin Ṣubḥî, "Khalîl Ḥâwî fî Muqâbala"*, in: *al-Fikr al-ᶜarabi al-muᶜaṣir,* May/June 1986, 148-154.
2. It was translated mainly by Buṭrus al-Bustânî (1819-1883) between 1848 and 1865 and published under the auspices of the American Protestant Mission to Syria and the American Bible Society. See Nadeem N. Naimy, *Mikhail Naimy. An Introduction*, Beirut 1967, 52 and cf. Sasson Somekh, *Genre and Language in Modern Arabic Literature*, Wiesbaden 1991 (=Studies in Arabic Language and Literature, vol. 1.) 79.

he says: "It is clear from the above that modernity in Arabic poetry in particular, and in the written language in general, has its roots in the Koran - the poetics of pre-Islamic orality represents the ancient in poetry - while Koranic studies laid the foundations of a new textual criticism, indeed invented a new science of aesthetics, thus paving the way for the growth of a new Arab poetics. If, moreover, we take account of the Koran's influence on the poetic quality of the writings of the mystics, we can see how the written language of the Koran gave birth to a new appreciation of artistic language, and how the Koran became, in the words of Ibn al-Athir (1162-1239), 'the wellspring of literature'. In this way Koranic studies have provided the most important source for the study of the poetical qualities of the Arabic language"[3].While the Koran is presented by Adonis as the source of the "modernity" of post-Jahiliyya poetry, one has to remember the evident Koranic subtext to this very statement. After all, the Koran contains a "Sura of the Poets", which warns believers at least about *some* poets: "And the poets - the perverse follow them; hast thou not seen how they wander in every valley and how they say that which they do not?" (Sura 26, 224ff.)[4]. Moreover, the Koranic revelation insists with a certain acerbity that it is definitely not poetry. "We have not taught him poetry; it is not seemly for him. It is only a remembrance and a clear Koran..." (Sura 36, 69), says the Koran with regard to the Prophet Muhammad, or even more emphatically in Sura 69, 41-42, in which God swears that the Koran is not the speech of a poet (*qawlu shâ^cir*): "No! I swear by that you see and by that you do not see, it is the speech of a noble messenger. It is not the speech of a poet (little do you believe) nor the speech of a soothsayer...". And finally,

---

3. Adûnîs, *al-Shi*ᶜ*riyya al-*ᶜ*arabiyya. Muḥâḍarât ulqiyat fi al-Collège de France,* Paris, Ayyar 1984, Beirut 50f.: *yatajallâ lanâ... anna judhûr al-ḥadâtha al-shi*ᶜ*riyya al-*ᶜ*arabiyya bi-khâṣṣa wa-al-ḥadâtha al-kitâbiya bi-*ᶜ*âmma kâmina fi al-naṣṣ al-qur'ânî;* the translation is taken from: Adonis, *An Introduction to Arab Poetics*. Translated from the Arabic by Catherine Cobham. London 1990, 49; see also Adunis, *Al-Naṣṣ al-qur'ânî wa-âfâq al-kitâba* 13-55, Beirut 1993.
4. The Koranic translations follow Arthur J. Arberry, *The Koran Interpreted.* Translated with an introduction, Oxford 1984. For Sura 26 see Michael Zwettler, "A Mantic Manifesto. The Sura of the 'The Prophets' and the Koranic Foundations of Prophetic Authority" in: James L. Kugel (ed.), *Poetry and Prophecy. The Beginnings of a Literary Tradition*, Ithaca and London 1990, 75-119, and more recently James E. Montgomery, "Sundry Observations on the Fate of Poetry in the Early Islamic Period" in: J.R. Smart (ed.) *Tradition and Modernity in Arabic Language and Literature,* Richmond 1996.

the Koran records the unbelieving Meccans as having said to the Prophet, "What, shall we forsake our gods for a poet possessed?" (Sura 37, 36).

Nevertheless, we know that the Prophet Muhammad did not abhor poetry as such and that the Koran did become a specific subtext for much of Classical Arabic poetry. Pious poetry, of course, from earliest Islamic times onwards abounds in references and allusions to the Koranic text. This includes short reminiscences of and references to the Koran; longer passages or quotations have to be slightly changed, if only to fit a metre. On a different level, Abû Nuwâs[5] was a master of irreverent, often blasphemous mockery which did not spare the Koran. Other Abbasid poets, like Ibn al-Rûmî and Ibn al-Muᶜtazz in a more neutral way, often allude to Koranic verses[6].

Perhaps as unexpectedly as Adonis, Nizâr Qabbânî expresses his appreciation of the poeticity of the Koran when he states:

> When God wanted to communicate with man, He took refuge in poetry, in the melting melody, in the beautiful word, in the graceful verse. He could have used

---

5. Ewald Wagner, *Abû Nuwâs. Eine Studie zur arabischen Literatur der frühen ᶜAbbasidenzeit, Wiesbaden* 1965 (= Akademie der Wissenschaften und der Literatur. Veröffentlichungen der orientalischen Kommission, Band XVII), 121ff.
6. For Koranic allusions in early Islamic poetry see: Ewald Wagner, *Grundzüge der klassischen arabischen Dichtung, vol. II* (Die arabische Dichtung in islamischer Zeit), 12; cf. also M. Rahatullah Khan, *Vom Einfluß des Korans auf die arabische Dichtung,* Diss. Leipzig 1938; Omar A. Farrukh, *Das Bild des Frühislam in der arabischen Dichtung von der Higra bis zum Tod ᶜUmars (1-23 D.H. / 622-644 n.Ch.),* Leipzig 71f.; A.M. Zubaidi, "The impact of the Koran and Hadith on medieval Arabic literature" in: A.F.L. Beeston et. al. (edd.), *Arabic Literature to the End of the Umayyad Period* (=CHAL), Cambridge 1983, 322-343; furthermore: Fred M. Donner, "Piety and Eschatology in Early Kharijite Poetry" in: Ibrahim as-Saᶜafin (ed.), *Fî Miḥrâb al-Maᶜrifah.*19. Mai 1998. Festschrift for Ihsân ᶜAbbâs, Beirut 1997, 13-19; Wadad Al-Qadi, "The Limitations of Koranic Usage in Early Arabic Poetry: The example of a Kharijite poem" in: W. Heinrichs & G. Schoeler (edd.), *Festschrift Ewald Wagner zum 65. Geburtstag, vol. 2, Studien zur arabischen Dichtung*, Beirut 1994, 162-181. A later example is a poem of al-Biruni (973-1048) on his genealogy, which contains an an allusion to Sura 111: "By God, I do not know my descent / I do not have certainty about my grandfather. / And how should I know my grandfather, knowing not even my father? / Yes, I am Abû Lahab, a Sheikh without culture / And my mother was the carrier of firewood"; see Gerhard Strohmaier, *Al-Bîrûnî. In den Gärten der Wissenschaft. Ausgewählte Texte aus den Werken des muslimischen Universalgelehrten*, Leipzig 1988, 7f..

> His power as the Lord to say to man:, 'Be a believer!' and he would have believed. But He took the more noble and beautiful way. He chose poetry.

After citing verses of Sûrat Maryam verbatim, Nizâr Qabbânî concludes: „This is one of God's poems. Shall I show you other poems? Open the gospel, read the psalms, then you will see how poetry flows from God's mouth"[7].

In what way, however, is the Koran a specific subtext for *modern* Arabic poetry? Is it - to rephrase Adonis' expression - also at the root of modern Arabic poetic modernity?

The selection of modern Arabic poetry which I have tried to analyse in this context is, of course, highly subjective and very limited. What I think may be a common link between all the poets quoted is that they in one way or another assume the role of the poet-prophet. In the following remarks, I want to point out three aspects of the question of how to define the exact position of modern Arabic poetry vis-à-vis the Koran. After a flashback to Amîn al-Rayḥânî, I will try, on the functional level, to distinguish two types of intertextual interaction with the Koranic text by offering short analyses of poems by Nizâr Qabbânî, Maḥmûd Darwîsh, Samiḥ al-Qâsim, Amal Dunqul, Muᶜîn Basîso and, as the youngest poet quoted, Aḥmad Ṭilib. A closing remark will deal with Adonis' poetry. There is, sometimes, the problem of ascertaining whether a specific Koranic subtext exists or not. To recognize a Koranic subtext seems at first glance a problem only for non-Arabs. How could anybody brought up in Arabo-Islamic culture fail to recognize a Koranic allusion? While conceding that in this non-Arabs are certainly at a disadvantage, the fact that Arabic in general is so heavily indebted to the language of the Koran may blind even the Arab literary critic. A good example of how the Koranic subtext can simply be overlooked is a recent study on the symbols of the *turâth* in modern Arabic poetry[8]. It concentrates on *Jâhiliyya* symbols and somehow manages to

7. Nizâr Qabbânî, *Al-Shiᶜr qindîl akhḍar* (Beirut 1963), containing an essay, *Allâh wa-al-shiᶜr,* which was written in 1957 = *al-Aᶜmâl al-nathriyya al-kâmila*, vol. 7, Beirut 1993, p. 59-70. See for the question of the aesthetic appreciation of the Koranic text: Navid Kermani, *Gott ist schön. Das ästhetische Erleben des* Koran, München 1999, passim.
8. Khâlid al-Karakî, *Al-rumûz al-turâthiyya al-ᶜarabiyya fî al-shiᶜr al-ᶜarabî al-ḥadîth*, Beirut-Amman, 1989.

disregard completely the Koran. But even if an intertextuality is recognized, there may be no agreement on whether it actually exists. For instance, Nizâr Qabbânî says in one of his many poems critical of Arab society:

Al-lafẓatu fî al-sharqi al-ᶜarabiyyi
arajûzun bâriᶜun
yatakallamu sabᶜata alsinah[9]

The word in the Arab world
Is a nifty marionette
Who speaks seven languages[10].

The translator adds in a footnote to explain the "seven languages": "A reference to the seven ways of reading the Koran". Not all Arabophones feel this intertextuality, and, of course, one man's intertextuality is not everyman's intertextuality. With regard to the poetic passages which I have chosen, I have tried to select only those whose link to a Koranic subtext is beyond reasonable doubt.

Historically, it is clear that this subtext has been with modern Arabic poetry from its very beginnings. One of the first Arabic writers to use it in an almost blatant way was Amîn al-Rayḥâni (1876-1940), who wrote a poem *al-Thawra* ("The Revolution") celebrating the victory of the Young Turks against Abdülhamid II, which was published first in New York in 1907[11]. This poem, one of the first instances of *shiᶜr manthûr*, closely resembles in its imagery and its composition some of the eschatological Suras of the Koran and is a pastiche of some of the main stylistic features of early Mekkan Suras: oaths, apocalyptic threats, eschatological promises,

9. Nizâr Qabbânî, *Murfîn* ("Morphium"), in *Diwân Lâ* (1970) = *al-Aᶜmâl al-shiᶜriyya al-kâmila,* vol. 2, 2nd. ed., 1980, 948.
10. Abdullâh al-Udharî (transl. & ed.), *Modern Poetry of the Arab World.* New York 1986, 102.
11. Amîn al-Rayḥânî, *Hutâf al-awdiya. Shiᶜr manthûr,* ("The Call of the Valleys. Prose-poetry") Beirut 1955, 18-22, first published in New York in 1907; cf. Carl Brockelmann, *GAL* S III 402; Shmuel Moreh, *Modern Arabic Poetry 1800-1970. The Development of its Form and Themes under the Influence of Western Literature,* Leiden 1976 (= Studies in Arabic Literature, Supplement to the Journal of Arabic Literature, vol. V), 292; Salmâ Khadrâ Jayyûsî, *Trends and Movements in Modern Arabic Poetry,* 2 vols., Leiden 1977 (=Studies in Arabic Literature, Supplement to the Journal of Arabic Literature, vol. VI) I 90.

formulaic expressions, etc. While the poem can scarcely be considered a masterpiece, it seems significant that the poetic revolution of introducing *shi*ᶜ*r manthûr* went hand in hand with a structure which was in every line indebted to the Koran. I am not sure that such a poem composed by a poet with a Christian background could at that time have been published in any part of the Ottoman Empire. I quote only a few lines:

Al-thawra

*Wa-yawmihâ al-qaṭûbi al-*ᶜ*aṣîb*
*wa-laylihâ al-munîri al-*ᶜ*ajîb*
*wa-najmihâ al-afîli tahdiju bi-*ᶜ*aynihi al-raqîb*
wa-ṣawti fawḍahâ al-rahîb
min hutâfin wa-lajabin wa-naḥîb
*wa-za'îrin wa-*ᶜ*andalatin wa-na*ᶜ*îb*
wa-ṭughâti al-zamâni yusâmûna nâran
w-akhyârihi yaḥmalûna al-ṣalîb
waylun yawma'idhin li-al-ẓalimina, li-'l-mustakbirîna wa-'l-mufsidîn...

The Revolution

By its dark and hot day,
By its wonderful bright night,
By its setting star at which the observer glances sharply,
By the sound of its terrible chaos,
And its crying and uproar and moaning
And its roaring and its songs of nightingales and ravens,
By the tyrants of time forced into a fire,
While their best men carry the cross -
Woe that day unto those who do evil, unto the haughty and the workers of corruption...

In the long run, this becomes monotonous, especially when the poet assumes the first person plural of divine speech in the Koran:

A-lam naquṣṣa ᶜ*alayhim qaṣaṣ Bârîs*
Yawma dukka al-Bastîlu wa-zaffat al-maḥâbîs
*Yawma quṭi*ᶜ*a ra'su al-maliki Louis*
Wa-ḥuzzat riqâbu kibâri al-faransîs

Have We not told them the story of Paris
The day the Bastille was levelled and the prisoners were hastened along,
The day the head of King Louis was cut
And the necks of the great of the French were wrung?

II. Functionalizing the Koranic subtext: the poet as prophet

There are, I think, two main types of intertextuality between the Koran and modern Arabic poetry.There is, on the one hand, Koranic language used as a means to intensify the religious impact; it is built on the common acceptance of the Koran as the fundamental text of Arabic culture and Arabo-Islamic religion. There is, on the other hand a use of Koranic language which distances itself from this traditional mode by a flippant, ironic, nostalgic or even destructive counterpoint to the context. This may serve to underline the incompatibility of the traditional Koranic diction and the poet's message. Sasson Somekh called the first function "linear", "that is drawing on the Koran with full acceptance of the framework of religious discourse", the second "ironic"[12]. It has to be admitted, I think, that this useful typology is not very rigid and there is much overlapping.

A. Let us start with flippancy. Nizâr Qabbânî (1923-1998) begins one of his long love poems with the words *ashhadu an lâ 'mra'atan atqanati al-lu^cbata illâ anti* ("I declare that there is no woman who can play the game to perfection but you")[13]. His playful subtext to this repeated beginning *ashhadu an la 'mra'atan... illa anti* is the *shahâda*, the Muslim declaration of faith. The closing verse of this poem is: *ashhadu an lâ mra^cata tamakkanat an tarfa^ca al-ḥubba ilâ martabati al-ṣalâti illa anti illa anti illa anti* ("I declare that there is no woman who could raise love to the quality of prayer but you, but you, but you")[14]. Apparently, the poet liked this idea so much that he called the poem and indeed the whole *Dîwân: Ashhadu an lâ 'mra'atan illa anti* ("I declare that there is no woman but you"). This is playful flippancy: for a rhetorical moment, the beloved becomes God-like, not in any Sufi sense but in a teasing tribute to her beauty. This is not

12. Sasson Somekh, *Genre* (s. footnote 2) 61.
13. Nizâr Qabbânî, *Ashhadu an lâ mra^cata illâ anti*, Beirut, 5th ed. 1983.
14. *Ibid.* 35.

completely innocent teasing - there is a certain aggressivity in it which was understood by most, loved and admired by many, and frowned upon and even hated by not a few. And if one remembers that the real *shahâda* consists of two parts ("I declare that there is no God but God and that Muhammad is His Prophet") - the invisible complete subtext of Nizâr Qabbânî's version could be: "I declare that there is no woman but you and that Nizâr Qabbânî is your prophet".

The weaknesses of Nizâr Qabbânî's poetry have often been mentioned[15]. One is that Nizâr Qabbânî is usually not satisfied with hints and allusions. His message is driven home, as it were and this weakens the poetic impact. Mild blasphemy frequently repeated loses much of its charm.

In a more somber mood, Nizâr Qabbânî says in his *Hawâmish ᶜalâ daftar al-Naksa* ("Notes to the book of defeat"):

julûdunâ mayyitatun
arwâḥunâ tashkû min al-iflâs
ayyâmunâ tadûru bayna al-zâri wa-'l-shaṭranji wa-'l-nuᶜâs
hal naḥnu khayru ummatin qad ukhrijat li-'l-nâs? [16]

We are a dead-skinned people
Our souls bankrupt
We spend our days practising witchcraft,
Playing chess and sleeping.
Are we the ,'Nation by which God blessed mankind'?[17]

The Koranic text of Sura 3, 110, *kuntum khayra ummatin ukhrijat li-'l-nâsi* ("You are the best nation ever brought forth to men"), is slightly adapted to fit the metre. In the context of Nizâr Qabbânî's scathing self-critique, the Koranic assertion is twisted into a rhetorical question which sardonically

15. They are not even completely neglected in the Festschrift-like homage to him: Muḥammad Yûsuf Najm (ed.), *Nizâr Qabbânî - A Poet for all Generations. Shâᶜir li-kull al-ajyâl.* Bi-ishrâf Suᶜâd Muḥammad Âl-Ṣabâḥ, 2 vols., Beirut 1998 (published shortly before his death), or in Adonis' somewhat reticent obituary *ᶜAlâ hadbaᶜ Nizâr* (in: *Al-Ḥayât* ???).
16. *al-Aᶜmâl al-siyâsiyya al-kâmila*, vol. 6, Beirut 1993, 487.
17. As translated by Abdullâh al-Udharî, *Modern Poetry* (footn. 10) 99, with slight adaptations.

belies its content. The ironic self-critique gains in acerbity by the Koranic grounding.

B. Whereas Nizâr Qabbânî's poetic prophethood is skilfully if sometimes simplistically playful, other poets strike a note of deadly seriousness. An example of such Koranic pathos is a passage from the poem *Marâthî* by the Palestinian Samîḥ al-Qâsim (born 1939): [18]

Lâm Nûn

wa-ḍarâᶜati rûḥî wa-ᶜimâdî fî al-ḥama'i al-masnûn
wa-'l-kafani al-ṭâliᶜi min jildî
wa-'l-tâbûti al-ṭâliᶜi min jasadi al-zaytûn
wa-'l-aslafi al-mawtâ al-aḥyâ'i al-mawtâ
wa-'l-aḥfâdi al-âtûn
ḥammalanî ahlî damahum ḥammaltu lisânî damaḥum
ṣâḥû min ḥanjaratî al-madhbûḥa

Lâm Nûn

By the supplication of my spirit and by my stay in mud moulded,
By the shroud coming out of my skin,
By the ark coming out of the olives' body
By the dead ancestors and the dead living
My people imposed the blood of the coming offspring on me
And I imposed their blood on my tongue.
They cried from my slaughtered throat...

This passage is a pastiche of different Koranic motifs. Its beginning resembles the beginning of many Suras. The *Lam Nûn* imitates the Koranic *ḥurûf muqaṭṭaᶜa* like *Nûn, Alif Lâm Mîm, Yâ' Sîn*, etc. at the beginning of some Suras. The oaths introduced by the *wâw al-qasam* echo the Koranic oaths sworn by God in the Koran. The allusion to these oaths was a technique which, as we have seen, was already used by Amîn al-Raiḥânî. Sura 68 (*sûrat al-qalam*) sounds especially close to Samîḥ al-Qâsim'

18. Quoted according to Ṣâliḥ Abû Iṣbaᶜ, *al-Ḥaraka al-shiᶜriyya fî Filasṭin al-muḥtalla. Mundhu ᶜâm 1948 ḥattâ 1975*. Dirâsa naqdiyya, Beirut 1975, 309: al-iqtibâs min al-kutub al-muqaddasa.

verses: *Nûn / Wa-'l-qalami wa-mâ yasṭurûn / ma anta bi-niᶜmati rabbika bi-majnûn / wa-inna laka la-ajran ghayra mamnûn...* ("Nun, by the pen and what they inscribe, thou art not, by the blessing of thy Lord a man possessed; surely thou shalt have a wage unfailing..."). The words *rûḥ*, *ᶜimâd*, *ḥama'*, *masnûn*, *tâbût*, *ẓaytûn*, *jasad* used by al-Qâsim are heavily impregnated with Koranic flavor. And the mysterious pseudo-Koranic *Lâm Nûn* stands in Samîḥ al-Qâsim's poem at the same time for Arabic *lan*, "never". The prophetic Koranic language conveys the political message of resistance. It is deadly serious - there is no irony, no disrespectful flippancy.

Close to this is a passage in Maḥmûd Darwîsh's *Ṭarîq Dimashq* ("The Way to Damascus")[19]. Towards the end of this long militant poem, praising Damascus and the Syrian role in supporting the PLO, the poet says:

Uᶜiddu lahum mâ staṭaᶜtu..
wa-yanshaqqu fî juththatî qamarun
sâᶜatu al-ṣifri daqqat
wa-fî juththatî ḥabbatun anbatat li-'l-sanâbili
sabᶜa sanâbila fî kulli sunbulatin alfu sunbula[20]

I make ready for them what I can
While in my body the moon is splitting.
Zero hour stroke
While in my body a grain has sprouted - in each ear
Seven ears, in each ear a thousand ears.

Again, there are different Koranic strands blended into each other. There is first Sura 8, 60: *wa-aᶜiddû lahum mâ staṭaᶜtum min quwwatin wa-min ribâṭi al-khayli turhibuna bihi ᶜaduwwa llâhi wa-ᶜaduwwakum* ("Make ready for them whatever force and strings of horses you can, so terrify thereby the enemy of God and your enemy"). This is how God exhorts the Prophet against his enemies. There is secondly the eschatological passage Sura 54, 1: *Iqtarabati al-sâᶜatu wa-nshaqqa al-qamar* ("The hour has drawn nigh; the moon is split"). And there is lastly the parable of Sura 2, 261: *mathalu*

19. = Maḥmûd Darwîsh, *Dîwân* . Beirut 12th ed. 1987, 535ff.: *Muḥâwalat raqm 7* ("Attempt no. 7", published 1973). See also Stefan Weidner, "Maḥmûd Darwîsh" in: Heinz Ludwig Arnold (ed.), *Kritisches Lexikon zur fremdsprachigen Gegenwartsliteratur*, 44. Nachlieferung, November 1997, 1-16.
20. Maḥmûd Darwîsh, *Dîwân* 544.

lladhîna yunfiqûna amwâlahum fî sabîli llâhi ka-mathali ḥabbatin anbatat sabᶜa sanabila fi kulli sunbulatin mi'atu ḥabbatin ("The likeness of those who expend their wealth in the way of God is as the likeness of a grain of corn that sprouts seven ears, in every ear a hundred grains").

Maḥmûd Darwîsh weaves these three Koranic verses into seven short lines of poetry. He amalgamates eschatological Meccan verses with militant Medinan verses. And with characteristic boldness he makes of the hundred ears in the Koran "a thousand ears"; the hour of the Day of Judgment, "the Hour", becomes "zero hour", thus changing the stylistic register by imitating a broadcasting voice announcing the hour in radio-like fashion. This whole secularized eschatology is placed in the poet's body, ready for martyrdom to liberate Palestine[21]. The Koranic subtext assures pathos. Poet and prophet blend into one speaker, the political message gains religious intensity. The Koranic subtext enforces the poet's standing as a poet-prophet: this is a link which is common to Amîn al-Rayḥânî, Samîḥ al-Qâsim, Maḥmûd Darwîsh, Muᶜîn Basîsû, and Amal Dunqul. The poet-prophet is a favorite Arabic lyrical ego. It may also rest on a biblical subtext as can be seen in poetic works from Jibrân Khalîl Jibrân to Khalîl Ḥâwî and Yûsuf al-Khâl.

C. Even more intricate is Maḥmûd Darwîsh's poem *Lidînî, lidînî li-aᶜrifa* ("Give birth to me, give birth to me, that I may know"). Written in November 1983 for the fighters of the PLO who had to leave Lebanon, Maḥmûd Darwîsh invokes a multitude of Koranic concepts:

> *Lidînî ..., lidînî li-aᶜrifa fî ayyi arḍin amûtu wa-fî ayyi arḍin sa-ubᶜathu ḥayyan*
> *Salâmun ᶜalayki wa-anti tuᶜiddîna nâra al-ṣabâḥi, salâmun ᶜalayki, salâmun ᶜalayki*

> "Give birth to me. Give birth to me that I may know in which land I will die, in which land I will come to life again.
> Greetings to you as you light the morning fire, greetings to you, greetings to you."[22]

The poem's subtext are two Koranic verses. The first is: *Wa-mâ tadrî nafsun fî ayyi arḍin tamûtu* (Sura 31, 34) ("No soul knows in what land it

21. Cf. Abû Iṣbaᶜ, *Al-Ḥaraka al-shiᶜriyya* (footnote 18) 310.
22. As translated by Abdullâh al-Udhari (ed.), *Victims of a Map*, London 1984, 21f.

shall die"). In this case, Maḥmûd Darwîsh evidently counterplots the Koranic message. His verse flagrantly contradicts the subtext. The poet does demand to know. He demands from his mother, i.e., his country: "give birth to me that I may know in which land I will die". The relation Koranic subtext - poetic text is hardly ever completely innocent, but in this case it is especially full of tension. The second Koranic verse is Sura 19, 33, *wa-al-salâmu ᶜalayya yawma wulidtu wa-yawma amûtu wa-yawma ubᶜathu ḥayyan* ("Peace be upon me, the day I was born and the day I die and the day I am raised up alive"). Thus speaks the prophet Jesus miraculously from the cradle to Maryam's unbelieving relatives. And Maḥmûd Darwîsh similarly speaks from his exile to the Palestinians despairing of their fate.

Maḥmûd Darwîsh's poetical cycle *Aḥada ᶜashara kawkaban ᶜalâ âkhir al-mashhad al-andalusî* ("Eleven stars on the last Andalusian Scene")[23] alludes in its title to Sura 12, 4, "When Yûsuf said to his Father: 'Father, I saw eleven stars, and the sun and the moon, I saw them bowing down before me'". The cycle is shaped in eleven poetical fragments - and the Koranic subtext for the title is the whole of Sura 12, which depicts the prophet Yûsuf's exile. This story begins with Yûsuf's dream of the eleven stars and, of course, climaxes in Yûsuf's final triumph. The title of the Dîwân juxtaposes the Koranic subtext with the historical Arab loss of Cordoba to the Spanish reconquista, one of Darwish's favorite symbols for the Arab loss of Jerusalem and Palestine.

This secularized play on Koranic imagery and allusion to Koranic verses and suras is an important emphatic device. In Maḥmûd Darwîsh's language, there is not a hint of mockery or flippancy. Religiously coloured language is in Arabic culture a primary device for commanding serious attention. It reinforces the role of the poet-prophet dear to many an Arab poet's heart.

The larger the audience, the more likely a negative traditionalist reaction. Yûsuf's dream in Maḥmûd Darwîsh's version was set to music by the renowned Lebanese singer Marcel Khalifeh. When his song Anâ Yûsuf yâ abî ("I am Joseph, o my father") based on one of Maḥmûd Darwîsh's earlier poems which included the Koranic quote of Sura 12, 4, came out in 1996, the chief prosecutor of Beirut, ᶜAbdallah al-Biṭâr, charged the poet with

---

23. Beirut 1992. See the interesting analysis of Ali J. al-Allaq, "Tradition as a Factor of Arabic Modernism: Darwish's Application of a Mask" in: J. R. Smart (ed.), *Tradition and Modernity in Arabic Language and Literature*, Richmond 1996, 18-26.

blasphemy for having included a verse from the Koran in his song (19 September 1996) . The case was later dropped. One might also compare the reception of Yûsuf Shâhîn's film *Al-Muhâjir*, which was based on the story of the Koranic Yûsuf and was for a time banned in many Arab countries[24]. Leftist Arab poets had and have a special predilection for the Koranic subtext. The communist poet Muᶜîn Basîsû (1930-1984) wrote an elegy on Yûsuf Salmân, the Secretary General of the Iraqi Communist Party who had been executed in 1949, and called it *Surat Yûsuf Salmân*, celebrating in this "Sura" the "prophet" Yûsuf Salmân and his message, communism[25]. The same poet foreshadows Mahmûd Darwîsh's *Aḥada ᶜashara kawkaban*, which was just quoted, in his poem *Aḥada ᶜashar firâsha fi daftar al-mâ'* ("Eleven butterflies in the notebook of water"), a poem which in eleven short stanzas is directed to the poet's bride, Palestine. The eleventh and last stanza of this poetical cycle abounds in direct Koranic allusions[26]:

tusâfirîna fi kitâbi al-mâ'
sûrata Iqra'
Tarjaᶜîna fî kitâbi al-nâri
Sûrata Uktub
Taktubîna sûrata al-Muqâwamah
wa-al-arḍu qâdimah

You depart in the Book of Water
As the Sura Iqra' ("Recite!").
You return in the Book of Fire
As the Sura Uktub ("Write"!).
You write the Sura of Resistance
And the land will come back.

---

24. For the complex question of the representation of the Prophet Muhammad and other prophets in Arab films see Werner Ende, "Mustafa ᶜAqqad's 'Muhammad'-Film und seine Kritiker" in: Hans R. Roemer & Albrecht Noth (edd.), *Studien zur Geschichte und Kultur des Vorderen Orients. Festschrift für Bertold Spuler zum siebzigsten Geburtstag,* 32-52.
25. Muᶜîn Basîsû, *al-Aᶜmal al-shiᶜriyya al-kamila*, Beirut 1979, 694-701; cf. Stefan Wild, "Judentum, Christentum und Islam in der palästinensischen Poesie" in: *Die Welt des Islams* 23/24 (1983/1984) 293f.
26. Muᶜîn Basîsû, *Aᶜmâl* 589ff.

In the following four examples, the tension between the Koranic subtext and the poetic content approaches the breaking point. It is difficult to see where exactly the fault line is, where the super-text comes to sound so aggressive that it turns into something approaching either parody or blasphemy.

1. In 1982, the PLO, after having been forced out of their sanctuary Beirut, convened for its National Congress in Algiers. For this occasion, Maḥmûd Darwîsh wrote and read his long and grim poem *Madîḥ al-ẓill al-ᶜâlî* ("Praise of the high shadow") to them. Here the Koranic subtext is embedded in an explosion of passion, rage, and grief. At one point the poem runs:

Naḥtallu mi'dhanatan wa-nuᶜlinu fî al-qabâ'ili
anna Yathriba ajjarat qur'ânan li-Yahûdi Khaybar?
Allâhu akbar.
Hâdhihi âyâtunâ, fa-qra':
Bi-smi al-fidâ'îyi lladhî khalaqâ
min jazmatin ufuqâ.
Bi-smi al-fidâ'îyi lladhî yarḥal
min waqtikum li-nidâ'ihi al-awwal
Al-awwali al-awwal
'Sa-nudammiru al-haykal'.
Bi-smi al-fidâ'îyi lladhî yabda'
Iqra':
'Bairûtu ṣûratunâ,
Bairûtu sûratunâ'.[27]

Shall we occupy a minaret and proclaim among the tribes that Yathrib let out its Koran to the Jews of Khaybar?
God is great.
These are our verses, so recite:
In the name of the Fedai who created
a horizon out of a shoe.
In the name of a Fedai who departs
from your time to his first call,

27. Maḥmûd Darwîsh, *Madîḥ al-ẓill al-ᶜâlî*, Beirut 1983, 27f. I have quoted this poem in S. Wild, "Judentum..." (footnote 25) 294.

his very first call:
'We will destroy the Temple.'
In the name of the Fedai who begins,
Recite:
'Beirut is our image.
Beirut is our Sura.'

Here, the manifold Koranic reminiscences are so obvious that it would be tedious to enumerate them. The angry poet-prophet appropriates the Koranic text tradition; the *bi-smi llâhi* becomes *bi-smi al-fidâ'i,* the fedai takes the place of God..

2. One of the more famous poems of Amal Dunqul (1940-1983) is his *al-Bukâ' bayna yaday Zarqâ' al-Yamâma* [28] ("Weeping before Zarqa' al-Yamama"). In this poem full of "verses, psalms and hymns", we find[29]:

Kalimât Spartakus al-akhîra

al-Majdu li-al-shayṭâni ma^cbûdi al-riyâḥ
Man qâla "lâ" fi wajhi man qâlû "na^cam"
man ^callama al-insâna tamziqa al-^cadam
Man qâla "lâ" fa-lam yamut
Fa-ẓalla rûḥan abadîyata al-alam

Spartakus' Last Words

Praise be to Satan, adored by the winds,
Who said "no" in the face of those who said "yes"
Who taught man the tearing of nothingness,
Who said "no" and did not die
And remained a spirit of eternal grief.

This passage, formally and by virtue of its rhyme an evident allusion to the opening verses of Sura 96, takes up the Sûfî topic of Iblîs as the only true

28. *Diwân* Beirut 1985, 110; the poem is reproduced in Amal Dunqul's handwriting in ᶜAbla Ruwaynî, *Amal Dunqul al-Janûbî*, Beirut-Cairo 1992, 34.
29. See Fatima Moussa-Mahmoud, "Changing Technique in Modern Arabic Poetry: A Reflection of Changing Values?" in: J. R. Smart (ed.), *Tradition and Modernity* (footnote 23) 61-74.

believer. Iblîs did not obey God when He ordered the angels to fall down before Adam (Sura 18, 50ff.); Iblis thereby became the only true monotheist *muwaḥḥid*, a tragic role[30]. But *al-majdu li-al-shayṭâni* as counterformula to *al-ḥamdu li-llâhi* can make a believer shiver.

3. My third example is Amal Dunqul's poem *Muqâbala khâṣṣa maᶜa Ibn Nûḥ* ("Special interview with Noah's Son)[31], written in 1976. The Koranic subtext is Sura 11, 42ff.: the prophet Noah bids his son to embark with him on the ark but the son refuses whereupon the son is drowned. After the flood, Noah argues with God about his son's death, but God comforts him by assuring Noah that what he whom he had thought his son in reality was not[32].

The translation of the Koranic subtext runs:

> He said: 'I will take refuge in a mountain, that shall defend me from the water.' Said he, 'Today there is no defender from God's command but for him on whom He has mercy'. And the waves came between them, and he was among the drowned ... And Noah called unto his Lord, and said, 'O my Lord, my son is of my family, and Thy promise is surely the truth. Thou art the justest of those who judge.' Said He: 'Noah, he is not of thy family, it is a deed not righteous. Do not ask of Me that whereof thou hast no knowledge. I admonish thee, lest thou shouldst be among the ignorant'.

In Amal Dunqul's poem, the disobedient and sinful son disavowed in the Koran becomes the hero: his father, the prophet Noah, becomes the villain. Noah flees, cowardly, with the corrupt elite of the city to the Ark. The singers, the marechal, the usurers, the Chief Justice and his page, the sword

---

30. For the historical context see Peter J. Awn, *Satan's Tragedy and Redemption: Iblis in Sufi Psychology*. With a foreword by Annemarie Schimmel (= Studies in the History of Religion - Supplement to Numen - vol. XLIV) Leiden, 1983, passim; for a more modern context: Ṣâdiq Jalâl al-ᶜAẓm, *Ma'sât Iblîs* in: id., *Naqd al-fikr al-dînî*, Beirut 7th ed. 1994, 55-87, and Khalîl Shaikh, *Der Teufel in der modernen arabischen Literatur. Die Rezeption eines europäischen Motivs in der arabischen Belletristik, Dramatik und Poesie des 19. und 20. Jahrhunderts*, Berlin 1986.
31. *Muqâbala khâṣṣa maᶜ Ibn Nûḥ*, in: *Dîwân* 393ff.; see for the biographical context Ruwaynî (footnote 28) 61f. Cf. the analysis of this "most daring" poem in Fatma Moussa Mahmoud (s. footnote 29) 68ff.
32. See for the whole context *Encyclopedia of Islam* (2nd. ed.), s.v. *Nûḥ* (B. Heller).

bearer and the temple dancer, the tax collectors, the arms dealers, the effeminate lover of the princess - they all flee into the Ark. Only Noah's son along with the youth of the city stay to build a dam (an allusion to the Assuan high dam?), and carry water away so that they may save their country. In the *ᶜallahumu yunqidhûna mihâda al-ṣabâ wa-al-ḥaḍârati / ᶜallahumu yunqidhûna al-waṭan*, I see a clear allusion to the *laᶜallahum yaᶜlamûn* clauses of the Koran. The poet who had been imprisoned several times for his leftist opinions anticipates censorship and sardonically leaves three censured verses to his reader's imagination.

Ṣâḥa bî sayyidu al-fulki qabla ḥulûli al-sakînah:
unju min baladin lam taᶜud fîhi rûḥ!
Qultu: ṭûbâ li-man ṭaᶜimû khubzahu
Fi al-zamâni al-ḥasan
Wa-adârû lahu al-ẓahra yawma al-miḥan
Wa-lanâ al-majdu naḥnu lladhîna waqafnâ
(wa-qad ṭamasa llâhu asmâ'anâ!)
Nataḥaddâ al-damâra
Wa-na'wî ilâ jabalin la yamûtu
(yusammûnahu al-shaᶜba)
na'bâ al-firâra
Wa-na'bâ al-nuzûḥ
kâna qalbî lladhî nasajathu al-jurûḥ
kâna qalbî lladhî laᶜanathu al-shurûḥ
yarqudu al-âna fawqa baqâyâ al-madîna
wardatun min ᶜaṭan
hâdi'an baᶜda an qâla Lâ li-'l-safînah
wa-aḥabba al-waṭan.

Then the lord of the ark cried out to me: before
The *sakîna* came down
'Save yourself from a city in which there is no more soul! '
I answered: "Blessed be who ate her bread
In prosperous times
And turn their backs on her
In the days of tribulation.
Praise be to us, who stayed - after God had wiped out our names".
We defy the destruction
And take refuge on a mountain which does not die (and is called: 'the people').

We refuse to fly
And refuse to be dispersed.

(Here censorship has deleted three verses.)

My heart which has been covered with wounds
My heart which has been cursed by books,
Is sleeping now over the wrecks of the city
A rose of putrefaction
Quietly
After having said "No" to the ark
And having loved the fatherland.

The whole Koranic subtext is twisted into its opposite: the true prophet is Spartakus, and his message is the cancellation of everything the Koran teaches.

In an article entitled "The War of Cassettes", the London monthly *al-Nâqid*[33] published in its first issue the text of an anonymous Saudi declaration of war against literary modernity, the authors being most probably adherents of a Saudi opposition group. The text condemned practically all modern Arabic poetry and prose writing between Naguib Mahfûz and Adonis. The article gives some interesting instances of what this group considers blasphemous use of Koranic subtexts in the poetry of Adûnîs, ᶜAbd-al-ᶜAzîz Al-Maqâliḥ, ᶜAbd al-Wahhâb al-Bayâtî, Samîḥ al-Qâsim, Ṣalâḥ ᶜAbd-al-Ṣabûr; Nizâr Qabbânî, etc.

Most of Palestinian poetry was and is for many more conservative circles scandalous. Characteristic is the following report about a Palestinian poet in an unnamed Arab country: he asks the censor for permission to have his *Dîwân* printed. The censor is agreeably surprised by the Islamic character of the *Dîwân* and puts his surprise into the following words:

This is the first time that I see an Islamic *Dîwân* written by a Palestinian poet. It is well known that all Palestinian poets are leftists. The Palestinian poets inside and outside Palestine are leftists, especially the poets of resistance. In the eyes of their admirers they have become like idols. Is it not strange that one of them in an

---

33. Al-Nâqid 1 (July 1988), p. 31-46, *Ḥarb al-Kâsît*.

Islamic country defames God, calls the prophets liars, and calls for the freedom of man which means the freedom to eat pork and to drink wine?[34]

4. The most scandalous use of a Koranic subtext so far was perhaps Ḥasan Ṭilib's collection *Âyât Jîm* (Cairo 1992). Ḥasan Ṭilib, one of the Egyptian angry young poets of the "generation of the seventies" and one of the founders of the literary magazine *Iḍâ'a* 77 ("Illumination 77"), lashed out at poetical tradition with his iconoclastic post-modern parody of Koranic style. "He skilfully uses the idiom, the ryhthm, and the tone of the Koran. Introducing his subject, the letter *jîm*, he wonders why it was not singled out in the Koran as in the case of *alif, lâm* or *sîn*. The five sections or suras present a brillant reconstruction of Arabic words and images using the letter *jîm;* one could not imagine there could be so many."[35] Of the final and fifth "sura" transcribed below Fatma Moussa-Mahmoud says:

> In the final sura, there is no attempt at versification; it is pure rhyming prose and has to be read in Arabic for the full power of its effect, its stark *muᶜâraḍa* (opposition) to some of the short incantationary suras that even children can learn to recite without necessarily understanding the meaning. [36]

Al-sûratu al-khâmisa
aᶜûdhu bi-'l-shaᶜbi min al-sulṭâni al-rajîm
Bi-smi al-jîm
Wa-al-jannati wa-al-jaḥîm
Wa-mujtamaᶜi al-nujûm
Innakumû al-yawma sa-tufjaᶜûn
Kam wadadtum law turjaᶜûn
Ilâ yawmi lâ jîmîn wa-lâ juyûm
Fa-idhâ jadda al-hujûm
Fa-ajḥashati al-jusûm
Fa-jasarati al-jîm
Wa-man adrâka mâ al-jîm
Fa-idhâ mazajnâ al-ajyâma mazâjâ
Thumma makhajna gurgahunna makhâjâ

---

34. Ma'mûn Furayz al-Jarrâr, *Al-ṣaḥwâ al-islâmiyya wa-al-ṭâqat al-muᶜaṭṭala*, in: *al-Umma* (Doha) 3/26 (Dec. 1982) 7-10; cf. S. Wild, "Judentum" (footnote 25) 295.
35. I follow and quote Fatma Moussa-Mahmud's article "Changing Technique in Modern Arabic Poetry: A Reflection of Changing Values?" (footnote 23) 61-74.
36. *ibid.* 71f.

Thumma majajnahunna majjâ
Qul yâ ayyuhâ al-mujrimûna innakum yawma'idhin la-fî wujûm
Tastanjidûna fa-lâ tunjadûn
Wa-qul yâ ayyuhâ al-râjûn
Innakum yawma'idhini al-nâjûn
Jâ'atkumû al-jîmu bi-mâ kuntum tastaᶜjilûn
Mâ lakum kayfa lâ tabtahijûn
Wa-li-âyâti al-jîmi lâ tujsidûn
Wa-bi-iᶜjâzihâ lâ talhajûn.
...
Al-jîmu jalla jalâluhâ. Ṣadaqa al-ḥarfu al-rajîm.

This parody with its abundance of Arabic roots containing the letter jîm defies translation. At the Cairo Book Fair in 1994, the religious establishment and the Azhar pressured the authorities into withdrawing the copies of this book[37].

III. The case of Adonis

As Adonis' poetical language is treated extensively elsewhere in this volume, I can limit myself to some short remarks. Whereas Adonis' poetic message is a Nietzschean declaration that God is dead, the poet is forever attracted by the divine as reflected by heterodoxy or radical Sufism. Some of his favourite poetical heroes are heterodox mystics like al-Ḥallâj or al-Niffarî. Adonis' reading of the Koranic Noah story in his poem *Nûḥ jadîd* ("The new Noah") is in its content remarkably like Amal Dunqul's poem "Special Interview with Noah" mentioned above. The lyrical first person in Adonis' poem is an Anti-Noah looking for a different God.

In his literary theory, Adonis has indicated the way in which he wants the Koranic subtext to be understood. Explaining the split in the Arab mind

37. G. Borg pointed out to me that in the Egyptian magazine *al-Funûn* there was a collection of similar albeit less venomous "Suras" like *Sûrat al-baqar*, *Sûrat al-amn*, *Sûrat al-Bulshifiq*, *Sûrat al-sittât*, *Sûrat al-quṭn* published anonymously in the late Thirties, and generally attributed to Bayram al-Tunisi (1893-1961). There does seem to be some resemblance between these "Suras" and the Maqamât Bayram, 2nd. ed. Cairo 1985. For biographical details see Martina Häusler, *Fiktive ägyptische Autobiographien der zwanziger und dreißiger Jahre*, Frankfurt/Main 1990, 80ff.

between a rational consciousness on the side of science and the future on the one hand and between the heart on the side of the past on the other, he goes on to say:

> From the perspective of this conflict, I started to see ... something inimical to the spirit of poetry in every move to make poetic creation subject to a rationalist scientific precept: one that seemed to say, the future before all else. I began to search for alternative forms which, while not rejecting the notion of the future, did not put an absolute ban on the past. There were forms which, on the contrary, embraced the past in some way: legend, mysticism, magical and non-rationalist elements of the literary tradition, the mysterious regions of the human soul[38].

Evidently, the Koran is part of this non-rationalist literary tradition. But it is insufficient to look for Koranic quotes or allusions. It is of only marginal importance that sometimes - rarely - a whole Koranic verse is quoted by Adonis, e.g., as a motto for a poem or for a collection of poems (Sura 2, 187) "Your wives are a vestment to you and you are a vestment for them" at the opening of *Taḥawwulât al-ᶜâshiq* ("The Transformations of the Lover")[39]. But decisive, even if much less easy to trace, is the opaqueness of the mystical religious language which is typically Adonis' language. Adonis is probably at present the most important model of the new Arab poet-prophet. His message is radically and deliberately new - but even as the Prophet Muhammad who transmitted a new message had to use the language of the *kâhin* and the *shâᶜir*, so Adonis cannot but use the prophetical ring of the Koranic language to proclaim his post-religious prophecy and message. There is more to this than the mere fact that no poet who expresses himself in Arabic can escape the Koranic language even when he does not choose the role of the poet-prophet. Part of the magic of Adonis' linguistic symbolism seems to me to lie in the fact that his language evokes a religious, Islamic, and inevitably Koranic spectre, only to immediately and deliberately counteract it, undermine it, and fight it. Stefan Weidner has rightly stressed the importance of Adonis' following characterization of al-Niffari's language:

---

38. Adûnîs, *al-Shiᶜriyya al-ᶜarabiyya* (footnote 3), English translation in: Adonis, *An Introduction to Arab Poetics.* Translated by Catherine Cobham, London 1990, 94f.
39. Adonis, *Taḥawwulât al-ᶜâshiq*, 000.

> Here, writing is change, renewal of the things in as much as it renews the images and the mutual relations between. And it is a renewal of the language inasmuch as it creates new relations between words and between words and things[40].

And this is, as Weidner points out, at the same time a description of Adonis' own linguistic program[41]. In this sense, one might call the Koran in Adonis' poetry a subtext twice removed.

---

40. *Al-Ṣûfiyya wa-al-suryâliyya* ("Sufism and Surrealism"), Beirut 1992, 186, quoted here according to Stefan Weidner 191, see footnote 197
41. For a more detailed analysis see Stefan Weidner's contribution in this volume.

RELIGIOUS MOTIFS AND THEMES IN NORTH AMERICAN MAHJAR POETRY

BY

CORNELIS NIJLAND

The literary scene of the North American Mahjar is dominated by one group of writers and poets who became known as *al-Râbiṭa al-Qalamîya* (The Pen League). This League came out into the open in 1920 after its members had already been closely working together since 1911. It counted ten working members three of whom produced a substantial literary oeuvre. They are: Gibrân Khalîl Gibrân (1883-1931), Mîkhâ'îl Nu^cayma (1889-1988) and Îlîyâ Abû Mâḍî (1890-1957).[1] The most productive poet was Ilîyâ Abû Mâḍî who produced five volumes of poetry, the first of which appeared in Egypt in 1911, followed in 1919 by *Dîwân Îlîyâ Abî Mâḍî, al-juz'u al-thânî* (The Diwan of Iliya Abu Madi, second part) and by the volumes *al-Jadâwil* (the brooks), 1927, *al-Khamâ'il* (the thickets), 1940 and *Tibr wa-turâb* (golddust and dust) posthumously published in Beirut in 1960. Mikhâ'îl Nu^cayma published one volume of poetry, *Hams al-Jufûn* (Eyelids whispering), Beirut, 1943, which comprises all his poems written between 1912 and 1931. Gibran began his career as a writer with prose poems which he published under the collective title *Dam^ca wa ibtisâma* (A tear and a smile) in the journal *Al-Muhâjir* (The Emigrant), from 1903 until 1908. They were republished in one volume with the same title in New York in 1914.[2] Gibran also composed other forms of poetry instances of which can be found in the journal *al-Sâ'iḥ (the Traveller)* in New York in the years 1916 and 1917, and he composed one long poem *al-Mawâkib* (The Procession), published in 1919.

This paper is based on all the poetical works by Gibrân and by Nu^cayma. As regards Ilîyâ Abû Mâḍî we have limited our research to the second part of his diwan which was published in 1919. This volume comprises

1. Personal names are the first time they occur transliterated with all the necessary diacritical signs. After that a simplified transcription without diacritical signs is being used. The name of Gibran is always spelled with a /g/ in conformity with the spelling used by the author on his books in English.
2. *Al-Majmû^catu al-kâmilatu li-mu`allafâti Gibrân Khalîl Gibrân al-^carabîya* (in the following quoted as *Al-Majmû^ca),* See Foreword by Mîkhâ'îl Nu^cayma, Beirut, 1964, p.19)

mainly poetry which he composed in the U.S.A. plus a few poems which he did not include in his first diwan in Egypt in 1911.[3] For a better understanding of his relation with the poets of *al-Râbiṭa al-qalamîya* the volume *al-Jadâwil* (the brooks), should have been included in this research but that would have swollen the amount of material for this paper.

The aim of this paper is to make an inventory of the religious motifs and themes used by these three poets in their poetry and to relate the use of those motives and themes to the religious formation of each of them. We should like to define patterns in their usage if they can be found and we should like to establish if the poet used these motives and themes in otherwise religiously coloured texts or if he also used them in otherwise profane texts.

Religious motifs in the works of Mîkhâ'îl Nuᶜayma

Mikha'îl Nuᶜayma was theoretician of the group. He formulated the rules by which the group was to operate as well as the principles of good poetry. Next to his criticism, his poetry, his stories, etc., he is also the author of an extensive autobiography which gives the reader interesting insights into his spiritual formation and into the actual circumstances under which he was writing and composing.

Nuᶜayma was born in 1889 in Biskinta (Lebanon) as the third son in a Russian-orthodox family. He had already been visiting the local orthodox school for one or two years when the Russian Orthodox Church opened an elementary school in Biskinta as part of an enterprise to open such school in Lebanon and Palestine. Nuᶜayma visited that school and was elected to receive further training in Nazareth and there he won a scholarship which allowed him to go to the Orthodox seminary in Poltava. He studied there from 1905-1910 during which period he disqualified himself for the priesthood by supporting a rebellion against the tightening rules of the seminary. In 1911 he joined his brothers in the U.S.A. and they permitted him to pursue his studies at the University of Washington in Seattle. With B.A.'s in Law and in English Literature he moved in 1916 to New York where he

3. ᶜÎsâ al-Nâᶜûrî, *Adab al-Mahjar*, 3rd. edition, Cairo, 1977, p.368: "Iliya included in it the nationalistic poems which he had not been able to publish in his first diwan *Tidhkâr al-Mâḍî* which was printed in Egyptin 1911".

worked in a variety of jobs. In 1932 he returned to Lebanon where he died in 1988.

It is clear from the above that when Nu^cayma began to compose poetry, he had acquired a rich treasure trove of religious symbols, from which he could borrow all the elements he needed for his poetry. An analysis of the contents of the trove might be helpful for the search for religious symbols in the poetry of Mikhâ'îl Nuᶜayma.

The source from which Nuᶜayma acquired the first symbols was, no doubt, his family. He tells about the daily prayers he had to say and about some experiences which were closely connected with popular religion. When a small boy his mother forced him to wear an earring to protect him from the evil eye. She also made him wear a silver neckband as a sign that his mother had to fulfil a pledge to the monastery (*Sabᶜûn,* I,31).

Popular religion plays a part in the story of the young bull his father had bought, but the down to earth approach by the father is the real issue of this story. The bull fell ill and some neighbours advised the father to promise a chunk of its meat to Saint George to make him cure the bull. Nuᶜayma tells with some relish that his father refused to do so. He quotes him as saying: "If Saint George can heal the bull but does not do so unless I promise him a part of its meat, I rather have no Saint George and no bull" (*Sabᶜûn,* I,62). He quotes his father as saying that religion is "good character and good conduct rather than the performance of the traditional duties and rituals." Nuᶜayma's father worked on Sundays and on religious feast days "because proper work is in itself proper worship"(*Sabᶜûn,* I,63).

During his schooldays Nuᶜayma acquired a rather good knowledge of both the Old and the New Testament. He tells in his autobiography that his first reading lessons consisted in spelling and reading a selection of Psalms. (*Sabᶜûn,* I,57) He further tells that, during his stay in Nazareth, he tried to locate all the places mentioned in the New Testament. He refers to Palestine as the promised land, overflowing with milk and honey, the dream of Moses, the prisoner of Joshua ben Nun, the beloved of David and Solomon, the inspiration of Isaiah and of the author of the book of Job.(*Sabᶜûn,* I,103) He concludes the first part of his autobiography by saying that he preferred the Gospel to the other books of the New Testament and that his most cherished piece was the "Sermon of the Mount".(*Sabᶜûn,* I, 278)

One may assume that Nu^cayma became thoroughly acquainted with the orthodox rituals during his studies at the orthodox schools in Biskinta, Nazareth and Poltava. There are a few instances in which he tells about going to church, but he never speaks about it or about the rituals in a positive sense. He writes in the diary he kept in Poltava: "I am not the only one who thinks that true Christianity does not consist in sitting in the church for two or three hours on Sundays, Saturdays and Feast days, but in the following of the teachings and guidelines of the Gospels" (*Sab^cûn,* I,85). In the same entry he writes: "What good is there in worship that turns your heart away from the worshipped one, in a Christianity that makes you forget Christ?" He compares the church with the stage and the priest with actors.

In the United States Nu^cayma was introduced to Free Masonry from which, he writes in his autobiography, he separated himself very soon, because the members cared more for the crusts and not for the kernels.(*Sab^cûn,*II,64) Theosophy and Buddhism had a more lasting influence on him. In more than one place he confesses to be a believer in the ultimate unity of all being, the transmigration of souls and the cycle of birth and death.

However, the religious imagery in the poetry of Nu^cayma is very traditional. His poetry abounds with Christian motifs and themes, like creation, paradise, the fall, resurrection and the last judgement, but there are also motifs from other religious sources. The question is if these motives and themes fit in with his acquired belief.

The poet alludes to the Old Testament story in which God "formed a man from the dust on the ground and breathed into his nostrils the breath of life." (The New English Bible, Genesis, 2;7) In *Afâqa al-qalbu,*(The heart awoke) the poet addresses his heart saying:

ilâ 'an dâra fî khaladî
bi'annaka lasta min jasadî
wa-'annaka ṭînatun lammâ
barânî Allâhu lam yanfuḥ
bihâ min rûḥihi al-'abadî

Until it occurred to me
that you are not part of my body
and that you were clay when
God created me into which He did not blow
some of his eternal spirit.

This is the fifth strophe of a poem which begins with two strophes in which the I-person says to be astounded that the heart was in fire after he thought it was stiff and frozen. The third and fourth strophes explain that feeling of astonishment, telling that so far the heart had been impervious to all sorts of advances. It leads the I-person to say what he said in the above-quoted strophe.

The poem *Ilâ M.D.B.* refers to another part of the creation story of Genesis:

Anâ al-sirru alladhî 'statarâ
Bi-rûḥika mundhu mâ khaṭarâ
bi-bâli al-kâ'ini al-'aᶜlâ
khayâlu al-ᶜâlami al-adnâ
faṣawwara min tharâ basharâ

I am the secret hidden
in your soul since there came
to the mind of the Supreme Being
the spectre of the lower world
and He formed man from mud (*Hams al-jufûn,* p.55-63)

The poem *Tarnîmatu al-rîyâḥ* (The singing of the winds) alludes to the story of the serpent tricking Adam and Eve into disobedience by promising them knowledge of good and evil, following which God drove them out of the garden of Eden (Genesis, 3).

kâna lî fî qadîmi al-zamân
martaᶜun fî riyâḍi al-jinân
biᶜtuhu bi-'l-wuᶜûd

I had in olden times
a pasture in the gardens of paradise
which I sold for promises (*Hamsu al-jufûn*, p.90)

The notion of being driven out from paradise is taken up again in the following strophe.The same root is used as in the book of Genesis, where the verb *ṭrd* is used. The poem uses the word *ṭarîd.* But here the connection with genesis seems to end. The I-person in the poem addresses the angel mentioned in the second strophe as "my angel" and asks him if there is no return for someone driven out who is exhausted from suffering. The angel was introduced in the second strophe as follows:

fa warâᶜa al-simâk
qad lamaḥtu malâk
bâsiṭan lî al-janâḥ

and behind the stars
I saw an angel
spreading to me its wings
(*Hamsu al-jufûn*, 88)

There is a notion of protection by the angel and this seems to be reinforced when the angel is addressed as "my angel" but I do not think that this can be stretched to mean "guardian angel."

There is another image taken from the Old Testament in the poem a*l-'Ân* (Now)

wa kam fataḥtu lahum qalbî fa mâ labithû
'an naṣṣabû baᶜlahum fî qudsi 'aqdâsî

How often I opened my heart to them and they did not tarry
to put up their Baal in my Holy of Holies *(Hamsu al-jufûn*, p.108):

There are also references to the New Testament in Nuᶜayma's poetry, but there are no allusions to Christ and his salvatory mission on earth. The small size of his oeuvre may be the cause for this. On the other hand there are a few allusions to the resurrection and the last judgment.

Following the order of *Hamsu al-Jufûn* we find p.26: *Ilâ sannatin mudbira* (To an outgoing year):

Wa-'l-yawma kaffu al-dahri taṭwîki
ᶜannâ wa man yadrî matâ tunsharîn?

Today the hand of time enfolds you
away from us and who knows when you will be re-awakened?

p. 37. *Ibtihâlât* (Supplications)

Speaking about his ear, the I-person of the poem says:

Wa-'idhâ mâ qaruba al-mawtu wa wâfâhâ al-ṣamam
akhtiman rabbî ᶜalayhâ raythamâ tuḥyâ al-rimam

And when death has drawn near and deafness has overtaken it
seal it, my Lord, when the bones are revivified

p. 39. Same poem

fal-yanam qalbî ilâ an yunfaḥu al-bûqu al-'akhîr

And let my heart sleep until the last trumpet is being blown

p. 61:

Afâqa al-qalb (The heart awoke)
waqumtu al-yawma wâ-ᶜajabâ
min al-amwâti multahibâ

Today o, miracle, you arose
from death, flaming

p. 93: The poem *Al-hamm* (Distress), opens hopefully:

dafantu fî al-ṣubḥi hammî
wa qawsahu wa sihâmah

I buried this morning my distress,
its bow and its arrows

However, at the end of the day the heart of the I-person begins to worry saying:

akhâfu an mâ dafannâ
yaqûmu yawma al-qiyâma

I fear that what we buried
will rise again on resurrection-day

In the poem *Law tudriku al-ashwâk* there is an allusion to heaven and hell, which the I-person in the poem rather sees as entities residing in himself than as places where one has to stay in eternal bliss or punishment:

idh lî fu'âdun qad ḥawâ jannatâ
wa-'llâhu adrâ kam ḥawâ min jaḥîm

Because I have a heart which contains a paradise
and God knows how many hells.

The references to the "Last Judgement" are in no way connected with the references to the day of the resurrection of the dead. They are in fact quite isolated. The lines, taken from the poem *Law tudriku al-ashwâku* (When thorns would understand), are more than simple allusions to the last judgment. The speaker in the poem remains fully within the religious concepts of the person he addresses, while saying that he will be deaf to his warnings:

yâ ḥâmila al-injîli yadʿû ilâ
nabdhi al-maʿâṣî mundhiran bi-'l-ʿiqâb
bashshir wa khalliṣ yâ akhî anfusâ
ḍallat likay talqâ jamîla al-thawâb
idh yanṣubu al-dayyânu mîzânahu

You, bearer of the gospel who summons to
do away with sins, warning of punishments
bring good tidings and, brother, save the souls
that erred so that you may find a good recompense
when the Judge sets up his scales.
(*Hamsu al-jufûn*, pp. 33, 34)

It should be noted that the balance or the scales are not mentioned in the Bible in connection with the Last Judgement, but there is the story of King Belshazzar having been weighed in the balance and found wanting (Daniel 5, 27). In Christian lore the Archangel Michael with the balance to weigh the souls is part of the visual presentation of the Last Judgment[4] In the Koran the Balance and the Last Day are intimately connected, but the word *dayyân* (Judge) which is used is this line does not occur in the Quran. Considering the religious formation of Nu^cayma it is more likely that he became acquainted with both motifs through Christian lore rather than through the Koran.

The poem *al-'Ân* (Now), p.109, is a protest against religious concepts like hell and paradise:

fa lâ turawwi^cunî nâru al-jaḥîmi wa lâ
majâlisu al-ḥûri fî al-firdûsi tughrînî

The fire of hell does not frighten me nor
do the company of maidens in paradise attract me.

With this last quotation we have left the terrain of the symbolic use of religious motives and themes, but that is almost inevitable in the case of Nu-^cayma, whose life was so immersed in religion.

Nu^cayma's motives and themes relate to creation, the fall, resurrection and the last judgment. All his motives and themes have been taken from the Bible, but apart from those that were taken from the first chapter of Genesis, it is difficult to tell from which verse, chapter or even book the image was taken. As little as they can be related to specific texts they can be related to Christian doctrine. None of the motives and themes seems to contradict or be at variance with his belief that man has to perfect himself during his stay on earth which is marked by a long chain of deaths and rebirths. On the other hand, all the poems in which the motives and themes are used do express religious feelings or at least have a religious undertone.

The Individual and the All-Soul in the poetry of Gibrân

We now pass to Gibrân who was born in 1883 in a Lebanese village in a Maronite family. His mother emigrated in 1894 to Boston, taking her children with her and leaving her husband behind. Gibrân returned in 1897 to

---

4. J. van Laarhoven, *De beeldtaal van de Christelijke Kunst.* Nijmegen, 1992, p. 80, describes the weighing of the souls as an ancient Egyptian motif, which came into Christian art through the intermediary of monks.

Lebanon to pursue his schooling there and to strengthen his knowledge of Arabic. He was back in Boston the autumn of 1899.[5] He made another trip to Lebanon in 1903 as the interpreter for an American family. In 1912 he settled in New York.

Little is known about his religious education except that he grew up in a Maronite family and that he visited Maronite schools. We may assume that reading the Bible, except may be the book of Psalms, was not a regular practice in his family nor in the schools he visited.

It is unlikely that Gibrân acquired any knowledge about Islam in his home village or in Boston, but he may have learnt something during his stay in Beirut. Be it as it may, in 1916 he was invited by the American Society of Religions in New York to give a lecture about Islam. The editor of the Arabic newspaper *al-Sâ'iḥ* wrote about it in the edition of 25.5.1916. According to this paper Gibrân began his lecture with the *shahâda*, the Muslim creed, adding that those words were the kernel of Arabness and that they were pronounced daily by 300 milion people.

Gibrân came into contact with theosophy in America and became a believer in reincarnation. This conversion created a distance with his Christian belief and made the difference between religions and creeds of minor importance. It is the individual approach to God, to the All-soul which counts:

"Uḥibbuka sâjidan fî jâmiᶜika,
râkiᶜan fî haykalika wa muṣalliyan fî kanîsatika.
faᶜanta wa-ᶜanâ ibnâ dînin wâḥidin huwa al-ruḥu".

"I love you, prosternating in your mosque,
bowing in your temple, praying in your church.
You and I belong to one religion, which is the spirit"[6]

One may expect that Gibrân made a free use of all sorts of religious symbols.

It should be noted here that Gibran sometimes made use of motto's in his work, two of which are Koran-verses (*Majmûᶜa,* 343, 574) and one is a quotation from the *ḥadîth,* (*Majmûᶜa,* 574). The other motto's are: one from

5. Khalîl S. Ḥâwî, *Khalil Gibran.* Beirut 1972, pp. 84ff.
6. (*Al-Majmûᶜatu al-kâmilatu li-mu`allafâti Gibrân Khalîl Gibrân al-ᶜarabîya* (in the following quoted as *Al-Majmûᶜa*), *Ṣawtu al-Shâᶜir*, Beirut, 1964, 347)

the book of Ecclesiastes, two from (an) unmentioned Indian poet(s), and one from John Keats.

It is possible to follow the same trail as was followed in the case of Mîkhâᶜîl Nuᶜayma, the trail of creation, fall, man being driven out of paradise, the resurrection of the dead, the final judgement and heaven and hell. It would have been the basic trail of a clergyman had the salvation of man by Christ been included. Gibrân follows the same trail as Nuᶜayma but he also ventured beyond that trail. Apart from the motives and themes taken from Genesis he used citations from the Psalms, the Song of Songs, Ecclesiastes and the Prophet Jeremiah.

Gibrân has his own versions of the creation in his prose poem *al-nafs* ("The Soul", in *al-Majmûᶜa*, 256) in which he tells that the God of Gods separated a soul from himself and that he took fire, air, sand and dust from which he formed man and gave him life. Another prose poem tells about "a kiss as the beginning of a joint sigh knitting the breathing God had breathed into the clay which then became man." (*al-Majmûᶜa*, 294) The prose poem *al-rafîqa* (the girl-friend) alludes to the creation story of the book of Genesis:

> "the first glance of my girl-friend resembled the spirit that hovered over the flood-water and from it sprang heaven and earth".[7]

Compare this sentence with Genesis 1,2: *wa rûḥu allâhi yaruffu ᶜalâ wajhi al-miyâhi.* The last sentence of this part of the poem runs as follows: [1] *Awwalu naẓratin min sharîkati al-ḥayâti tuḥâkî qawla 'llâhi: Kun* "The first glance of the partner for life resembles the word of god: Be".

The fall and its consequences occur in the poem *Ḥikâyatu Ṣadîq* (The story of a friend). The friend tells that a woman had entered his life and that: "she who had Adam ousted from paradise by the power of her will and his weakness returned me to that paradise".[8] There are other allusions to biblical motifs in this poem: "the woman has saved me from the darkness of hell and opened the gates of heaven for me and I entered. The real woman has taken me to the Jordan of her love and baptized me"[9]. Another allusion

7. *Awwalu naẓratin min al-rafîqati tushâbihu al-rûḥa alladhî kâna taruffu ᶜalâ wajhi al-ghamrati wa-'nbathaqat al-samâ'u wa-'l-arḍu.* (*al-Majmûᶜa*, 296)
8. *tilka allatî akhrajat Âdama min al-jannati bi-quwwati irâdatihâ wa ḍaᶜfihi qad aᶜâdatnî ilâ tilka al-jannati* .. (*al-Majmûᶜa*, 279)
9. *al-mar'atu ...qad anqadhatnî min ẓulmati al-jaḥîmi wa fataḥat amâmî abwâba al-firdûsi fa-dakhaltu. al-mar'atu al-ḥaqîqîyatu qad dhahabat bî ilâ urdunna*

to the consequences of the fall occur in the poem *Yâ Khalîlî al-faqîr* (My poor friend) saying: "You eat your dried out bread with sighing and you drink your muddy water mixed with tears"[10] The inspiration for these lines must rather be sought in Psalms 80,5 than in the book of Genesis.

There are one or two references to the resurrection, the day of reckoning and to recompense in heaven and punishment in hell. Like Nu^cayma Gibrân makes paradise and hell into innermost experiences of man instead of the abodes awaiting man after death:

Mâ al-na^cîmu bi-l-thawâbi innamâ al-jannatu bi-'l-qalbi al-salîm
Mâ al-jaḥîmu bi-'l-^cadhâbi innamâ al-qalbu al-khâlî kullu al- jaḥîm

"blessedness is not in recompence but paradise is in the pure heart
hell is not in punishment but the empty heart is all hell"

The biblical image of the burning bush occurs twice in Gibrân's poetry. One time a farmer's son falls on his knees before a prinsess, "like Moses did when he saw the burning bush".[11] The kneeling of Moses seems to be a free invention of Gibrân since it does not occur in the biblical story nor in the Koran. The second time the text runs as follows: "I knelt before you (my love) like the shepherd did when he saw the burning bush"[12]

The Psalms and the Song of Songs have been a source of inspiration for Gibrân. From it he borrowed motives and themes such as God's throne[13] and lines like: "Jubilate you upon whom the signs of beauty were sent down and rejoice for you should not fear and feel no sorrow"[14]. Jubilate and rejoyce occur in this combination in Psalms 40,17 and 70, 5, but the sending down of signs clearly is Koranic. The line: "until when will you lament, my soul"[15], leans against Psalm 42.

The poem *bayna al-kharâ'ib* (Amidst the ruins) relates the story of two shades sitting on marble columns one saying to the other:

---

maḥabbatihâ wa ^camadatnî

10. *al-Majmû^ca*, 281
11. *Ḥikâya* (story), *al-Majmû^ca*, 249
12. *Al-ṭiflu yasû^c*(the child Jesus), *al-Majmû^ca*, 322
13. *kursî majdi 'llâh(al-Majmû^ca*, 250)
14. *Tahallalû yâ ayyuhâ ^clladhîna unzilat ^calayhim âyâtu al-jamâli wa-afraḥû idh lâ khawfa ^calaykum wa lâ antum taḥzanûna (al-jamâl* (beauty), *al-Majmû^ca*, 261)
15. *Ḥattâ ma tanûḥîna yâ nafsî (Raḥmâki yâ nafsu raḥmâki*, (indulgence, o soul, indulgence), *al-Majmû^ca*, 268)

Hâdhihi baqâyâ hayâkila banaytuhâ min ajliki yâ maḥbûbatî . . . banaytu haykalan fî Ûrshalîma li-'l-ᶜibâdati faqaddasahâ al-kuhhânu thumma saḥaqathu al-ᶜayyâm. Wa-banaytu haykalan bayna aḍluᶜî li-'l-maḥabbati faqaddasahu Allâhu wa lan taqwâ ᶜalayhi al-quwwât. Ṣaraftu al-ᶜumra mustafsiran ẓawâhira al-ashyâ'a mustanṭiqan aᶜmâla al-mâddati faqâla al-insânu: mâ aḥkamuhu malikan! Wa qâlat al-malâ'ikatu: mâ aṣgharahu ḥakîman thumma ra'aytuki yâ maḥbûbati wa-ghannaytu fîki nashîda maḥabbatin wa shawqin fa-faraḥat al-malâ'ika ammâ al-insânu fa-lam yantabih!. . . wa lammâ ra'aytuki . . . asaftu ᶜalâ ᶜumrin ṣaraftuhu mustasliman li'-tayyârâti al-qunûṭi ḥâsiban kulla shay'in taḥta al-shamsi bâṭilan (al-Majmûᶜa, 263)

"These are the remains of the temples I built for you my love . . . I built a temple in Jerusalem for the worshippers, and the priests consecrated it and then time destroyed it. I built a temple within my chest dedicated to love and God consecrated it and the forces (of destruction) were powerless against it . . . I spent my life inquiring into the externalities of things, examining the workings of matter and man said: He is a very wise king! And the angels said: How little is his wisdom! Then I saw you my love and sang for you the song of love and longing and the angels rejoiced. Man, however, did not pay attention . . . and when I saw you . . . I deplored having spent a lifetime surrendering myself to the currents of despondency reckoning everything under the sun emptiness . . ."

It is not difficult to see that Gibrân based himself for this poem on the stories of Solomon in the first book of Kings and on the Song of Songs and Ecclesiastes. He borrowed from the Song of Songs also in other prose poems, like in *Ḥayâtu al-ḥubb* (The life of love) which opens with the line: "Come my love let us walk between the hills" (compare Song of songs 7,11). The second part of this poems opens with: "Come, my love let us go out into the field" (compare, Song of songs, 2,8), and the third part begins with the line: "Let us go to the vineyard, my love" (compare Song of songs, 7,12).[16]

This prose poem is different from the text of Ecclesiastes as the shade deplores having considered everything under the sun emptiness. In the poem *Taḥta al-shams* (Under the sun) the spirit of Solomon is addressed saying: "You know not that life is not a chasing the wind, and that there is

16. *Hallumî yâ maḥbûbatî namshi bayna al-ṭulûl* The second part begins as follows: *hayyâ binâ ilâ al-ḥaqli ya ḥabibatî.* The third part begins with the words: *la-nadhhab ilâ al-karmati ya maḥbûbatî (al-Majmûᶜa,* 244 and 245)

no emptiness under the sun"[17] (compare Ecclesiastes 2,11). The poet returns to this theme in *Ṣawtu al-shâʿir* (The voice of the poet): "Because the eternal wisdom did not create anything empty under the sun"[18]

The New Testament likewise was a source of themes and motifs for Gibrân. In the poem *al-ams wa-'l-yawm* (Yesterday and today) we read: "When he had arrived at the gate of the castle he looked to the city like Jeremia looked to Jerusalem and gave a sign with his hand in its direction as if he was bewailing it and said in a loud voice: O, you people walking in darkness, sitting in the valley of death".[19](Matthew 4,16 and John 12,35). There is a warning against false messiases (*al-Majmûʿa*, 265, Matthew 24,5) and in the poem *Ayyatuhâ al-rîḥ* (O, wind) has the line: "Are you dancing around the tombs of the nights whitewashed with snow".[20] The motif of the whitewashed tombs could have been borrowed from Matthew 23,27.

The poem *al-liqâ'* (The encounter) is clearly based on Revelation. It tells about a winged maiden with invisible wings sitting on a throne of clouds and spirits passing before her shouting: holy, holy, holy.[21]

Finally, some motifs seem to have their origin in the Koran or at least in Islam. In one of his poems Gibrân writes: "In the thirstiness of my heart is proof of the existence of Salsabîl"[22] In the poem *al-Mawâkib* (The procession) we find the line: "The rivers taste like Salsabîl."[23] (cf. Koran 76,18). Al-Kawthar, another river of Paradise, is mentioned in the line: "She (life) is beauty which gives those who obey her cups brimful of the Kawthar of joy"[24](Koran 108, 1). In another poem the river occurs as the "Kawthar of love" (*al-Majmûʿa*, 297).

---

17. *anti taʿlamîna al-'ân 'anna al-ḥayâta laysat ka-qabḍi al-rîḥ.(al-Majmûʿa*, 288)
18. *la'inna al-ḥikmata al-sarmudiyyata lam takhluq shay'an bâṭilan taḥta al-shams (al-Majmûʿa*, 345)
19. *wa lammâ waṣala ilâ bâbi al-qaṣri naẓara naḥwa al-madînati naẓrata Irmiyâ ilâ ûr-shalîma wa-awma'a biyadihi naḥwahâ yarthîhâ wa-qâla bişawtin ʿâlin: Ayyuhâ al-shaʿbu al-sâliku fî al-ẓulmati al-jâlisu fî ẓilli al-mawt. (al-Majmûʿa*, 267)
20. *"a-ghâḍibatan kunti ayyâma al-shitâ'i am râqiṣatan hawla qubûri al-layâlî al-mukallasati bi al-thulûj" (al-Majmûʿa*, 329)
21. *"taṣâʿadat min wâdî al-nîli ḥûriyatun maḥfûfatun bi-ajniḥatin ghayra manẓûra. wa jalasat ʿalâ ʿarshin min al-ghuyûmi murtafiʿin fawqa baḥri al-rûma mufaḍḍaḍin min ashiʿʿati al-qamr. . . fa marra jawqu al-arwâḥi sâbiḥatin fî al-faḍâ'i ṣâriḥâtin: qaddûsun, qaddûsun, qaddûsu ibnati miṣra" (al-Majmûʿa*, 300)
22. *wa fî ẓama' qalbî dalîlun ʿalâ wujûdi al-salsabîl (al-Majmûʿa*, 598)
23. *Inna bi-'l-anhâri ṭaʿman mithla ṭaʿmi al-salsabîl (al-Majmûʿa*, 358)
24. *Fa-hiya ḥusna'u tusqî muṭîʿîhâ min Kawthari al-lidhdhati ku'ûsan mufʿima (al-Majmûʿa*, 294)

The poem *al-Rafîqa* (The comrade) consists of three parts: *awwalu naẓratin* (The first glance), *awwalu qublatin* (the first kiss) and *al-qirân* (the union), which titles can also be read as *al-qibla* and *al-qurân*. That possibility may have inspired Gibrân to continue in this line of motives and themes in the sentence: "Here love begins to turn the prose of life into poetry and to compose from the meanings of life sura's which the days will recite."[25]

Gibrân's use of religious motifs and themes is in more than one aspect different from that of Nuᶜayma. He is more poetical is his preference for the poetical books of the New Testament. We might say that he has a predelection for expressive and dramatic texts. Different from Nuᶜayma all his motives and themes come from specific texts in the Bible, both from the Old and from the New Testament. Like Nuᶜayma, his Koranic motifs and themes rather come from common knowledge of Islamic culture and not from a specific knowledge of the Koran. The use of Koranic motto's need not to be based on Gibrân's own knowledge of the Koran. Like Nuᶜayma he does not use outspoken Christian motives and themes and he does not speak about redemption, though he does speak about the child Jesus.

The main difference with Nuᶜayma is that he used most of the motives and themes in otherwise profane texts, the most prominent of those being: love.

Last not least, the motifs and themes which Gibrân borrowed from religion do not seem to be in conflict with his own theosophically based conviction.

Îlîyâ Abû Mâḍî: Religious themes in a profane environment

The third poet we want to discuss is Îlîyâ Abû Mâḍî, the most productive poet of the group who enriched Arabic literature with five volumes of poetry and who composed Arabic poetry until his last breath. He did write prose pieces as the editor of his fortnightly and later daily *al-Samîr* (The companion) but these pieces were never collected in separate volumes.

Îlîyâ Abû Mâḍî was born in 1890 into an orthodox family in the Lebanese village of al-Muḥaydatha, the neighbour village of Bikfaya some 30 km. northeast of Beirut. He went in 1901 to Egypt where he was employed by his uncle as a sigaretvender. In his spare time he attended classes and there became infatuated with poetry. His first diwan was published in 1911,

25. *Hâhunâ yabtadî'u al-ḥubb an yanẓimu nathra al-ḥayâti shiᶜran wa yunshi'u min maᶜânî al-ᶜumri suwaran turattiluhâ al-ayyâmu.* (*al-Majmûᶜa*, 297)

the same year in which he left Egypt for the U.S.A. He settled in Cincinnati from where he moved to New York in 1916. There he published his second diwan in 1919. A small portion of the poetry in this diwan was occasional poetry, to mourn and to celebrate public persons or family members. He did compose quite a number of occasional poems as he probably had to being a celebrated poet in the community.

Most of these last poems appeared in dailies and were soon forgotten, whereas the poems to be rembered were collected in the diwans. However, many of the occasional poems deserve to be read and studied for their own sake, for their wit and for their role in the Lebanese Orthodox colony in New York. It is very well possible that the poet became less inclined to include this poetry in his diwan because the members of the group, especially Nu^c^ayma, considered it below the dignity of a poet to compose occasional poetry.

It should be remarked that Îlîyâ Abû Mâḍî was the only member of the group who lived ten years in an Arab country other than Lebanon and who became involved in Arabic poetry in a dominantly Muslim environment. We may assume that he acquired a profounder knowledge of Islam, or at least of its imprint on Arabic poetry, than the other members of the group.

Îlîyâ Abû Mâḍî differs from the Nu^c^ayma and Gibrân in his mixture of Christian and Islamic motives and themes and in the detachment and wit the poet sometimes displays in his verses.

One of the mixtures occurs in the poem *Bâ'i^c^atu al-ward* (The girl selling roses) in which is told what impression Paris makes on people:

idhâ ra'âhâ taqîyun ẓannahâ ^c^adanâ
wa 'in ra'âhâ shaqîyun ẓannahâ saqrâ

"when the devout believer sees her, he thinks her to be Eden
and when the scoundrel sees her, he thinks her to be hell"
(Dîwân vol.2, 72)

In the Koran *al-shaqîyu* (the scoundrel) is connected with hell (Sura 11,107), but hell is never called *al-saqaru. Taqîyun* does not occur in the Koran and ^c^*Adanu* only once.

Another mixture occurs in the words *al-ilâhu tâᶜâlâ*[26] in which the well-known Islamic combination *allâhu tâᶜâlâ* (God, he is supreme) is changed in a Christian sense by using *al-ilâhu* instead of *allâhu.*

Îlîyâ Abû Mâḍî's knowledge of the Old and New Testaments does not seem to have been as profound as that of Nuᶜayma and Gibrân. There are no direct quotations in his poetry, but there are references to biblical stories and to Christian religious practice and beliefs.
Describing his anxiety, the I-person of a poem says:

fa râḥa ka'annamâ huwa shaᶜbu mûsâ
ghadâta al-tîhi fî al-qafri al-yabâbi
Na'â ᶜan 'arḍi miṣra

"It went in the morning of scorn into the waterless desert as if it were the people of Moses. It went away from the land of Egypt . . ."
(*Dîwân, vol.*2, 94)

The Arab rebellion against the Ottoman overlord and the following conquest of Jerusalem and of Syria was celebrated by the poet in two poems in this volume. The first one is *Fatḥ Urushalîm* (The conquest of Jerusalem): The commander is praised saying: "You have made things pleasant for Moses, the Messias and Ahmad and all people and God, he is supreme".[27]

The poem in which the conquest of Syria is celebrated is titled: *Ilâ al-fâtih* (To the conqueror). The poem opens with the name of Allenby. The last two lines of this poem are:

Fa-kâna al-jundu kulluhum yaṣhûᶜa /
wa kânat kullu Sûriyâ "Arîḥâ"
fa'in yakun al-masîḥu fidâ al-barâyâ
fa'innaka anta anqadhta al-masîḥâ
(Dîwân vol.2,176)

"All the soldiers were Joshua / and all of Syria was Jericho
when the Messias is the redeemer of men / then it was you who rescued the Messias."

---

26. *Dîwân Îlîyâ Abû Mâḍî, al-juz'u al-thânî,* 174
27. *arḍayta Mûsâ wa al-masîha wa 'Aḥmada wa al-nâsa ajmaᶜa wa al-ilâha taᶜâlâ/ (Dîwân Îlîyâ Abû Mâḍî, al-juz'u al-thânî,* 170)

There are more metaphores in this poem than the ones in these two lines but they are certainly the most significant. "You rescued the Messias" borders on blasphemia but we might see it as a hyperbole, or we might take "the Messias" as standing for the Holy Land, a rather peculiar pars-pro-toto.

The poem *al-ᶜâshiq al-makhdûᶜ* (The betrayed lover) is more homely. The betrayed lover pledges to spend the rest of his life in the church:

lâzamtuhâ badrayna mâ 'ltafatat
ᶜaynî ilâ shamsin wa-lâ badrî
'atlû anâshîda al-nabîyi ḍuḥâ
wa-'uṭâliᶜu al-injîla fî al-ᶜaṣrî
ḥînan maᶜa al-ruhbâni âwinatan
waḥdî wa-aḥyânan maᶜa al-ḥabrî
fî al-ghâbi fawqa al-ᶜushbi muḍṭajiᶜan

"I stayed there two months without turning my eye to sun or moon.
I chanted the songs of the prophet (Anâshîda al-nabîyi) in the morning
and read the gospel in the afternoon, sometimes with the monks,
then alone and then again with the clergy, in the woods lying on the grass . . ."
(al-Sâᶜih., 21.09.1916, frontpage and second page)

It is most probable that with this *Anâshîda al-nabîyi*, the Psalms were meant, rather than the Lamentations of the prophet Jeremiah. That means that King David to whom the Psalms are ascribed, is seen as a prophet, as he is in the Koran (Sura 4,161) but not in the scriptures. In the same poem occurs the line: "She recites for lovers sura's which are not in verse and not in prose". [28]

Adam, Eve and paradise do occur in the poem *al-Ṭayarân* (Aviation) in a hyperbolical way: "When Adam had known the guy his anger against Eve would have disappeared from his heart. He would have made the earth a paradise, to which paradise in beauty, radiance and loveliness would have been inferior." [29]

There are other poems is which Christian religious lore plays a role. One poem deals with the fall of Erzurum praising the conqueror: "You clad them in clothes of shame which hellfire will not purify even not when they

---

28. *tatlû ᶜalâ ahli al-hawâ suwaran laysat bi-manẓûmin wa-lâ nathrî*
29. *ṣayyara al-'arḍa jannatan dûnahâ al-jannatu fî al-ḥusni wa-'l-bahâ wa-'l-rawâᶜ* *(Dîwân Îlîyâ Abû Mâḍî, al-juz'u al-thânî,* 81.)

would wash themselves in its heat"[30] The other poem is titled: "The lost paradise or the vision of the German Emperor"[31]. The Emperor sees himself knocking at the door of heaven and being denied entrance and then he is denied to enter hell.

Îlîyâ Abû Mâḍî celebrates the town Milford in one of his poems calling it "Beautiful Milford".[32] That, however, is the second line of the title, the first line being "The mother of towns" (*Umm al-qurâ*), which is the Koranic name for Mecca. To describe the beauty of the place the poet more than once reaches out for religious motives and themes current in Islam or in Christianity. The following lines contain religious motives and themes which could have been taken from either religion. The city is seen as hell whereas the village is a very pleasant place.

Bi'sa al-madînatu innahâ sijnu al-nahî
Wa-dhawî al-nahî wa jahannamu al-aḥâr

How evil is the city, it is the prison of interdiction
and of those who prohibit and it is the hell of free people
(*Dîwân, vol.2,14*)

The poet then enumerates other evil aspects of the city telling that anyone who would have seen what I have seen would not envy the city-dwellers except Bashshâr.[33] In the next line the poet asks for God's forgiveness for his rashness. The first hemistich could have been said by Moslim and Christian but the second hemistich shows that the speaker is not the devout believer as suggested by the first part.

Ghufrânuka Allâhumma mâ anâ kâfirun
falima tuᶜadhdhibu muhjatî bi-'l-nâr

Forgiveness, O God, I am not an unbeliever
why then you torment my brain with hellfire
(*Dîwân, vol.2,14*)

---

30. *'albastahum thawba ᶜârin la taṭhuruhu nâru al-jaḥîmi wa law fî ḥarrihâ 'ghtasalû (Dîwân Îlîyâ Abû Mâḍî, al-juz'u al-thânî,*121)
31. *Al-firdawsu al-dâ'iᶜu aw rû'yâ al-qaysari al-Almânî (Dîwân Îlîyâ Abû Mâḍî, al-juz'u al-thânî,*144)
32. *Milford al-Jamîla (Dîwân Îlîyâ Abû Mâḍî, al-juz'u al-thânî,*13-16)
33. Bashshâr= Bashshâr ibn Burd (714-784) the blind poet, who grew up in Basra and then moved to Baghdad.

Describing the falls of Milford the poet says: It endlessly sprinkles its rocks with its tears, do you think it washes away its sins (*awzâr*).[34] The *awzâr* are Koranic but the connection between the sprinkling of water and the cleansing of sins seems a clear reference to the use of holy water in Christian churches. The top of the falls is compared with a *minbar* (the pulpit in the Mosque).

On p.15 the sixth line takes up the title of the poem: "O mother of towns" preceded by the words: "you sister of paradise"[35] (cf. Koran 41,28)

A religious connotation also has the line where the I of the poem is standing in awe before the river, as if I were in a temple, as if it were one of the holy books.[36]

The last line of the poem begins as follows: "A night and a morning amongst the brethren of purity"[37], which is a clear allusion to the famous Islamic brotherhood that lived and worked in the tenth century a.D in Basra.

The poet does not shrink from using themes which have a central significance in Islam, like the night-journey of the prophet: "Winter has covered the ground: When there had not been ice (the horse) would have flown impassioned, like Buraq with the lad of the nightjourney."[38]

The last poem to be mentioned here is a four-liner which runs as follows:

baynî wa bayna al-ᶜuyûni sirrun Allâhu fî al-sirri wa-'l-ᶜuyûn
idhâ'asat fikratî al-qawâfî awhat li-nafsî bihâ al-jufûn
hâti 'sqinî al-khamra jahran wa-lâ tubâli bimâ yakûn
in kâna khayrun aw kâna sharrun innâ ilâ 'llâhi râjiᶜûn

"between me and the eyes is a secret, God is in the secret and the eyes
when my thoughts find the rhymes difficult, the eyelids reveal them to my soul
come here, pour out the wine openly and do not mind what will happen
be it good or be it bad, to God we will return"
(*Dîwân vol.2, 92*)

---

34. *A-tarâhu yaghsuluhâ min al-awzâr* (*Dîwân Îlîyâ Abû Mâḍî, al-juz'u al-thânî,* 14)
35. *yâ ukhta dâri al-khuldi*
36. *Mutahayyiban faka'annanî fî haykalin wa-ka'annahu sifrun min al-asfâr* (*Dîwân Îlîyâ Abû Mâḍî, al-juz'u al-thânî,* 16)
37. *Laylun wa ṣubḥun bayna ikhwâni al-ṣafâ.*
38. *mithlu al-burâqi bi-fatâ al-miᶜrâj* (*Dîwân Îlîyâ Abû Mâḍî, al-juz'u al-thânî,*97)

The openly pouring out of wine may have some nasty consequences and that may refer to the fact that drinking of wine is forbidden in the Koran, but that need not have been intended here. The last hemistich, however, is a clear reference to Koranic verses (sura **2**,26,246 and **3**,77).

Looking back on the poetry of Îlîyâ Abû Mâḍî one sees that almost all the motifs and themes taken from the Bible and the Koran are set in an otherwise profane environment. Abû Mâḍî hardly uses such motifs and themes for religious purposes. It is not insignificant that Abû Mâḍî spent his youth in Egypt where he must have become thoroughly acquainted with popular Islamic culture in which the religious and the profane are intimately interrelated. He may also have picked up his wit in that environment.

BETWEEN HEAVEN AND HELL: SIN AND SEXUALITY IN THE POETRY OF ILYÂS ABÛ SHABAKA(1903-1947)

BY

ROBIN OSTLE

The most significant names in Arabic poetry in the first half of the 20th century tend to be associated either with the neo-classical mode in Egypt (Ḥâfiẓ Ibrâhîm, Aḥmad Shawqî) or Iraq (Maᶜrûf al-Ruṣâfî, Jamîl Ṣidqî al-Zahâwî, Muḥammad Mahdî al-Jawâhirî), or with romantic poetry which saw the peaks of its development in the *Mahjar* (Îlyâ Abû Mâḍî, Mikhâ'îl Nuᶜayma), in Egypt (Ibrâhim Nâgî, ᶜAlî Maḥmûd Ṭâhâ) and in Tunisia (Abû al-Qâsim al-Shâbbî)[1]. The work of other poets such as Khalîl Muṭrân are difficult to place within convenient categories of stylistic classification because of the manner in which particularly innovative parts of his creative output go well beyond the predominantly neo-classical style in which he wrote[2]. Rather in the same way, the poetry of Ilyâs Abû Shabaka is usually thought of as belonging to the romantic category both in period and style[3]: this is completely justified in terms of his ideas about the poet and poetry, and one could also describe his famous narrative poems *The Silent Invalid* (*al-marîḍ al-ṣâmit*, 1928) or *Ghalwâ'* (1945) as springing from the very centre of the romantic tradition. Yet the most unique quality in his poetry is one which has little to do with the dominant features of any particular literary style: this is his willingness to confront fearlessly and frankly issues of sin and sexuality, and to explore in his work the depths of degradation and depravity to which the human spirit can sink. The readiness to confront squarely such taboo issues in a deeply personal manner has been relatively rare in Arabic literature in the 20th century, and the fact that Abû Shabaka did so prior to 1940 is nothing short of remarkable.

Ilyâs Abû Shabaka was actually born in Providence in the USA in 1903 of Christian Lebanese parents, but his family did not settle there and they re-

---

1. See M.M.Badawi: *The Cambridge History of Arabic Literature: Modern Arabic Literature*. (Cambridge 1992), pp. 36-131
2. *Ibid*. pp. 84-88.
3. *Ibid*. pp. 122-26.

turned to Lebanon while Abû Shabaka was still in early infancy[4]. His education as a teenager in the ᶜAyntûra Institute was to provide one of the main formative cultural influences on his subsequent life, namely his knowledge of the French language and culture. Throughout his varied career as a teacher, writer, journalist and translator, his francophone enthusiasms were clear: all his translations were from French and covered a wide range of literary material from the 17th-19th centuries. In his book *Intellectual and Spiritual Links' between the Arabs and the French* (*Rawâbiṭ al-fikr wa-al-rûḥ bayna al-ᶜarab wa- al-firanja*, 1943) he sought to demonstrate the centrality of French influence on a range of world literature, while his first *dîwân* of poetry, *The Lyre* (*al-Qîthâra* , Beirut 1926) contained a number of poems translated from French. This collection is dedicated to the spirit of Abû Shabaka's dead father: he had been murdered when the poet was only ten years old, and the dedication sets the tone for the melancholy and pessimism which pervade the volume.

The period 1926-1938 saw the composition of Abû Shabaka's most important poetry, although the publication dates of of the relevant collections are misleading: his narrative poem : *Ghalwâ'* was not published until 1945, but was written between 1926 and 1932, while the thirteen poems which make up the collection *Serpents of Paradise* (*Afâᶜî al-firdaws*) date from 1928 until the date of publication in 1938. The poet's first excursion into narrative poetry came with *The Silent Invalid* in 1928.

Crucial to the appreciation of Abû Shabaka's work during these years are the biographical details revealed by Razzûq Faraj Razzûq in his book *Ilyas Abû Shabaka and his Poetry* (*Ilyâs Abû Shabaka wa shiᶜruh)*, Beirut 1956): *Ghalwâ'* is a scarcely veiled reference to Olga, the woman to whom Abû Shabaka was engaged for ten years before they were finally able to marry, and in the course of this lengthy engagement, in 1928 he had a torrid affair with a married woman.[5] These are the autobiographical sub-texts to *Ghalwâ'* and *Serpents of Paradise* in which the poet engages with constant conflicts between lust and love, duty and transgression, and vain struggles to reconcile human animality with spirituality. M.M. Badawi's *Critical Introduction to Modern Arabic Poetry* (Cambridge 1975) provides an admira-

4. The best source for biographical details on Abû Shabaka is still Razzûq Faraj Razzûq: *Ilyâs Abû Shabaka wa-shiᶜruhu* (Beirut 1956).
5. *Ibid.* pp.180ff.

ble and comprehensive study of *Ghalwâ'* [6], but less attention is devoted to *Serpents of Paradise* on which this brief study will now concentrate.

The rather gloomy and pretentious juvenilia of *The Lyre* provide little indication of the tortured obsessions with sin and sexuality which are to come. It is true that the love poems in this collection emphasise more the pains, the problems, deceits and disappointments which can mark such realms of human experience, but there is nothing here which is dramatically different from the sour misogyny of much of the work of 'Abd al-Raḥmân Shukrî, for example:[7]

> Beware of love! In love is evil, it is a fire in the heart which melts.
> If there is a deceitful heart in men, then the hearts of women are more so.

At this early stage in his development, the poet seems to accept life's evil and the duality of love almost as one who is not directly involved but who stands apart and observes. What we have here are merely the seeds of Abû Shabaka's later obsession with the opposing forces of good and evil. The transition to *Serpents of Paradise* is as shocking as it is surprising: the naive and puritanical morality of an inexperienced young man now gives way to a sense of sin and spiritual debasement as he struggles to come to terms with the effects of the love affair which cut across his engagement to Olga. He identifies on a grand scale with Biblical archetypes of sexual deceit and masculine weakness: while his version of the story of Samson and Delilah owes much to the model of Alfred de Vigny, it is the profound sense of the shocking nature of Samson's downfall that adds sinister dimensions to the poem which go far beyond anything achieved by the French romantic. The noble strength of the lion-like Samson is flawed by the lascivious heat of his lust[8]:

> The burning lusting heat drips from him, as though he is in the heat of the noon.
> He beats the ground angrily with his claws, and despair echoes in the darkness.
> The sparkle of flame fills his eyes, and his eyes are the mouth of the furnace.

---

6. M.M. Badawi, *A Critical Introduction to Modern Arabic Poetry* (Cambridge 1975), pp. 147-50.
7. *Al-Qîthâra* (Beirut 1926) p.35.
8. *Afâᶜî al-Firdaws*, (2nd edition Beirut 1948) p.21. All subsequent references are to this edition.

Much of the power of Abû Shabaka's verse depends on constant antithesis: the strength and power of Samson cannot prevent his downfall and betrayal; the beauty of Delilah co-exists disturbingly with her treachery and deceit; the morning of love is succeeded by the night of death; the beautiful fruits of Delilah's lips are poisons; the space between her breasts which affords softness and repose to Samson gradually leads him to the abyss of destruction:[9]

> The flame died in the master of the forest, the victorious prince of the caverns.
> And the great one, the great one, is weakened by a female, he is led by the lowly, the lowly.
> Flatter him, for in the rays of your eyes is the morning of love and the night of the tombs.
> On your beautiful lips are fruits which concealed the lust of death in their juice.
> Flatter him for between your breasts the abyss of death yawned on the comfortable bed.

Bitter ironical antithesis informs even the titles of a number of the poems: with "In the Temple of Lusts" ("Fî haykal al-shahawât") Abû Shabaka might almost have been satirizing the purity of the title of the well known poem by Abû al-Qâsim al-Shâbbî, "Prayers in the Temple of Love"("Ṣalawât fî haykal al-ḥubb")[10]. Far from venerating the female ideal, for Abû Shabaka woman is the "serpent of Paradise"[11]. As he gazes at his beloved, he is painfully aware that the passion which they have for each other is a source of danger and evil. The strength of their love is as much an urge to bestiality as it is to life enhancing nobility[12]:

> In the night I am afraid of a ghost which floats upon the surgings of your eyes for a time and disappears.
> A ghost of red lust which is woven by the wine of nights; it has ruin in its depths............

9. *Ibid.*p.22.
10. Abû al-Qâsim al-Shâbbî: *Aghânî al-ḥayât* (Tunis 1966), pp. 183-87.
11. *Afâᶜî al-firdaws*, p. 32.
12. *Ibid.* pp.32-33.

> You take the night by force, strenuously, unceasing, until weariness congeals in your eyes.
> The black in your eyes is but the remains of innards which have been ravished.

The colour red which appears in the second line of this quotation is one of the recurrent motifs in Serpents of Paradise and always in association with evil and sin. The poem "Red Lust"("al-shahwat al-ḥamrâ")[13] moves from the heat of passion, the red of wine, to the burning of the lust which tortures him like a flame[14]:

> I feel in my body a lust which tortures me, and in my blood a vehemence like the wine in my bowl.

The poet has a constant sense of his body as a vessel which needs to be voided of the elements which create love and passion. Only in this way can he avoid the degradation of the weakness from which he suffers in the face of these overwhelming forces[15]:

> I have a heart which I have emptied, so leave it empty of love, do not fill it.

The City of Sodom is yet another Biblical reference which presents the opportunity to mould this archetypal symbol of human vice in the evil fires of redness.[16] The city arises on the crests of flames of lust and passion before in turn it is destroyed by the purifying fire of divine wrath[17]:

> Oh Sodom. You were raised up amidst the flames, glowing red in your ingrained lusts.

As Abû Shabaka demonstrates again his talent for horrifying descriptions of the city teeming with evil, it is clear that he sees himself as very much part of the overall scenario:[18]

---

13. *Ibid.* pp.41-44.
14. *Ibid.* p.41.
15. *Ibid.* p.49.
16. *Ibid.* pp.35-37
17. *Ibid.* p.35.
18. *Ibid.* p.37.

Oh child of fornication. Your fire is in my blood, so blaze away as much as you will.
I do not fear the fire-brand of hell, as long as my body, oh Sodom, is my hell.

In his first collection, *The Lyre*, there are numerous references to the poet's disenchantment with existence and humanity - especially women - but there was always a certain distance between the poet and the objects of his jaundiced observation. In *Serpents of Paradise* this sense of detachment disappears as the language and imagery plumb new depths of sinister force. Nowhere is this clearer than in the poem "Defilement" ("al-Qâdhûra")[19]which opens with the poet emerging from a dream which he has had of a world of enchantment and delights. As he awakes and looks around him, the contrast is horrific[20]:

I wandered in a flood of night as obscenity dinned around, and filth fumed and foamed about.
There is a simmering in the in the boiling mire, and a lather, as if men were a bog which sighed.
I thrust my glance into the solid gloom, with a rasp of lashes in each of my eyes.

There is a shocking physicality in the imagery which the poet reinforces with powerful onomatopoeic vocabulary as he gazes on the people around him wallowing in the disgusting mire of their filth and sin. Here one has the rare experience in Arabic poetry written before 1950 of the poet impressing not by the sanitized beauty and and attractiveness of his lines, but by the vivid impressions of disgust and loathing which they create. His vision is one of horror and death which is constantly at hand[21]:

Filthy things walk around joyfully in life, singing, and the echoes of tombs call back.
They are human beings, stuffed phantoms. I wept for them in my hell, and they made merry.

---

19. *Ibid.* pp.26-29
20. *Ibid.* pp.26.
21. *Ibid.* p.27.

Young and beautiful women who had once inspired him have now undergone grim transformations[22]

> Women who were stingy with their breasts as wet nurses, their rosy lips are a fountain of sin.
> Harlots who have wasted their youth in whoring, their spirit is hag-like, servile.

Nature which had once been so attractive to him, now has become something grim and horrendous. A wind blows through the forests with a shrieking clamour like the shrilling voice of the Jinns in the valley of Hell. The vision ends with the poet wondering how the soul could have descended so far from its former purity.

It is apparent from "Defilement" that the poet feels himself very much part of what he describes ("my hell"), and this saves the work from the charge of self-centred arrogance. Abû Shabaka does not stand apart from his subjects in splendid isolation commenting on them in a self-righteous manner, a feature that was much too frequent in Arab poetry of the romantic period. There is no suggestion of moralising on the part of the poet, or self-serving withdrawal from the world. In contrast to much of the ivory-tower speculation about the evils of man and civilisation popular with Jibrân and the *Mahjar* poets or with ᶜAbd al-Raḥmân Shukrî, Abû Shabaka himself is part of the pictures of sin and corruption. He despairs on his own account as well as for others. "The Red Prayer"("*al-Ṣalât al-ḥamrâ*"[23]) is one of the most moving expressions of his individual agony. It is a desperate prayer addressed to God by the poet who, even while asking for forgiveness, recognises his inability to conquer his sin and his lust. Again the poem is imbued with the association between the colour red and evil. He begins by confessing his knowledge that he is a sinner, and describes his attempts to repent and reform. The pace of the poem alternates between the two different metres of *basîṭ* and *mujtath*, the former being slower and heavier[24]-:

> These past nights still leave their traces in the ruins of my eyes.
> Oh dread! My heart still has desires and hopes for the delight of shame.

---

22. *Ibid.*
23. *Ibid.* pp.50-55.
24. *Ibid.* p.50.

When my eyes awoke to my degradation, to my depravity,
I determined to root out lust, but I was dissuaded.

At the end of each section comes the despairing refrain of the hopeless confession:

Oh God! Pardon, for I am a wicked sinner.

Sadly he tells the story of his life of sensuality and sin, making reference to the great figures in history who have come to nothing through the sins of the flesh. He is vividly conscious of his own identification with all this human corruption, yet he cries out for mercy in the midst of his own lustful suffering[25]:

I call to you while the red darkness burns me; no reply, you turn away and do not save me.
When I awoke in shame from the drunkenness of passion, I sought you, almost hidden by shame.

In spite of his numerous appeals to God, and his desires and resolutions to repent and reform, he always relapses into sin and succumbs to lust. When the final refrain occurs at the end of the poem, it is by now more a statement of immutable fact than a plea for deliverance based on any hope of redemption. The poet remains firmly within the toils of his own vices

I went asking my soul for defence from my sins,
But found none to defend me save my own lies.
Oh God. Pardon. For I am a wicked sinner..

Of all the collections produced by Abû Shabaka between 1926 and 1945, *Serpents of Paradise* is the most consistent and the most ruthless in its explorations of the human capacity for self- destruction through an inability to reconcile the conflicting ranges of emotion in love, and to achieve an equilibrium between duty and natural instinct. To be sure one of the dramas which faced, and which still faces, individuals in Near and Middle Eastern societies is how to reconcile the desires for emotional liberation which had

25. *Ibid.* p.54.

been encouraged by the impact of the European enlightenment, with the reality of the strict control over sexual relations which dominates most social contexts. Other romantic poets of the period reacted to the problem in various ways: the *mahjar* writers concentrated on the neo-Platonic concept of the dualism of body and soul, al-Shâbbî created the female ideal which he venerated through a language of religious liturgy, while ʿAlî Maḥmûd Ṭâhâ's verse of hedonistic sensuality reached widespread audiences via music and the spoken word.[26].
Ilyâs Abû Shabaka is a lone voice in his generation both in laying bare the dark sides of sexual repression and the extent to which he himself contributes to the darkness. There is a world of difference between these thirteen poems of *Serpents of Paradise* which take one through the poet's own tortured struggles, and the gloomy moralizing of ʿAbd al-Raḥmân Shukrî whose apparent problems with his own sexuality were laid entirely at the door of the opposite sex.

It is with something of a sense of relief that one discovers in the later *dîwâns* of Abû Shabaka a process of reconciliation and redemption through love: *The Melodies* (*al-Alḥân*, 1941), *To Eternity* (*Ilâ al-abad*, 1944) and *Call of the Heart* (*Nidâ' al-qalb,* 1944) all tend in this direction. While the sadness and pains of love are not absent from these works, it is now seen as much more of a saving grace by the poet who had written of the perfidy of Delilah and the destructive forces of animal passion. Looking back over the span of Abû Shabaka's poetry from *The Lyre* until the collections published shortly before his death in 1947, it is possible to see an individual odyssey in verse from profound spiritual crisis to ultimate redemption. Yet in spite of the undoubted originality of his narrative of his *The Silent Invalid*, *Olga*, and *To Eternity*, it is *Serpents of Paradise* which has ensured Abû Shabaka's special place in the history of Arabic poetry. Scholars have noted the model of Baudelaire and *Les Fleurs du Mal*[27] which may well have encouraged the Lebanese *poète maudit* in his turn to extend the limits of the modern Arab poetic sensibility in such precocious fashion.

---

26. *Ibid.* p. Robin Ostle: "The Romantic Imagnation and the Female Ideal" in Allen, Kilpatrick and de Moor (Eds.), *Love and Sexuality in Modern Arabic Literature* (London 1995), pp.33-45.
27. M.M. Badawi: *A Critical Introduction To Modern Arabic Poetry*, pp. 145ff.

THE HUMANIZED GOD IN THE POETRY OF A TAMMUZIAN: BADR SHÂKIR AL-SAYYÂB

BY

ED DE MOOR
University of Nijmegen

Introduction

Modern Arabic Poetical schools have been described in accordance with standard critical analysis and have been given qualifications such as "neo-classical", "romantic" or "modernist"[1] (see *The Cambridge History of Arabic Literature*). In this list of qualifications the qualification *Tammuzians* seems to be an exception. Originally this name was given to five important Greater Syrian poets of the fifties: al-Khâl, Adûnîs, Ḥâwî, al-Sayyâb and Jabrâ. We might add other contemporary minor poets who followed them in exploiting this thematic field in their poetry, and later poets, like the Palestinians, who used this thematic field to introduce their political ideas as has been demonstrated recently in Abu Hashhash's study on Palestinian poetry[2]. When we consider the Arabic poetry of the fifties, we are astonished by the outburst of poetical talent in those years, like desert flowers abundantly sprouting in "the waste land" of ever repeated images and motifs of the classical and neo-classical poetry.

It was a very young generation that opened its mouth and cried its message of renewal all over the Arab world. It is no exaggeration to say that most stars on the poetical firmament of today started sparkling in the fifties. Nor is it an exaggeration to conclude that their most important source of inspiration is to be found in the mythical field and thus closely linked to the general societal feeling of renewal, liberation and political independence in the Arab world. It was, as it were, a happy coincidence of political, societal and literary inspiration that caused this sudden outburst of talent and created the so-called "New Poetry" in which we might, if we look at principles of form and prosody, easily distinguish a Baghdadian and a Beirutian current. It is recieved wisdom that what was started in Baghdad by al-Malâ'ika, al-

1. See as an example The Cambridge History of Arabic Literature: Modern Arabic Literature, 1992.
2. Ibrahim M. Abu Hashhash, Tod und Trauer in der Poesie des Palästinensers Maḥmûd Darwîsh, Berlin 1994 .

Sayyâb and Bayâtî, was worked out in Beirut by the team of *Shi*ᶜ*r*. Al-Khâl, Adûnîs and al-Ḥâjj had been impressed strongly by western free verse poetry; in this they followed their Lebanese predecessors of the Mahjar School. But they went much further in liberating themselves from the shackles of convention. Here I shall say no more about matters of form in the poetry under discussion. Although we certainly must pay attention to formal aspects, especially in the poetry of Badr Shâkir al-Sayyâb, the main thrust of our reading will be semantic and I shall focus on the mythical content of Sayyâb's poetry in the historical context of the fifties.

I will first devote some attention to this historical context and then discuss some examples taken from the poetry of al-Sayyâb which in my opinion deserve our special attention within the framework of this study.

For the historical context I can refer to some important studies mentioned in Leslie Tramontini's dissertation on Sayyâb's Collections *Azhâr wa asâṭîr* and *Unshûdat al-maṭar*[3]. The main source for this remains of course Iḥsân ᶜAbbâs' study[4], which combines biographical and analytical approaches. An extended structural analysis was presented in 1983 by ᶜAbd al-Karîm Ḥasan in a Sorbonne dissertation, supervised by André Miquel. It is a detailed study of the vocabulary, themes and motifs, based on statistical methods. But the book does not offer much insight into the textual context and even less into the historical context[5]. As far as mythology in the work of al-Sayyâb is concerned, we have at our disposal studies written by ᶜAbd al-Riḍâ ᶜAli and ᶜAlî ᶜAbd al-Muᶜṭî al-Baṭl[6]. More general are the studies of Asᶜad Razzûq and Rîtâ ᶜAwaḍ that deal with the meaning of myth in modern poetry, esp. the Tammuzian poets, and the theme of death and resurrection in modern Arabic poetry, respectively[7]. Studies of al-Sayyâb written in

3. Leslie Tramontini, *Badr Shâkir al-Sayyâb. Untersuchungen zum poetischen Konzept in den Diwanen azhâr wa-asâṭîr und unshûdat al-maṭar*, Wiesbaden 1991.
4. Iḥsân ᶜAbbâs: *Badr Shâkir al-Sayyâb, dirâsa fî ḥayâtih wa-shi*ᶜ*rih*, Beirut 6th edition 1992.
5. Mansour Guissama, *Badr Shâkir al-Sayyâb, essai sur la créativité poétique,* Publications de la Faculté des lettres de Manouba, Tunis, 1989
6. ᶜAbd al-Ridâ ᶜAli, *al-Usṭûra fî shi*ᶜ*r al-Sayyâb,*Baghdad, 1978, and ᶜAlî ᶜAbd al-Muᶜṭî al-Baṭl, *al-Ramz al-usṭûrî fî shi*ᶜ*r Badr Shâkir al-Sayyâb,* Kuwait 1982.
7. Asᶜad Razzûq, *al-Usṭûra fî-al-shi*ᶜ*r al-mu*ᶜ*âṣir. Al-shu*ᶜ*arâ' al-tammûziyyûn.* Beirut 1959; Rîtâ ᶜAwaḍ: *Usṭûrat al-mawt wa al-inbi*ᶜ*âth fî al-shi*ᶜ*r al-*ᶜ*arabî al-ḥadîth*, Beirut 1978.

Arabic are numerous and western studies are scarce. Tramontini's book is therefore useful and may serve as an introduction to the work of al-Sayyâb. Thus much on the secondary sources. Our main source remains of course Sayyâb's *Dîwân* edited by Dâr Shiᶜr, later Dâr al-ᶜAwda[8].

Let us now consider the literary historical context of Sayyâb's emergence as a Tammuzian poet within the poetical renewal of the fifties.

The Tammuzians and the review *Shiᶜr*

The poetic revival of the fifties with its strong mythical implications is linked inseperably with the names of the Anglo-American poet T.S.Eliot and that of the author of the anthropological goldmine *The Golden Bough*[9], Sir James Frazer. It is in their works that one has to look for the cultural background of the "Tammuzi movement". Both Eliot and Frazer deeply impressed the young poets of the free verse movement belonging to the Beirutian *Shiᶜr* group and those who sympathised with the idea of Greater Syria, so popular in that circle.

It was the critic Jabrâ Ibrâhîm Jabrâ who translated parts of *The Golden Bough* and gave poets who used the myth of Tammuz in their poetry the name of "Tammuzi poets". He was the first who theorized, as it were, their poetry. In his criticism of al-Khâl's *al-Bi'r al-ûlâ* in *Shiᶜr* no. 7/8 1958, p.58-59, we read:

> Earth and water are Tammuz. Tammuz is Christ and Christ is mankind. This symbolic equalization is the fundament of nearly every poem, but every poem is a new experiment of tracing this fundamental equalization... it is the return of man to God, sc. the return to life and justice and the light passing by death.

Tammuz is the answer to the "*mafâza*" ("desert") and "*jadb*" ("bareness") which modern man experiences in all aspects of life (Jabrâ speeks of "*mafâzat al-wujûh, mafâzat al-mudun, mafâzat al-zaman*"). It is the poet who tries to find "rebirth and resurrection" (p.57). Al-Khâl was one of the

8. *Dîwân Badr Shâkir al-Sayyâb*, Dâr al-ᶜAwda, Beirut 1971. With an Introduction by Nâjî ᶜAllûsh.
9. The book was first published in 1890 and had a tremendous impact on evolving concepts of modernism in the first part of the 20th century. In 1922 Frazer published a shortened version of his work which has been translated into many languages.

first to use the ancient symbol of Tammuz, "like most religious symbols" results of man's first experience with life, fear, belief and death, symbols that open a door to liberation/salvation and save man from despair and darkness. The waste land *("al-arḍ al-kharâb")* is sprinkled with blood at the end in order to raise the wheat and the grapes, and the earth is not only a graveyard but also "*bayt raḥim*" and a place of rebirth and harvest.

Jabrâ informs the reader of *Shiʿr* that although this Tammuzian symbolism is wholly new in Arabic poetry, western poets like T.S.Eliot, well aware of great cultural changes taking place, took refuge in the twenties in Babylonian myths. Further on Jabrâ also refers to *The Golden Bough* of James Frazer in which the myths that nourished Eliot's reading and poetry were collected.

In the same article (p.60) Jabrâ mentions the Tammuzi poets Adûnîs, Yûsuf al-Khâl, Badr Shâkir al-Sayyâb and Khalîl Ḥâwi; to these may be added the name of Jabrâ Ibrâhîm Jabrâ himself. They are generally considered to be the innovators, but, as Kheir Bek argued in his dissertation on modernist poetry, they were inspired by poets like Jibrân Khalîl Jibrân and Fu'âd Sulaymân who had already cherished Syrian mythology as a means of stressing Lebanese identity.The Iraqi al-Sayyâb, the most sensitive of all, was familiar with the idea of Greater Syria and with Babylonian mythology. He sympathised with the *Shiʿr* group, although he was of a different political orientation. So al-Sayyâb, after having published some of his poems in the first issues of *Shiʿr*, read his poetry along with "*Khamîs Shiʿr*" in July 1957. The Lebanese Khalîl Ḥâwî joined them, whereas the Palestinian Jabrâ contributed to *Shiʿr* from the beginning, as did the others. Although Ḥâwî soon came into conflict with the editors of the review and Sayyâb later cut off his relations for political reasons, they were all connected by their daring approach to poetical traditions and their use of the mythology of death and resurrection. In the first year of the review we find the theme of death and rebirth already worked out in a poem by Ḥâwi *al-Sajîn*:

Shahwatu al-ʿanqâ'i mâtat fi rifâtin
Hiya wa-'l-dunyâ ʿalâ ḥaqdin dafîn
The passion of the Phoenix died in a corpse
together with the world in bitter resentment" (Sh I, 2, p.7)

Christ, easily annexed by those poets to the Syrian mythological field, is present in Adûnîs' poem *Samʿatuhu wa famuhu hijâra* (SH I, 2, 47). Jabrâ speaks in the same issue of *Shiʿr* of the death of his home town Bethlehem in the poem *Bayt min ḥajar*. Al-Khâl published his poem *al-Biʿr al-maḥjûra* and al-Sayyâb's poem *al-Nahr wa-'l-mawt* deals with a theme that will be recurrent in the whole of his poetical work: the desire for death, always connected with the desire for life, with explicit references to the myth of Adunis, the Syrian god who gives of his blood to create new life.

What strikes us in these first references to the Tammuzian myth is the accent laid on the theme of death, most evidently in the poem of Sayyâb:

> *Fa-'l-mawtu ʿâlamun gharîbun yaftanu al-ṣighâr*
> *Wa bâbuhu al-khafîyu kâna fîka, yâ Buwayb*
> "Death is a strange world appealing to young people
> and its hidden gate was in you, Buwayb" (Sh I,2,p.11)

but even in the summer issue of 1957 we already find the evocation of new life:

> *Awaddu law gharaqtu fî damî ilâ al-qarar*
> *li-aḥmila al-ʿib'a maʿa al-bashar*
> *wa abʿatha al-ḥayâta, inna mawtî 'ntiṣâr!*
> "I want to be drowned in my blood, sinking unto the bottom
> to bear the burden with the people
> and to give life again: my death is a victory".(Sh I,2, p.12)

In the next issue of *Shiʿr* we find two of the most quoted and translated Tammuzian poems. The first one is *al-Baʿth wa-al-ramâd* ("Resurrection and ashes") in which Adûnîs exploits the myth of Adunis and the myth of the Phoenix together.[10] The other poem is Sayyâb's sensitive elaboration of the Christ theme: *al-Masîḥ baʿd al-ṣalb* ("Christ after the Crucifixion"), and this poem will deserve our special attention.

Atif Faddûl published recently in Beirut a dissertation entitled *The Poetics of T.S.Eliot and Adunis*. In this comparative study attention is paid to the intercultural exchange between the *Shiʿr* group and the Anglo-American New Poetry movement in which especially Eliot and Pound played a domi-

10. This has been translated and discussed by Joseph Zeidan in his article: "Myth and Symbol in the Poetry of Adûnîs and Yûsuf al-Khâl" in *JAL*, X, 1979, pp.70-94. See also I. Boullata, *Modern Arabic Poets*, London, 1976, pp.57-62.

nant rol. Without any doubt al-Khâl's role in this process was crucial. He spent nearly eight years, 1948-1955, in the United States and came back to Lebanon with the idea of establishing a movement similar to that of the Imagists. It is no coincidence that it was the Christian al-Khâl who became impressed by Eliot's defence of European Christian civilisation. He himself could boast of a philosophical background thanks to Charles Malik's teaching at the AUB in the 1940s. That also explained his political standpoint: Malik emphasized political freedom and saw Lebanon as the cradle of Western civilisation and Christianity as one of Lebanon's fundamental characteristics. Al-Khâl therefore could not share *al-Âdâb*'s enthusiasm for Arab nationalism. In his view the civilisation of Lebanon and of Greater Syria was not Arab but Western and Mediterranean. There was only a marginal place for Islam in this civilisation. A new Arab poetry could only be realized by "an intercultural fusion between the Arab World and the West".

Eliot's poetical principles started from his deep consciousness of the crisis in Western civilization, in the twenties, so well expressed in *The Waste Land,* leading to the spiritual barrenness of the life of Western man.

What Eliot wanted to suggest was a return to Christian belief in original sin and the innate imperfection of man, "the return to a religious world view, instead of a humanistic one" (Faddul p.90). One wonders whether the young Arab poets understood this point of view. What startled them was the rich imagery of myths proposed by Eliot, which fitted so well into their political and cultural education in the Greater Syrian movement of Anṭûn Saᶜâdah and their dreams of a new world. For a short while they succeeded in finding and identifying with a cluster of values, after which they resumed their feelings of unrest and fragmentation.[11]

A careful reading of al-Sayyâb's poems makes us realise that he started using Tammuzian symbols of death and resurrection in 1953/4 in an optimistic and hopeful mood, but after 1958, more and more disillusioned with the political deterioration in Iraq, he started using the myth to express his despair and succumbed to an ironic approach. Then Tammuz became a symbol of hopelessness.

Symbolism made its debut in Arabic poetry in the thirties. al-Khâl and Adûnîs were inspired by Saᶜîd ᶜAql who insisted on the concept of "unconsciousness" as the highest state of poetry. In this state the poet "unites with the eternal truths of the Universe". Jibrân's poetry was strongly influenced

11. Razzûq, *Uṣṭûra*, pp. 17-26.

by Romantic ("School of Jena"), Symbolist and modernist movements. In the poetry of *Shi*ᶜ*r* and the Tammuzians Symbolism enjoys dominance.

To follow Eliot meant to choose symbolism, modernism and romantic idealism, based on the so-called mythical method of writing. This approach is greatly at variance with the traditional approach to reality. The poet creates his own reality and this is essential for understanding the way a poet like Sayyâb used reality and memory. It explains why in this poetry a small village like Jaykûr could become Paradise and a place of supreme happiness and why the city could become hell.

Sayyâb's poetical imagery

Nâjî 'Allûsh, in his introduction to the *Dîwân Badr Shâkir al-Sayyâb*, distinguishes four periods in the life and poetry of Sayyâb. The first period is characterized as "romantic"(1943-1948). The second period (1949-1955) is marked by "realism". In this period Badr frees himself from traditional ᶜ*arûḍ* poetry and experiments with the *taf*ᶜ*'îla*. In exile in Kuwait he feels more and more involved in the Arabic cause and gets into trouble with the Communist Party. This period ends politically in 1954 when Sayyâb leaves the Communist Party and engages himself in the pan-Arabic movement.

The first poem in which the myth of Tammûz is used is *Ughniyya fî shahr âb* ("Song in the month of August", *Diw*. 328):

Tammûz yamûtu ᶜ*alâ al-ufuqi*
*Wa taghûru dimâhu ma*ᶜ*a al-shafaqi*
*Fî al-kahfi al-mut*ᶜ*ami....*
....Tammûz yamûtu wa marjânah
ka-'l-ghâbati tarbuḍu bardânah

Tammûz dies on the horizon
his blood seeps away with the evening glow
in the dark cave...
Tammûz dies and his coralline (blood)
lies cold down like the forest

As happens in the myth, Tammuz is killed like by a wild boar, but in the middle of the summer. His death brings a chill to the life of the women of the city, a symbol of their empty life.

These poems belong to the third period, the period of "*al-tammûziyya*" or "*al-wâqi^ciyya al-jadîda*" (1956-1960). In this period al-Sayyâb wrote his best poems, brought together in the collection *Unshûdat al-maṭar*.
The figures of Tammûz, Christ, Ishtar, the village Jaykûr and the city of Bâbil dominate the poetry of this period.

The Tammuz theme is cyclical: the blood of the dying god runs in the earth every year when nature dies and brings new life in springtime. This blood motif combines with the water-motif, rain pouring and falling down, bringing life but death as well. This is best illustrated in *Unshûdat al-maṭar*, which is so familiar to all of us that it does not need illustration. Most striking are the symbolic connotations of motifs taken from Sayyâb's childhood: the village he was born in: "Jaykur" seems to symbolize happiness and heaven, and its river "Buwayb" becomes the grave in which man waits for new life. The "water" symbolises death and new life together, like "the rain" in *Unshûdat al-maṭar*. These symbols assume archetypical dimensions when connected with the world of the gods of fertility.

Christ dying on the cross becomes Adunis whose blood drenches the earth of the mountains and colours the river. We see it in the poem *Marḥâ Ghaylân* were the lyrical I is drowned deep in the river and speaks to his father as a young child:

"Bâbâ yâ Bâbâ"...
ka'anna rûḥî
fî turbati al-ẓalmâ'i ḥabbatu ḥanṭatin wa ṣadâka mâ'u
wa-a^clanti ba^cthî yâ samâ'.
Hâdhâ khulûdî fî al-ḥayâti takunnu ma^cnâhu al-dimâ'u
"Bâbâ" ka'anna yada al-Masîḥ
fîhâ, ka'anna jamâjima al-mawtâ tubar^cimu fî al-ḍarîḥ
Tammûz ^câda bi-kulli sunbulatin tu^câbithu kulla rîḥ
Anâ Ba^clu: akhṭuru fî al-Jalîli...
^calâ al-miyâh, anuththu fî al-waraqâti rûḥî wa-'l-thimâr
wa anâ Buwaybu adhûbu fî faraḥî wa arqudu fî qarârî...

"Papa"...my soul is like a grain of wheat
in the dark soil and your echo is water.
You announced my resurrection, O heaven,
This is my immortality in life
whose meaning is hidden in the blood
"Papa"...Christ's hand seems to be in it,

sculls of death seem to sprout in the grave
Tammuz brought back every ear of wheat playing with the wind
"I am Baal: in Galilee I walk ... on the water
and I spread my soul among the leaves and the fruits ...
I am Buwayb melting of joy and resting in the deep

Who is "Papa" in this poem. A Father with mythical dimensions? A God-father? Perhaps even God the Father, as Christians say? There is a reference to the miracle of Christ (Baal) walking on the Sea of Galilee. The last line reveals Sayyâb's tendency toward mysticism, but the whole poem represents a strongly felt relationship between life and death, earth and heaven.

It is not surprising that a man who stressed the idea of personal sacrifice for the liberation of the people came to use the figure of Christ, the Son of God, who died to save mankind, as Christians believe, and whose dying was interpreted by Arab Muslim poets as martyrdom for a new world. As for Christian symbolism, it seems that al-Sayyâb was deeply impressed by the poetry of Edith Sitwell in which the biblical figures of Jesus, Judah and Eliazer and others feature prominently.

As an example of this we may look consider his poem *al-Masîḥ ba^{c}d al-Ṣalb*, "Christ after Crucifixion" published in Shi^{c}r summer 1957 (Dîwân p.457-462). Christ, in Sayyâb's poetry, is a symbol of sacrifice *per se* (Tramontini). But who is Christ in this poem?

The text can be divided into 6 sections

Section 1: l.1-11
The text opens with of a lyrical I which comments on its crucifixion. As in "*Unshûdat al-maṭar*" palm-trees in the early morning figure in the first image. Here they are part of the narration of a man's crucifixion and burial by people who left him to the winds and the loneliness of the grave. Intriguing is the fact that the "I-figure" is presented alive and listening to what is happening in the outside world. It seems that people are complaining loudly. Their voices connect the buried one with the city. The complaints in line 2 and 8 create an image of sadness but are also signs of life in the darkness. But also these sounds stop and the city/people fall asleep.
It seems to me that this first passage refers to two symbolic layers:

firstly to the narration of Christ's burial, familiar to al-Sayyâb from his contacts with Christians in South Iraq and his reading of the Gospel;
secondly to the political situation in Iraq. The first layer is obvious, the second more oblique. It is explained by the tension between the person in the grave and the people of the city (in Sayyâb's poetical language always the place of danger and disintegration). This tension is expressed by the image of the complaint seen as a line connecting the grave with the city, the depths with the surface. And around the grave winter and the cold dominate.

<u>Section 2: l.12-30</u>

The second passage, lines 12-30, contrasts strongly with the former. The historical site of Jerusalem is replaced by the symbolic place of happiness that justifies life: Jaykûr.

Images of youth, fertility and summer are evoked in five lines preparing the venue with the I-person whose heart is the centre of life and whose blood pours into the earth. Here too, the lyrical I seems to be underground, at the same time he is the sun, he is the earth, he is water, he is wheat and he is bread that has to be eaten. He dies in order to give life. If his heart (the ear) dies, then resurrection is assured for everyone who eats. The Christian reader can not help seeing here a reference to Holy Communion. Line 26 underlines this perspective: "I died so that the bread would be eaten in my name" The Tammuzian aspect follows: "so that they could sow me (sc. the grain) at the season". In line 24 there may be a reference to the Phoenix myth:"I died by fire...but the god remained." The round form of the bread suggests the image of a girl's breast and of the feeding breast, a recurrent image in Sayyâb's poetry. Christ-Tammuz gives himself totally in lines 28-30 and becomes one with mankind and nature. In this vision, sacrificing one's life becomes a highly worthy act.

<u>Section 3: l.31-42</u>

This section (lines 31-42) is puzzling. Here the poet evokes the bafflement of people about resurrection: "you can die only once and you will not return to life". Judas, the apostle who betrayed Christ, is upset when he sees his master again. In a few words he is characterised as a black shadow of Christ, a *timthâl* of ideas, who lost his spirit. If Christ is bread, he is stone. He cannot express his feelings and is afraid of warmth:

> "Is this you? or is it my shadow that became white and spread light? You come from the world of the dead. But death comes only once! So said our ancestors!"

Section 4: l.43-61

The structure of passage four (43-61) is reminiscent of the use of the refrain "*maṭar, maṭar, maṭar*" in *Unshûdat al-maṭar.*

Here we read "*qadamun ta*ᶜ*dû qadamun qadamu*" (line 43, line 46, line 52). These repeated rhythmic expressions intensify the feeling of oppression of Christ in his grave threatened by soldiers. What do they mean, these steps on the grave? Christ has been crucified ("*a-wa-mâ ṣallabûnî ams?*" l. 48). The poet stresses the helplesness of Christ/Tammûz. Helplessness is also signified by "*anâ al-âna* ᶜ*uryânun fî qabrî*". Theologically we could say that here the *kenosis* of the God is completed.

But divinity is regained by doing well to others, by dividing the self, by sharing clothes and warmth with the poor. This giving is parallel to the image of nature in wintertime when the seeds and grains start to sprout and germinate. This is a generous God who hides himself in poverty and shows his nature by giving. By showing his vulnerability Christ/Tammuz razes the wall between divinity and humanity:

57 *Thumma fajjartu nafsî kunûzan fa*ᶜ*arraytuhâ ka-'l-thimâr*
ḥîna faṣṣaltu jaybî qimâtan wa kammî dithâr
ḥîna daffa'tu yawman bi-laḥmî ᶜ*iẓâm al-ṣighâr*
ḥîna ᶜ*arraytu jurḥî, wa ḍammadtu jurḥan siwâh,*
ḥuttima al-sûru baynî wa baina al-ilâh

We notice the deliberate use of the intensive second form in these five lines and the typical insistence on the socialist values of sharing and equality. One could say that Sayyâb's God is a socialist one.

Section 5: l.62-71

This section (lines 62-71) reiterates the opposition between soldiers and people. Against the violence of the soldiers the hero (Christ) is defenceless. They employ all means to violate his integrity (line 62-68). "Like a hungry swarm of birds in a deserted village".

To the violence of the soldiers are opposed the looks of "my people, from the lights of heaven full of memories and love". They take away the burden and moisten the cross (like a young plant, so that it can sprout again for new life). With "my people" we are back in the paradise of Jaykûr.

Section 6: l.72-78

This section (lines 72-78) is surprising. Christ is presented on his cross but when we follow his glance over the plains and the city, we see a large forest of crosses and under every cross a mother weeping. It seems that the crucifixion of Christ has been followed by many others. Therewith this crucifixion looses its uniqueness and Christ becomes one of many and it is projected on the prevailing political terror who killed the martyrs of the revolution. The poet expresses his astonishment by a "*Quddisa al-Rabb*" and for the first time we hear the name of God so familiar to Arab people, Muslims and Christians alike: "*al-Rabb*". Bless the Lord! This is the labour pains of the city". So ends this beautiful poem in an apocalyptic image of pain and violence: For new life, as the labour pains tells us.

If we consider the way al-Sayyâb uses the story of Christ here, we realise that it is far from the Christian interpretation we might expect or perhaps would like to expect. Certainly, the poet writes with compassion about Christ in his grave, having been submitted to the tribulations of the soldiers of the state, but he is not dead, nor is He with the Father. There is no angel or Holy Spirit to comfort him. He is in a state of expectation and is connected to the people of the city who wait for the start of a new season. What makes him divine is his capacity to share everything and to be in everything after sacrificing his life (lines 18-30). That passage seems to me the most exciting of the poem. This is the Sayyabian wording of a unique uttering: "this is my body for you to take and eat", as we hear in the Christian ritual of the Eucharist.

Of course, al-Sayyâb did not formulate this idea of Salvation which is the creed of traditional Christianity. But he did combine it with the repetitiveness of the myth of Tammûz connected with the passage of the seasons. The end of the poem, an expression of Sayyâb's socialist vision of the world, strikes me as very personal: the suffering of Christ on the cross was not unique, his suffering is everywhere. Christ symbolises Everyman.
But this ending can be interpreted as the beginning of new life.

There is no place here to Consider the application of the Tammuzian theme in Sayyâb's later poems. Tramontini has studied a number of the poems and has concluded that the poet used the myth more and more in an ironic way, when he realised that the political ideals which he believed in did not lead to the new Iraq he dreamed of. When in 1958 Qâsim becomes for him the new Tammuz he soon discovers that all the statues made of him are useless. After the massacre of Mosul in 1958 in particular he is deeply depressed and uses the myth to express his disillusion:

"Is this Adunis, this emptiness, this paleness, this waste?
Is this Adunis? where is the light, where the harvest?
sickles that don't earn
blossoms without fruits
black lands without water
What do we have to expect after so many years?
Is this the scream of men?
Is this the complaint of women?
Adunis, what kind of heroism
you came with false glances, emptyhanded
There is no return of Adunis, no resurrection of Christ

In *Ru'yâ fî ᶜâm 1956* (1960) al-Sayyâb once again combines his hope and despair. All the sacrifices of the revolution have been in vain: Sterility ("*ᶜaqm*") is the ultimate result. Thunder and lightning yes, but no rain. Ishtar's kiss does not revive Tammuz. Tammûz (Qâsim) becomes a symbol of terror and his ubiquitous image a symbol of death. The Tammuzian symbol of red anemones, blood that gives new life, becomes a symbol of terror in a shocking image of the Mother of the North (Mosul) whose breasts are cut off and whose eyes are pulled out (?). al-Sayyâb uses the image of the godhead to attack the communist terror in Mosul and Kirkuk in 1959.

In *al-ᶜAwda li-Jaykûr* (1960) (Diw.426) Christ speaks about "vinegar and blood pouring from his heart" instead of "water and blood" as the traditional image celebrates. He is presented as a miracle-worker who changes water into wine:

"Water becomes wine and the cup is full of food".

But the use of the symbol is ironic again:

"This is the springtime of disease!"

The poem is a cry for justice and compassion. The poet himself becomes Christ crying for justice.

"Agony, not death
words, no voice
labour pains, no birth
Who crucifies the poets in Baghdad?
Who buys his eyes and hands?
Who makes a crown of thorns for him
Jaykûr O Jaykûr
Strings of light
hang up the cradle of morning
Prepare the birds and ants
a meal from my wounds

This is my meal, O hungry people
these are my tears, O poor people
this is my prayer, O believers:
may the vulcano burst out in flames
may the Euphrates send its streams
so that we can enlighten the darkness
and learn what mercy is:
Jaykûr...O Jaykûr
Vinegar and water
are coming out of my heart
from my burning wound
from all my deepness
O my people...
Jaykûr, O Jaykûr, do you listen?
Open the door for those who want to go in
Collect your children playing in the village garden
This is the Last Supper
This is the harvest of years:
Water became wine, and the cups
are filled with food
This is the spring of
Disease.

When Tammuz can not longer be used for the sake of the people, Sayyâb gives a role of redemption to Ishtar who collects the dead body of Tammuz to give it new life. We find her in the poem "Cerberus in Babylon" as a mourning goddess commiserating with the poor. In the poem "*Ru'yâ fî ᶜâm 1956*" Ishtar is like Christ crucified. The poem is cruel and horrifying and the images not always free of bombastic exaggeration.

Ṣallabûhâ, daqqû mismâran
fî bayt al-mîlâd, al-riḥm
They crucified her putting nails in
the home of birth, the womb

At the end the waste land is everywhere:

al-mawt fî al-shawâriᶜ
al-ᶜaqmu fî mazâriᶜ
wa-kullu mâ nuḥibbuhu yamût
al-mâ'u qayyadûhu fî al-buyût

The city and the countryside are taken by destruction and fire:

wa-yarquṣu al-lahîbu fî al-bayâdir

and even Christ is not able to save man:

wa-yuhliku al-Masîḥu qabl Eliᶜâzir

Jaykûr itself, the paradise of dreams, is at last infected by the disease of which Sayyâb speaks in "*al-ᶜAwda li-Jaykûr*". Jaykûr becomes a deserted place and Sayyâb leaves the Tammuzian symbolic world.

At this point in his life, Sayyâb suffered in prison. Upon his release, he experienced a nervous breakdown, which may explain the tone of his poem *Amâma babi 'llâh* (dated 26 August 1961).

In this poem we hear a disillusioned and tired man (Sayyâb was already ill) praying to his creator. As in his Tammuzian poetry the poet refers to the course of the seasons but he ceases to mention Tammuz, Astarte, Christ and other mythical figures. This poem seems to be a return to the traditional God Creator and the poet prostrates himself before the gate of heaven. It is the prayer of a tired believer who expresses his feelings with irony but yearns to see Him:

> The tone is reminiscent of the Book of Psalms. The greatness of God almighty is contrasted with an overwhelming feeling of impotence and humility.

Passage 1 (lines 1-16)

The poem opens with a *compositio loci*. The poet stands or better lies prostrated (*muntariḥan*) before God the Almighty and asks in the dark for help (*astajîru*)[12]. God is called a pastor of ants, who hears the sound of pebbles in the deep (irony!). But the poet doubts if God hears him shouting and screaming:

> *A tasmaᶜ al-nidâ'? yâ-bûrikta*
> Do you hear the appeal, O Sanctified One?

If he hears him, will he answer?

The text proceeds with qualifiers of Gods power and arbitrariness. He is called *ṣâ'id al-rijâl* (hunter of men) and *sâḥiq al-nisâ'* (a violator of women) and *mufajji'* (horrifying), the one who destroys people (*muhlik al-ᶜibâd*) with stones and earthquakes and makes their houses empty (*mûḥish al-manâzil*). In his situation the poet is overwhelmed by contrary feelings of contrition (*uḥissu bi-'nkisârat al-ẓunûn fî 'l-ḍamîr*) and revolt.

Passage 2 (lines17-47)

This passages opens with *lâ abtaghî min al-ḥayât ghayr mâ ladayya*, an understated way of saying, "I am tired of everything". In the following lines we find 5 times the expression "*taᶜibtu*": I am tired of the middayheat, I am tired of my great struggle, I am tired of my latest springtime, I am tired of the artificiality of life, and surprisingly: "I am tired like a child tired from his weeping."

In this passage the poet seems to look back at the struggle for life and with life, with numerous references to vegetation that recall the Tammuzian poet. The whole has for him artificial dimensions:

> *aᶜîshu bi-'l-ams wa-adᶜû amsî al-ghadâ'*

12. *G.J. van Gelder has drawn my attention to the presence of this motif in classical kalâm.*

ka'annî mumaththil min ᶜâlam al-radâ

I live in yesterday and I call yesterday tomorrow morning
like an actor in a world of destruction (lines 42-3)

Passage 3 (lines 48-69)

This passage is in the form of a prayer in two parts. The first part concludes in line 57:

"I want to sleep in your sanctuary
under a cover of sins and mistakes
on a bed of intercourse with whores
scoffing me for your hand which touches me
I wish I could see you
I hasten myself to your great gate
on the ship of sinners and outcasts
yelling with our broken voices
like daggers cleaving the air with their mourning:"

In the second part the daggers assume voices which speak and the poet expresses in a highly romantic way his feelings of loss, spleen and his desire for beauty:

"our sharp (?) faces are like
children's designs in the sands
they don't know what beauty and charm is
Gone is childhood, dimmed is the lustre of youth
faded away like clouds
and we have our own faces to bear
they don't escape from the eyes, they appear to them
but they don't reveal our souls nor reflect
their movements
towards you O creator of beauty
we roam, thirsty for the gardens of the noble
from a world that sees the lilies on the water
but fails to see the oister in the deep
and the incomparable pearl in it"

Passage 4 (l. 70-71)
This passage serves as epilogue and reiterates the desire for death.

At the Congress of Rome that followed soon after the writing of this poem, in October 1961, Sayyâb spoke in glorious terms of the Tammuzi experiment, as ʿAbbâs tells us: "He praised the Tammuzi poets who were afflicted by despair and abstained from commitment..." and Sayyâb admitted to the audience that he belonged to the "*ʿuṣba*" of poets who are named the Tammuziyyîn. But the glorious time of his Tammuzian poetry was long gone.

THE DIVINITY OF THE PROFANE: THE REPRESENTATIONS OF THE DIVINE IN THE POETRY OF ADÛNÎS

BY

STEFAN WEIDNER
University of Bonn

The notion of "Modernity" has been used to cover a multitude of complex, often very different phenomena in the history of, roughly speaking, the last two hundred years. It has been applied for such different purposes that it is probably more misleading than helpful, and we should be careful not to regard it as a hallmark for good or bad. One of the phenomena, however, which is usually linked with modernity in the domain of culture is the crisis of religions and a growing scepticism as far as the belief in God in general is concerned. Even if the questioning of traditional religious beliefs has never been as widespread as social or technical phenomena of modernity, it has been one of the most decisive factors of intellectual life in the 20th Century, not only in the West, but also, to a smaller extend, in the Islamic world. The work of Adûnîs[1], a naturalized Lebanese citizen born in the costal region of northern Syria in 1930 and one of the foremost contemporary Arab poets, has to be seen in the context of this development. Like hardly any other modern Arab author he immediately tackles the crisis of the Divine and tries to solve it by means of poetry.

Adûnîs's preoccupation with the Divine can be traced back until the early fifties; it is in his famous collection "*Aghânî Mihyâr al-dimashqî*" ("The songs of Mihyâr the Damascene")[2], published in Beirut in 1961, that the Divine appears as the main issue of his poetry. Not surprisingly, the word "*Allâh*" (and its derivations including "*rabb*" ["Lord"]), which occurs

---

1. Adûnîs is the pen name of ᶜAlî Aḥmad Saᶜîd Asbar. For a general overview of Adûnîs's work cf. Weidner, Stefan: "Adonis". In: Arnold, Heinz Ludwig (editor): *Kritisches Lexikon zur fremdsprachigen Gegenwartsliteratur*. München: Edition Text und Kritik, 1996, 41. Nachlieferung, pp. 1 - 11.
2. Poems from *Aghânî Mihyâr al-dimashqî* are quoted according to the most widely spread edition of Adûnîs's poetry: Adûnîs *al-Aᶜmâl al-shiᶜrîya al-kâmila*: Beirut: Dâr al-ᶜAwda 1988[5], vol. 1, pp. 245 - 430. This edition is referred to as "*Aᶜmâl vol. 1*". For a bilingual Arabic-German edition of "*Aghânî Mihyâr al-dimashqî*" with a commentary cf. Adonis: "Die Gesänge Mihyârs des Damaszeners". Gedichte 1958 - 1965. Translated and edited by Stefan Weidner. Zurich: Ammann, 1998.

53 times according to my count, is the most used proper noun in the volume.

The importance of the Divine and the superhuman becomes obvious from the very first pages. The protagonist, introduced in the grammatical third person, but not yet named, is presented in the introductory "Psalm"("*Mazmûr*")[3] — the title itself, of course, already hints at the religious dimension of this prose poem — in terms of qualities and characteristics which clearly transcend the human. He is not only said to encompass the opposites ("he is the reality and its contrary, he is the life and its other", "*Innahu al-wâqiᶜu wa-naqîḍuhu, al-ḥayâtu wa-ghayruhâ*"), thereby escaping any definitions, but has neither a bodily outward appearance ("He has the shape of the wind", "*lahu qâmatu al-rîḥi*") nor an ancestry ("he has no ancestor and his roots are in his footsteps", "*lâ aslâfa lahu wa-fî khuṭawâtihi judhûruhu*"). Furthermore, he has abilities which are marked by power over life and death: "He fills life and no one sees him. He whips it into foam and drowns in it" ("*yamla'u al-ḥayâta wa-lâ yarâhu aḥadun. Yuṣayyiru al-ḥayâta zabadan wa-yaghûṣu fîhi*), and: "he scares and vivifies (...) he peels man like an onion." ("*yurᶜibu wa-yunᶜishu (...) yaqshiru al-insâna ka-al-baṣalati*").

So far, the character described here shares a lot of attributes with God as conceived in the Islamic theological tradition. According to this theology, God's main characteristics are his undefinability, his being uncreated and having no predecessors. Other indications also seem to imply that a god-like character is presented here. Thus, it is said that "he creates his kinds starting from himself" ("*yakhluqu nawᶜahu bad'an min nafsihi*"), an idea which is close to the creation of man according to Genesis 1.26/27, though it is rather contradictory to the Islamic notion of God[4]. Moreover,

---

3. *Aᶜmâl* vol. 1, p. 251-252.
4. According to the Islamic tradition, God is not supposed to create his own kind, because God has to be uncreated. The question if God can create his own kind seems to have been subject to a controversy in the early Islamic theological thought: in his "*Ṭabaqât al-Muᶜtazila" Aḥmad ibn Yaḥyâ ibn al-Murtaḍâ* tells the story of a theological dispute between a Muslim judge and an unbeliever at the court of Sind. The Muslim was asked, if Allah were able to create his own kind - for if he were really omnipotent, he should be able to do so. This judge who was sent to Sind by Harûn al-Rashîd failed to answer it, so that Harûn al-Rashid cried out: "*A-laisa li-hâdhâ al-dîni man yunâdilu ᶜanhu*?" ("Isn't there anybody to defend our religion?"). Harûn was told that those who are able to do so were not allowed to dispute and were imprisoned. Harûn ordered them to appear at his court, and among them there was a young man who said: "This question is logically impossible, because what has been

when he is said "to have the shape of the wind", ("wind" ["*rîḥ*"], being the last word of the psalm), one is reminded of the conception of God as a 'pneuma' or of the 'spirit' of God as being comparable to the 'wind' in the biblical tradition. The etymological link of "*rîḥ*" and "*rûḥ*" ("spirit") with the "*ruakh*" ("spirit") of the Hebrew Bible further stresses this idea. In the literary tradition, Western and Eastern, only gods have been said to have "the shape of the wind".

Quite obviously, however, it is not a God who is presented here. The subject of the poetic speech shows at least some traits which contradict the notion of God most decisively. He is, like no God ever would,"dancing for the mud so that it yawns and to the tree so that it falls asleep" ("*râqiṣan li-al-turâbi kay yatathâ'aba, wa-li-al-shajari kay yanâma*")[5]. More importantly, he shows signs of being "at a loss", as if he were lacking something. It is said that, after having turned "the morrow into game", he runs after it "in despair" ("*yuḥawwil al-ghada 'ilâ ṭâridatin wa-ya*ᶜ*dû yâ'isan warâ'ahâ*"). His words "are chiseled into the direction of loss" ("*maḥfûratun kalimâtuhu fî al-tijâhi ḍiyyâ*ᶜ*i*") and "perplexity — a well known mystical term denoting a degree of the spiritual states ("*aḥwâl*") of the Sufi — is his homeland" ("*al-ḥayratu waṭanuhu*"). The protagonist, thus, appears as a god-like creature, a demi-God or someone who, despite all his divine attributes and also some kind of omnipotence, is not without needs and distress. He represents the sphere of the human and the profane as much as he represents the Divine.

The second poem "He is not a star" ("*Laysa najman*")[6] takes us closer to the protagonist, who is once again depicted in terms common to the sphere of the religious. His divine character, however, is now rather explicitly denied: "He is not a star, not the inspiration of a prophet" ("*laysa najman, laysa iḥâ'a nabî*"). The distance of the protagonist from the

---

created can only be new, and what is new can not be like the old (i.e.God)". This young man then was sent to Sind instead of the judge. Cf: Aḥmad ibn Yaḥyâ ibn al-Murtaḍâ: "Die Klassen der Muᶜtaziliten". Ed. by Susanna Diwald-Wilzer. Beirut: Imprimerie Catholique, 1961, pp. 55 - 56.
It is not clear, though, if Adûnîs had this anecdote in mind when he wrote the Psalm. Nonetheless, the anecdote underlines the theological repercussions Adûnîs's text must have for those readers who are aware of the history of Islamic theology.

5. A dancing God can be found in Nietzsche, however. Zarathustra says: "Ich würde nur an einen Gott glauben, der zu tanzen verstünde" ("I will only believe in a God who knows how to dance"). In: Nietzsche, Friedrich: *Sämtliche Werke*. Kritische Studienausgabe. Vol. 4, p. 49. München: Deutscher Taschenbuch Verlag, 1980.
6. *A*ᶜ*mâl* vol. 1, p. 253.

traditional notion of the Divine is further stressed by saying: "he is coming like a heathen spear, invading the earth of the letters" (*"ya'tî ka-ramḥin wathanîyin / ghâzîyan 'arḍa al-ḥurûf"*). It is only in the third poem of the volume, that the protagonist is named - and given a status: he is called "King Mihyâr" (*"Malik Mihyâr"*)[7]. The domain of this king, however, is not real, but a symbolic one — he shares his domain with the poet: his castle is the dream, he lives in the kingdom of the wind and rules in the country of secrets. The figur of Mihyâr has been compared to the ancient Persian God Mithra[8]. The name Mihyâr, therefore, bears, although in a rather remote way, divine connotations.

The whole range of transformations and aspects of the person of Mihyâr cannot be explained here. It should be noted, however, that he has a considerable amount of Divine traits, but that he is not impervious. The Divine as represented by him is mingled with the human. In one of the following poems it is made clear that it is the Divine in the traditional Islamic sense that the "heathen spear" is most pungently directed against. Mihyâr is said to transgress "the frontiers of the Caliphate" and "to reject the Imamat", thus expressing his disregard for the wordly order of Islam (*"huwadhâ yatakhaṭṭâ tukhûma al-khalîfa (...) huwadhâ yarfuḍu al-imâmah"*)[9].

This 'transgression' of the religious order and value system is worked out and illustrated in several other poems. In poems like "The Holy Barbarian" (*Al-barbarî al-qiddîs*), "The New Noah" (*Nûḥu al-jadîd*) or "Shaddâd" (the name of a legendary person), the heretical tendency is already hinted at in the titles. In "The Holy Barbarian"[10] Mihyâr is presented with attributes of sainthood as well as paganisme: "This is Mihyâr, your holy barbarian[...]/ He is the suffering creator" *("dhâka*

---

7. *A^cmâl* vol. 1, p. 254
8. Cf.Krystyna Skarzynska-Bochenska does so in her article: "La symbolique du bien et du mal", in: Skarzynska-Bochenska, K.: "*Adonis. Obrazy, mysli, uczucia*". Warsaw: Wydawnictwo Akademickie Dialog, 1995, p. 176. Mithra, Skarzynska-Bochenska argues, is Mihir in Persan and thus close to the name "Mihyar". This insightful suggestion is further emphasized by the fact that light and darkness play an important role in the poetic imagery of "The Songs of Mihyâr". Mithra, as is well known, was partly identical with Apollon and Helios.
   'Mihyâr the Damascene" is, by the way completely independent from the historical '*Mihyâr al-dailamî*". Adûnîs has stressed this recently in an interview with the author of this article (forthcoming in the German literary review "Neue Rundschau").
9. *A^cmâl* vol. 1, p. 268. The poem is: "*Wajhu Mihyâr*" ("Mihyars face").
10. *A^cmâl* vol. 1, p. 274.

Mihyâru qiddîsuki al-barbarî — [...]/ *"Innahu al-khâliqu al-shaqî"*). As a creator he belongs to the sphere of the Divine, but he also suffers and thus belongs to the human.

In the poem "Shaddâd"[11] the heresy is more deeply rooted in the Arabic-Islamic tradition. The poem alludes to the myth of "'Iram *dhât al-ᶜimâd*" ("The many columned city of Iram"), which is mentioned in the Koran 89:6-7 as having ignored the orders of God. " *Iram dhât al-ᶜimâd*" is also the title of the chapter of which "*Shaddâd*" is the last poem. Shaddâd, the ruler over 'Iram "has come back" ("ᶜ*âda Shaddâd ᶜâd*"), the poem tells us in the first line. The age of rebellion against the orders of God, the reader is led to conclude, begins anew. The city of 'Iram, which was condemned by God in the Koran, is, according to the poet-speaker, "the homeland of those who are desperate and those who refuse" ("*Innahâ waṭanu al-râfiḍîn / Alladhîna yasûqûna 'amârahum yâ'isîn*"). It seems to be the same refusal which has been connected to the character of Mihyâr in the former poems, the same desperation and the same perplexity. The inhabitants of 'Iram do not care for salvation or the menace of God. Whereas the Koran condemns the city and its inhabitants, in the poem "Shaddâd" the city is presented as a home for all those who agree with the poet-speaker in his attitude of refusal. In the last two verses this becomes even more obvious. The poet speaker now uses the first person plural "we", that is he comprises himself among those he has addressed before[12]. The poet-speaker calls 'Iram "our land and our only heritage" ("'*Innahâ 'arḍunâ wa-mîrâthunâ al-waḥîd*"). Then, in the following and final line, he says: "We are its sons who are reprieved until the day of resurrection" ("*Naḥnu 'abnâ'ahâ al-munẓarîna li-yaumi al-qiyâmah*"). The full meaning of this line can only be realized when one is aware of its Koranic background. For in the Koran (eg. in 15:37-38) it is Satan who is said to be among the reprieved: "You [Satan] are reprieved till the Appointed Day" ("*Qâla fa-'innaka mina al-munẓarîna / 'Ilâ yawmi al-waqti al-maᶜlûmi*"). By saying "we (...) are reprieved until the day of resurrection", "we" is paralleled to Satan: We, the last line of the poem tells us, are condemned like Satan and subjected to the punishment of God at the Day of Judgment. We are only reprieved until then. In the poem, this is stated as a rather neutral fact, but it is clear from the poems before that the

11. *Aᶜmâl* vol. 1, p.379.

12. In the second and third line of the poem: "So raise the banner of yearning / And leave your refusal as a sign" *("Fa-rfaᶜû râyata al-ḥanîn / Wa-trukû rafḍakum 'ishâra")*.

poet regards our being “munẓar” (“reprieved”) as a conditio humana and accepts it as such.

Heresy and the longing for a new worldly or religious order become also obvious from the poem “The New Noah”[13]. According to the Islamic tradition, Noah is regarded as one of the first and most important prophets of the one and single God. This Islamic Noah is replaced by a new Noah, the speaker of the poem. In the final verses of the poem, this new Noah says that he does not listen to the words of God, but “long[s] for another, for a new Lord” (“*Namḍî wa-lâ nuṣghî li-dhâka al-'ilâh / Tuqnâ 'ilâ rabbin jadîdin siwâh*”). Again, the heretic impact of the poem is quite obvious. It is remarkable, however, that the notion of God is not completely dismissed; instead, the traditional God is replaced by a new one, and the most important role of the new Noah is to be one of his prophets. The meaning of God and Noah and the worldview they convey have changed, but the divine structure, if I may say so, has remained: There is still a god, and there are still prophets, they only symbolize new values.

Another highly interesting poem for our purposes seems to be at first glance a homage to one of the most venerated persons of early Islam: “Elegy to ᶜUmar ibn al-Khattab” (“*Marthiya ᶜUmar ibn al-Khaṭṭâb*”)[14]. It is, however, rather obscure, owing to the fact that it refers to a story told in the “Kitâb al-'aghânî”, which might not be known or recognized by every reader.

The story in the *Kitâb al-aghânî*[15] tells of the encounter of ᶜUmar and Jabala, — rendered as “*Jibilla*” in the poem, for reasons of rhyme, I guess. Jabala is a Byzantine nobleman and leader who has converted to Islam and renders his visit of duty to the caliph and the holy places in Mecca. During the circumambulation of the Kaaba, a Beduin inadvertently tears Jabala’s robe. Jabala gets upset and beats him. Consequently, ᶜUmar allows the beduin to ask for satisfaction or to take revenge, justifiying this to the surprised Jabala by telling him that in Islam everybody is equal. Jabala’s response, that under these conditions he prefers to become a Christian again, worsens the situation: As an apostate, he is now threatened by death. ᶜUmar, however, tolerates that Jabala leaves, probably fearing a clash between his adherents and Jabala’s.

13. *Aᶜmâl* vol. 1, p. 418
14. *Aᶜmâl* vol. 1, p. 424
15. Cf. Abû al-Faraj al-Isfahânî: *Kitâb al-Aghânî.* Edited by ᶜAbd A. ᶜAlî Muhanna and Samîr Jâbir, Beirut: Dâr al-fikr, 1995 3 vol. 15, p. 158 -159.

If the poem is read against the background of this story, its meaning becomes apparent. The question: "When are you beaten, o Jibilla" ("*Matâ tuḍrabu yâ Jibillah*"), posed by "a voice", makes possible an interpretation according to the story in the "*Kitâb al-Aghânî*". Jabala has not yet been beaten, but he should have been if the promise of Islam to treat every Muslim equally regardless of his origin had been fulfilled. It is this promise which is alluded to in the last two lines: "And we are waiting/for your promise which comes from heaven" ("*wa-naḥnu fî ntiẓâr / mawᶜidika al-âtîyi min al-samâ*'"). Being pronounced by the religion of Islam, the promise is of Divine origin. But it has been unfulfilled until now, justice has not been done. The striking feature of this poem, to my mind, is that this failure is attributed to such a venerated figure as ᶜUmar. It should have been his task (and was his chance) to fulfill this promise, but he preferred a more diplomatic solution. Reading this poem, the reader is witnessing the deconstruction of the myth of the so called rightly guided caliphs, of the Golden Age of Islam, and thus one of the most popular of all Muslim creeds.

The destruction or deconstruction of established religious orders and creeds is not the only way the Divine is treated in the "Songs of Mihyâr". The impulse of destruction is, in most cases, matched or accompanied by a creative act or by setting up positive values. Thus, the poem about ᶜUmar, is, of course, not only a deconstruction of the myth of early Islam and the rightly guided caliphs, but also the acknowledgement of the value of equality among men regardless of their origin. The dialectic of destruction and creation is also at work in the short poem "Death" ("Mawt")[16]. It says in its first two lines: "We dịe, if we do not create gods/ We die if we do not kill gods —" ("*Namûtu 'in lam nakhluqi al-âliha / Namûtu 'in lam naqtuli al-âliha* —"). By talking of gods and their creation by men, the poem is already beyond the sphere of the Islamic or Christian conception of the Divine. The constant creation and destruction of gods and all that is implied by them, i.e. the worldly and religious order, is presented as the conditio sine qua non of life. While this is quite obvious, the last of the three lines of the poem is comparably obscure. It is an apostrophe which adresses the "Kingdom of the straying rock", "straying" forming a significant rhyme with "Gods": "*Yâ malakûta al-ṣakhrati al-tâ'iha*". I cannot help but be

16. *Aᶜmâl* vol. 1, p.389

reminded here of Matthew 16.18.-19. which reads in Arabic translation as follows:

> "*Wa-anâ aqûlu laka 'aiḍan 'anta Buṭrus wa-ᶜalâ hâdhihi al-ṣakhrati 'abnî kanîsatî wa-'abwâbu al-jaḥîmi lan taqwâ ᶜalaihâ. Wa-'uᶜṭîka mafâtîḥa malakûti al-samawâti.*"[17]

The rock is the symbol of stability. What is built on this rock will last forever and remain where it was put, will stay what it is. The notion of a straying rock, thus, is quite a paradox. I tend to regard this poem as the quintessence of how the Divine and God are represented in "The Songs of Mihyâr". It seems to encapsulate the whole world view of this diwan. As we will see, it is helpful even for the understanding of the later works of Adûnîs. The metaphysical security guaranteed by the rock is only that of a fragile equilibrium. It is the equilibrium between creating and killing gods. We still need gods, the poem tells us, and we still need the kingdom, the worldly oder set up by God. However, as a very condition of our life, that is, I am inclined to add, of the conditio humana in modernity, this order is no longer built on stable grounds. Moreover, the poem seems to imply that the function of the Divine is more important than its particular form, its realisation in a specific religion. The latter, together with the belief in a particular God, may and must differ and change, but that there always has to be a power comparable to the Divine which 'produces' a religion and a "kingdom", is presented as an anthropological necessity. The poem, if I may say so, expresses a Copernican change in the field of the Divine: the Divine moves.

I hope I did not go too far in reading all this into a very short poem. I feel entitled to do so, however, on the grounds that, as we have already seen, the notion of God or the Divine in general is by no means dismissed, but kept or rebuilt from the very beginning. The notion of particular gods in the traditional sense or of traditional world orders is, as we have also seen, attacked and demystified. Thus, "The Songs of Mihyâr" themselves practice what they preach according to this little poem, namely destroying and creating Gods.

The volume of poetry written after the Mihyâr "The Book of Transformations and of Emigration in the Regions of Day and Night"

---

17. Ed. Dâr al-Kitâb al-muqaddas fî sharq al-awsaṭ (without place [Beirut?] and date).

("*Kitâb at-taḥawwulâti wa-al-hijrati fî 'aqâlîm an-nahâr wa-al-lail*")[18] is also obsessed with the Divine. Of special interest for our purpose is the treatment of the Divine in the part "The transformations of the lover" ("*Taḥawwulât al-ᶜâshiq*")[19]. Here, for the first time in Adûnîs's poetry, the body shifts to the center of the poet's attention; the Divine, on the contrary, seems to be completely absent. Both on the level of language as well as ideas, however, a thorough analysis reveals the importance of the Divine even in this poem.

The 30-page poem is to a large degree a collage. As far as I know, not all of Adûnîs's sources have been worked out so far, but thanks to some studies by Arab scholars we have come to know the most important ones[20]. The technique Adûnîs uses is rather simple. He takes chosen classical texts with a certain religious meaning, puts them into a profane context and, moreover and most decisively, he changes precisely those words and expressions which denote the former religious context. The religious, thus, is replaced, usually by locutions somehow connected to the body or sexuality. This replacement of the religious can be seen most clearly in the following three examples which I have picked out of a whole list of analogous ones. In the first example, Adûnîs changes a text by al-Aṣmaᶜî. Instead of a pilgrimage "to the holy house of God via Syria" ("*ilâ baiti Allâhi al-ḥarâmi ᶜan tarîqi al-Shâmi*"), Adûnîs talks about a journey "fi tarîqi al-nisâ'"[21], while the rest of the story is, more or less, identical[22]. Another striking example is based on a saying by al-Niffarî. In *al-Mukhâṭaba* 57.9 al-Niffarî says: "The Lord stayed me, and said to me: Say to the Sun, O thou that wast written by the Pen of the Lord, (...)." ("*'Awqafanî al-rabbu wa-qâla lî qul li-al-shamsi 'ayyatuhâ al-maktûbata bi-qalami al-rabbi*")[23]. In Adûnîs version, it is not the Lord ("al-rabb") who says this, but "*al-sayyid al-jasad*", "Mister Body". Instead of the sun, the

18. In Aᶜmâl pp. 431 - 597.
19. Ibid. pp. 505 - 540.
20. The results of these studies are collected and summarized by Kâẓim Jihâd in his book: *Adûnîs muntaḥilan*. Kairo: Maktabat Madbûlî, 1993. By accusing Adûnîs of plagiarism, Jihâd misses the central point of Adûnîs's technique of collage, namely the profane reinterpretation of the classic religious texts he uses.
21. *Aᶜmâl* vol. 1, p. 531.
22. A synoptic version of al-Aṣmaᶜî's and of Adûnîs's version can be found in ibid. p. 91.
23. Arberry, Arthur J. (ed.): *The Mawáqif and Mukhátabát of Muḥammad ibn ᶜAbd al-Jabbár al-Niffarí*. London: Cambridge University Press, 1935, p. 182 (Arberry's translation).

beloved is addressed, and she is not, like the sun, written by the pen of the Lord, but by the pen of the lover: "*Ayyatuhâ mar'ata al-maktûbata bi-qalami al-ᶜâshiq*"[24]. We do not have to be adherents of the psychoanalytic school of literary analysis to state that the highly venerated Koranic "*qalam*" ("pen", e.g. in Koran 96:4) here is nothing but a name for the phallus. The heretic impact of this reinterpretation of the Divine can hardly be matched.

A rather subtle example which might easily pass unremarked is the following allusion to a Koranic expression. In a description of the act of love Adûnîs writes: "I am torn while descending into the depths of the body which are filled with creatures burning, dying down, moaning and wailing."[25]. The expression "moaning and wailing" is used in Koran (11:106) to describe the cries of those who are cast into the fire of Hell. In Adûnîs's version, these cries become somehow part of the sexual activity. In incorporating these words into a description of lovemaking, however, Adûnîs does nothing but revive another meaning of these words: "*shahîq*" and "*zafîr*" also mean the cries of rutting donkeys. As before (cf. note 4), we cannot know if Adûnîs has used this expression consciously. Those Arab readers who know the Koran well, however, are most likely to be reminded of the Koranic use of these words. Hell and Heaven, we migth interpret Adûnîs's provocative use of Koranic language, are located in the body, not in a transcendental sphere.

The Divine, thus, is literally replaced by the profane, the traditional notion of God by an adoration of the body. This method, simple as it is, is even more striking if we realize that the Divine as a function or system of thought and approach to the world is, to a large degree, retained. It is founded now on the body instead of God, but it functions the same way as if there were still God. There is still a pilgrimage, we are led to conclude, but it leads to the other gender, to women. There is still a mystical experience, but instead of being concerned with God, it is rooted in sexuality. (A change, which is, by the way, the inversion of the Sufi technique, which consists of using the profane terminology of love to describe love of God). There is even a direct and explicit adoration of specific gods. Several times in the poem the poet says "Liber, Libera, Phallus", thus invoking the ancient pagan Gods Liber and Libera, who,

24. *Aᶜmâl* vol. 1, p. 514.

25. "*Atamazzaqu anfaṭiru nâzilan ilâ aghwârihi / malî'an bi-khalâ'iqa tashtaᶜilu tanṭafi'u tashhaqu wa-tazfuru.*" Ibid. 520.

according to Augustine in his "De civitate dei" (Book 7, chapter 21), were celebrated in processions exposing giant Phalli. Fortunately for the poet, this subtext has been largely unnoticed.

To summarize, we may say that the structure of the Divine is kept while its traditional outward shape is replaced by the notion of the body. "The transformations of the lover" is, therefore, the first decisive attempt of Adûnîs to "create" or determine a new God from the profane and to use the tradition to bestow it with divine traits. Whereas the demi-god Mihyâr was a rather diffuse, untangible figure and was sometimes interchangeable with the poet-speaker or other figures like Odysseus, the body is now presented as the legal successor to the Divine — and the poet is its herald. From now on, the body remains at the center of the poet's attention and is, in some poems more, in some less, bestowed with divine attributes.

In some poems written during the Lebanese Civil War the relationship between the body and the Divine gains a new quality. To show this, I am going to analyse briefly two poems, one written in 1977 and the other in 1982. The first poem is "Unintended worship ritual" ("*Quddâs bilâ qaṣd, khalîṭ iḥtimâlât.*")[26] Right from the beginning, the text presents itself as a follow-up to "The Transformations of the Lover", saying: "And thus, she was an unintended worship ritual" ("*'Idhan kânat quddâsan bilâ qaṣdin*")[27]. Instead of God, the worship ritual is directed towards a woman. In the following, however, it is not a woman who is portrayed, but the city of Damascus, where the poet lives. The city is described in terms of a body and in the whole poem city and woman are largely synonymous. Several times, the poet calls his beloved "woman-city" ("*al-mar'atu al-madîna*"). Making love and writing, i.e. finding the right words and the language to express his love are also paralleled: "Her body being his language by which he spoke/ he listened to her body speak about a travel between ink and paper/ between member and member" ("*Aṣghâ' 'ilâ jasadiha [jasaduha lughatuhu wa-bihi yatakallamu] / yatakallamu ᶜalâ al-safari bayna al-ḥibri wa-al-waraqi / bayna al-ᶜaḍwi wa-al-ᶜaḍwi*")[28]. Moreover, Damascus here is not only an image of the beloved, but the symbol of the Arab world, the

26. In: Adûnîs: *Al-Aᶜmâl al-shiᶜrîya al-kâmila*. Beirut: Dâr al-ᶜawda 1988[5], vol. 2, pp. 369 - 391.

27. Ibid. p. 371. I am using the translation by Issa Boullata, which has appeared together with his insightful article on this poem in Middle East Studies 21 (1989), pp. 541 - 562.

28. Cf. Adûnîs: *Al-Aᶜmâl al-shiᶜrîya al-kâmila*. Beirut: Dâr al-ᶜawda 1988[5], vol. 2, p. 377.

political division of which becomes apparent in the Lebanese Civil War. The poet regards it as his task to heal the Arab nation by his poetry, the beloved by his body. This redemptive task of the poet is expressed quite clearly in the last part of the poem: "your (i.e. Damascus') name is being doubled now/ and, by the glory of your other name,/it is now poetry/ that recasts you letter by letter / in order that you will be in people's reach, / in order that you will be at hand so long as there is poetry."[29] In short, the task of poetry is to reconcile and to heal the Arab nation from its defects. This task, I think, is rooted in an almost religious conception of poetry. The model character of the religious in the poet's struggle becomes obvious when he calls his act of love "*'Iᶜjâz*":

> I exclude you (sc. the beloved) from
> how, why, and where,
> and I practice my inimitable miracle.[30]

The transcendental poetical power of the Koran, which has been laid down as a dogma in the term "*'Iᶜjâz*" (miracle), is, by using this term for the sexual act, now projected onto the body, the powers of which are said to be as miraculous as the Koranic verses. The body of the poet thus becomes the symbol for the powers of poetry, which now seems even to compete with the Koran in its promise to heal and redeem, in short, to exercise its divine powers.

As in "The Transformations of the Lover" and "The Songs of Mihyâr", the traditional religious concept of Islam or any other religion is discarded. Frankly, the poet says that he is "embraced by heresy" ("*Yaḥḍunuhu zuhâ'a harṭaqatin*")[31]. The main characteristics of the religious, however, are maintained and transposed onto the poet, his body and his language. the Divine as a system of thought or alleged powers remains as in the former poems.

The poem "The Time" ("*Al-Waqt*")[32], written in response to the Israeli siege of Beirut in 1982, shows a pattern comparable to "Unintended worship

29. *Hâ huwa smuki yazdawiju al-âna, / Lâkin, bi-majdi smiki al-âkhar, huwa al-âna/ al-shiᶜru lladhî yuᶜîdu shabkaki / Ḥarfan ḥarfan, / Li-takûnî ᶜalâ marmâ al-khalqi / Li-takûnî qarîbatan ᶜalâ madâ al-shiᶜri.* Ibid. p. 390.
30. *Astathnîki min / Kaifa wa-lima wa-'ain /Wa-'umârisu 'iᶜjâzî*, ibid. p. 389.
31. Ibid. 384.
32. The poem can be found in Adûnîs: *Kitâb al-ḥiṣâr*. Beirut: Dâr al-âdâb, 1985, pp. 5 -

ritual". The poet overcomes the vicissitudes of the war and the omnipresent destruction by his magic poetical powers. In contrast to his age, which is marked by destructive forces, the poet embodies the reconciliating forces of poetical language, as is stressed in the last lines of the poem. There he writes (in extracts):

> My skin is not a cavern of thoughts, (...)
> my weddings the grafting of two poles; this epoch is mine
> the dead God, the blind machine — (....)
> I am the Alpha of water and the Omega of fire — the mad lover of life.[33]

The religious dimension of the last phrase is obvious; by calling himself "the Alpha and the Omega", the poet identifies himself with what formerly was the Divine, with the only difference being that the Divine, here, is not located in the other world, is not transcendental but tellurian, elemental. As in "Unintended worship ritual" the definition of what the Divine is has obviously changed, but, nonetheless, the stance of the Divine is again adopted. The poet, so to speak, usurps the Divine.

Quite naturally, the question of credibility and acceptance of such a stance poses itself. We can enjoy the poem aesthetically, — it is, I think, one of the most perfect of Adûnîs' later poems — and can admire the poet's determination to fight war by means of poetry. The impact of the poem,

---

19. The title of the poem itself has an explicit religious dimension. In the Koran, the expression *al-waqt* is often used to denote the time of the final judgement (e.g. 15, 38; 38, 81), and the Apocalypse of John often mentions that the time of the final judgment has come or is about to come (e.g. 1,3; 22,10). It is also a Sufi - expression denoting a degree of ecstasy (in this context cf. Schimmel, Annemarie: *Mystische Dimensionen des Islams*. München: Diederichs, 1992, p. 190). I have recently presented a more extensive discussion of "*al-waqt*" in my article "A Guardian of change? The Poetry of Adûnîs between Hermeticism and Commitment", in: Bürgel, J.C. and Guth, S.: *Conscious Voices. Concepts of Writing in the Middle East*. Beirut: Beiruter Texte und Studien, 1999.

33. "*Laisa jildî kûkha afkâri, (...) / Wa-'aʿrâsî liqâḥun/ Bayna qutbayni, wa-hadhâ al-ʿaṣru ʿaṣrî / Al-ilâhu al-mayyitu, wa-al-'âlâtu ʿumyâ'a (...)/ Wa-'annî 'alifu al-mâ'i wa-yâ'u al-nâri — majnûnu al-ḥayât*". Cf. Adûnîs: *Kitâb al-hiṣâr* . Beirut: Dâr al-'âdâb, 1985, p. 19.
The translation is based on the translation of "Al-Waqt" by Amyuni., In: *Journal of Arabic Literature 21* (1990). Instead of "the Alpha" and "the Omega", however, Amyuni translates "'Alif" and "Yâ'", not realizing the allusion to the Apocalypse of John 22.13.

however, is, to my mind, partly spoilt by the highly pathetic, overrated claim of the poet, and it is not clear how poetry can manage to overcome war, or how it should reconcile the Arab nation, as in "Unintended worship ritual". To assess this problematic trait of the poems, we should be aware of the following: If modernity has brought about a crisis in religious beliefs and notions, a crisis that is impressively mirrored in Adûnîs' *The Songs of Mihyâr*, it is most probably not only a crisis of a specific religious system, but of the Divine itself, of a certain pattern or system of thought which organizes and guarantees the credibility of the Divine. It is such a system which makes dogmata as the '*Iʿjâz* or phrases like "I am the Alpha and the Omega" (as a word of God in the Apocalypse) a truth beyond doubt and discussion. Such truths, however, have been severely questioned from the end of the last century up until our days. And this questioning concerns the whole of religious thought, the whole of the belief in the Divine, not just a particular dogma in a particular religion. This same impulse which makes people question dogmas and other beliefs, also nourishes our incredulity and scepticism if somebody, may he be the best poet, confronts us with an allegation we have to believe in. The problem we have with this resides not so much in what we are asked to accept by the poet, but precisely that the poet asks us to give up our scepticism, to trust and follow him in his attempt to change the world by means of poetry. Only to a public of disbelievers can a poet say that his body performs the *Iʿjâz* or that he is the Alpha and the Omega of the elements, but, strangely enough, the same public of disbelievers is asked then to accept the re-establishing of the Divine from the poet. Maybe the poet has reckoned with a different audience, i.e. a public for whom this remains unnoticed or unproblematic, and not with sceptical orientalists who do not even believe in poetry. In any case, the Divine is not only one of the main issues of Adûnîs' poetry, but its main problem, the unresolved center of the poet's preoccupation and one of his main motivations in writing. The question which haunts this poetry and could already be detected in the *Songs of Mihyâr*, is how to present, how to found the Divine anew and give it a new shape without subjecting it to the same fate as the established religions. For Adûnîs, poetry is the means of introducing this new type of the Divine and to grant it the necessary credibility.

One of the most gifted poets of the Arab world uses all his powers of expression to try to save the Divine by inventing a modern shape for it and thus trying to make it acceptable again. Although this Divine has lost most of its traditional appearance, its most important functions are retained. We may regard this as an impressive attempt to fuse modernity and tradition. We might read it as a first hand testament as to how the Divine is still rooted the Middle Eastern societies, represented here by one of its foremost and most libertine intellectuals. Both, I think, is true. If we want or not, we have to accept that even the most perfect poetry is sometimes subjected to contradicting forces which multiply its meanings and possible readings. The treatment of the Divine in Adûnîs' poetry is one of the best examples for this. And, last, but not least, it is an invitation to debate.

THE CHRIST FIGURE IN ṢÂYIGH'S POETRY

BY

ROGER ALLEN
University of Pennsylvania

With due acknowledgement to the wealth of divine symbols in the work of such modern Arab poets as al-Sayyâb, ᶜAbd al-Ṣabûr, and Adûnîs, all of whom were major participants in that movement of change in Arabic poetic sensitivity that followed the Second World War (to which Jabrâ Ibrahîm Jabrâ's translation of sections of Frazier's *The Golden Bough* made a major contribution), I have chosen to search for the expression of the divine, and more particularly the use of the Gospel narratives, among the Christian poets and especially those whose education made them particularly aware of the tradition of English poetry. In such a context, the name of Tawfîq Ṣâyigh comes inevitably to the fore. Born to a Christian father (a Presbyterian minister) in Syria in 1923, he grows up as a Palestinian in Tiberias, the venue of so many of the events in the life of Christ. Exiled from his adopted homeland after the Dayr Yâsîn massacre in 1948, Ṣâyigh shares in the agonies of the continuing Palestinian exile. His wanderings in the wilderness of alienation and his quest for meaning through suffering afford his poetry a universality that transcends his own personal experiences. Finally, his education in English and its literary tradition brings him into close contact with the towering figure of T.S. Eliot and his poetry, most especially "The Wasteland"--that combination of personal desolation and public expression of malaise at the fate of Europe in the wake of the Second World War that, with all the weighty "anxiety of influence" that strong predecessors like Milton and Coleridge could bring to bear on an English poet, was to become emblematic of an entire era and is arguably the most influential poem of this century. Ṣâyigh's translation of Eliot's "Four Quartets" (1971, but first published serially in the 1960s), poems marked by their strongly confessional tone, is merely the clearest illustration of an influence that is evident in Ṣâyigh's own poetry.

These elements--the Palestinian struggle and a Christian identity--combine with the theme of a passionate, yet tortured love to form the principal matrices of Ṣâyigh's poetic output. Frustration, memory, longing, alienation--both literal and psychological, and challenges to the seemingly inexorable logic of reality, often orchestrate Ṣâyigh's poetic voice with different configurations resulting in an intensity that is akin to obsession. A process of questioning leads the poetic persona to challenge the very nature of his devotion. In what follows I propose to focus on two poems in which the sacred, the Christian, and particularly the life of Christ are especially prevalent, but I will preface my comments with the provision of the briefest of contexts. In his earlier poems Ṣâyigh's poetic persona can stroll along the Corniche in Beirut, musing about poetry and love[1]. Indeed, a sizeable proportion of his earliest collection, *Thalâthûn qaṣîda* (1954), consists of reflections on the theme of love. And yet, the intermingling of the secular and divine that is to be so much a feature of his later poetry is already present. The traveller "On the road to Damascus"[2] who announces in the first line that he can see, "yet the blind man pities my condition," has a revelatory encounter:

Halumma azîḥu al-qushûr ᶜan ᶜaynayka
wa-urîka mabâhija al-ḥayâ

Come, let me remove the crust from your eyes,
then I can show you the glories of life...

---

1. For the purpose of this study, I have used Tawfîq Ṣâyigh, Al-Aᶜmâl al-kâmila, London: Riad El-Rayyes Books, 1990. Page references in the notes that follow are to that edition. Ṣâyigh 's poems appear in English translation in a number of anthologies, of which the following are currently available: *Modern arabic Poetry: an anthology* ed Salma Khadra Jayyusi, New York: Columbia UNiversity Press, 1987; *An Anthology of Modern Palestinian Literature* ed. Salma Khadra Jayyusi, New York: Columbia UNiversity Press, 1992; and *When the Words Burn: an anthology of modern Arabic poetry 1945-1987* trans. John Mikhail Asfour, Dunvegan, Ontario: Cormorant Books, 1988. For biographical details on Ṣâyigh, samples of his writing and correspndence, and photographs of him and many modern Arab poets, see Maḥmûd Shurayḥ (Mahmoud Shureih), *Tawfiq Ṣâyigh: sîra shâᶜir wa-manfâ*, London: Riad El-Rayyes Books, 1989. For further details on Ṣâyigh's life and poetic career, as well as for insightful analyses of many his poems, see Issa J. Boullata, "The Beleaguered Unicorn: A study of Tawfiq Sayigh," *Journal of Arabic Literature* Vol. IV (1973): 69-93; and Mounah A. Khouri, "The Paradise Lost in Ṣâyigh's Poetry," in *Studies in Contemporary Arabic Poetry and Criticism*, Piedmont, California: Jahan Book Co., 1987, pp. 139-47.
2. Ṣâyigh, *al-Aᶜmâl al-kâmila*, pp. 62-65.

Enjoined to get the best out of life and its beauty, the traveller, now empowered with vision, can proceed along the road to Damascus.

Adopting a more defiant and frustrated tone Ṣâyigh can also use this same love theme in order to add his particular voice to those of other poets who challenge the moral underpinnings and fate of the Arab nation; for him it now has all the attraction of an old woman, formerly beautiful perhaps and married to a ruler who has provided lavishly for her needs, but reduced to a haggard state of irrelevance and humiliation.[3] Burdened by the weight of the past, squeezed like a genie into tradition's bottle and wondering if he should shout out to Solomon like the genies of legend (and of the "City of Brass" tale *in A Thousand and One Nights),* Ṣâyigh questions his God about the nature and purpose of freedom.[4] As his life becomes more complex and the mood darkens on all fronts, these questions not only become more insistent, but also challenge God to meet him at least halfway. A particular feature of "Poem 1" in *Qaṣîda K* (1960) is the repeated use of "*urîdu*" ("I want"):

Lâ, lâ urîdu an atamassaka anâ bi-ḥablika
wa-urîduka wa-ḥablaka an tatashabbathâ bî

No, no! To be the one to grab hold of Your rope, that is not my wish.
That both You and Your rope should cling to me, that is what I desire....

and later

*Aah! urîduka al-sâ*ᶜ*î*
wa-urîdunî al-âtîka murghaman mukhtâran

Ah! I wish You to be the seeker
and me the one who comes to You, compelled, yet by choice...[5]

As is well known, one of the most complexifying factors in Ṣâyigh's period in exile was to be his prolonged and agonising love-affair with an English woman named Kay who becomes an overpowering force in his personal life and his poetry. Reports of his personal distress that come from colleagues

3. ibid., pp. 51-53.
4. ibid., pp. 43-45.
5. ibid., pp 114, 116. The translations are my own.

and friends like Jabrâ Ibrâhîm Jabrâ who share his exile find ample corroboration on the pages of his *Dîwân*:

wa-yunkirunî man kâna alîfî
wa-akâdu ajhalu dhâtî

Former colleagues fail to recognize me.
I hardly know my self.[6]

The title of Ṣâyigh's second volume of poetry, *Qaṣîda K* (1960), is inspired by this love relationship, yet the collection still includes within it continuing concerns with the political issues of the day: a poem in praise of the Algerian fighter, Jamîlah Buḥayrid, and the renowned 24th poem in the collection beginning with the phrase "*Iqtirâb wa-lâ-dukhûl*" (Approach, but no entry), which can serve as a manifesto of the exiled Palestinian, stateless and transient, condemned to wander the seas like the Flying Dutchman without ever experiencing the joys and comforts of arrival and welcome.[7] This collection also contains one of Ṣâyigh's most remarkable poems, one in which identities of speaker and poet seem especially closely linked: "*Min al-aᶜmâq ṣarakhtu ilayka yâ mawt*" (From the Depths I have Cried to You, O Death)[8]. The title, of course, immediately reminds the listener of the 130th Psalm of David, which begins:

Out of the depths have I called unto Thee, O Lord: Lord, hear my voice!
Let Thine ears consider well the voice of my complaint.

In Ṣâyigh's poem however the Psalmist's cry does not appear in the text of the poem, and the speaker's cry of despair is not to God but to Death itself. The combined weight of exile, tortured love, and sin lead the poet to contemplate the direst of thoughts:

aᶜrifu an ᶜalayya al-laylata mishwârun
yufattitu qalba abî
wa-yufarriḥunî

6. ibid., pp. 159-60
7. ibid., pp. 133-38, 222-28.
8. ibid., pp. 229-41.

I know that I must make a trip tonight
that will devastate my father's heart
and delight me...

He invites his beautiful filly to carry him away at a gallop from all the hatred, the blood, and the agony, and "to vault the final stream."[9]

It is not however in the volume that carries Kay's name, but in Ṣâyigh's third collection, *Muᶜallaqa Tawfîq Ṣâyigh* (1963), that the full impact of her apparently perverse and destructive behaviour on his poetic inspiration is fully evident. In the title poem, London, the city of rain, becomes the site of maximal alienation and destructive despair. The emotional connotations of the word "passion" are now transmuted into the passion of Christ's agony, as the speaker is nailed to the Cross and hoisted high; yet there are no women to mourn and none to roll back the stone from the tomb. The two Marys are transformed into mother and lover:

Maryam al-badhl wa-al-wiqâyah
wa-Maryam taṭlubu kulla yawmin ḍaḥiyyah
Maryam al-qalb wa-Maryam al-jasad...

the Maryam of giving and nurture,
the other Maryam demanding a fresh victim each day,
the Maryam of the heart, the Maryam of the body...[10].

Among this complex mixture of emotion, agony, and quest that go to make up Ṣâyigh's poetic persona (and of which the above is intended as the briefest of surveys), there are poems in which the environs of Tiberias and their central function in the creation of the myths of early Christianity become a particular focus. It is to a reading of two of those that I now turn.

---

9. ibid., pg. 241. I cannot help commenting on how uncannily, eerily similar this motif is to that of Ṣâyigh's close friend and supporter at this troubled time, Jabrâ Ibrâhîm Jabrâ, in his own poem "Urkudî, urkudî, ya muhratî." (Incidentally, Jabrâ's own translation of this poem into English, "Run, run, my lovely mare," is published in *Edebiyat* Vol. 1 no. 2 [1976], 146-47.) Those who know both poets well may be able to shed light on the circumstances surrounding the composition of both poems, but I can only assume that the disarming resemblances are deliberate and, in some way, the result of the close friendship between the two poets, especially during Ṣâyigh's period in England.
10. ibid., pg. 120.

Ṣâyigh's first collection, *Thalâthûn qaṣîda*, contains a poem whose title establishes an immediate link to the Gospel accounts: "*Al-Maw*ᶜ*iẓa* ᶜ*alâ l-jabal*" (The Sermon on the Mount).[11] The voice of the speaker is brought prominently to the fore in the very first line: "*Anâ ayḍan ittaba*ᶜ*tuhu.*" Seated on a hill overlooking "our drowsy lake" (*buḥayratinâ al-na*ᶜ*sâ'*), he is confident that Christ will return and once again intone the words of the Beatitudes: "Blessed are...." (*ṭûbâ*). This all-important theme of "return" (ᶜ*awdah*) is clearly one that must resonate loudly in the poetry of a Palestinian; one thinks also of its prose expression through the name Yuᶜâd adopted by Emile Ḥabîbî in his memorable narrative, *Al-Waqâ'i*ᶜ *al-gharîba* (1972-74; *The Secret Life of Saeed the Pessoptimist*, 1982. For Ṣâyigh's speaker Christ's return to a hill overlooking Lake Tiberias is an aspiration,

*wa-a*ᶜ*rifu annahu sa-ya*ᶜ*ûdu*
wa-antaẓiru ᶜ*awdatahu*

And I know he will return;
I await his return.

Such an aspiration for the speaker, and, by extension, for the future of the region, is placed at the conclusion of a poem in which memories of his participation in events far back in the past are invoked, the feeding of the multitude and the rapt attention to Christ's words. As the striking opening line tell us, the speaker was present among the crowds and partook of the marvellous meal. Yet, in spite of the crowds or perhaps because of them, he withdrew:

waḥdî labithtu ᶜ*alâ al-tallah...*
waḥdî labithtu, antaẓiru ᶜ*awdatahu*

Alone I lingered on the hill
alone I lingered awaiting his return.

The crowd witnessed the miracles, but the speaker was in need of a more personal communion. In an echo of the opening line we learn that:

anâ jurribtu ayḍan

---

11. ibid., pp. 33-36.

fî ghayr barriyyah jurribtu

I was tempted also
in no wilderness was I tempted.

And to the speaker Christ did indeed return, bringing personal counsel and comfort:

hal sami^c ahu siwâya? ẓanantu
annahu kâna yusirru lî
lam yunâdinî wa-kharajtu

Did anyone hear him save me? I thought
he was confiding in me alone;
he did not call me, but I came out.

The memory of these events and their impact on the crowd, but most especially on the speaker, leads him to hope, indeed to assume, that Christ will return again. Things have changed, needless to say. The "hill" now has another function, in that friends, relatives, and colleagues have died in the fighting: a parenthesis --a favourite device of Ṣâyigh--informs us that "our graveyard is now on the hill" (*maqbaratunâ al-âna ^c alâ al-tallah*). But the hope and expectation is that the returning Christ's very words will exert the same power as they did during His lifetime.

The second poem I wish to consider is found in the collection, *Qaṣîdat K.* Here the title does not reveal any obvious link with the Gospels, and yet its tone and content reveal not only the speaker's continuing sense of communication with his Messiah but also the increasingly questioning, indeed angry, tone that is to become so characteristic of Ṣâyigh's later poetry. "*Arba^c ughniyyât lâ ḥubb*" (Four songs, no love) is addressed directly to "the buried Messiah." Once again, our contemporary speaker is concerned to link and contrast the current Christ with the historical accounts in the Gospels. And, whereas previously there seemed to be understanding, now there are other emotions:

amsi lam abki
wa-al-yawm lâ aqwâ ^c alâ kaff al-bukâ'
ḥuznan wa-khawfan:
wa-ḥaqnan Masîḥi ^c alayk

Yesterday I did not weep
but today I cannot stop weeping
in sorrow and fear
and in hatred of You, my Messiah...

The speaker has witnessed the events of the Passion, but in the past he had complete confidence that Christ would return:

wa-ᶜudtu masâ'an li-baytî
mûqinan annaka lâḥiqun bî
wa-'ntaẓartu al-ṣafîr al-rafîq
aw ḥaṣâtan ᶜalâ zujâj al-nâfidhah

In the evening I returned home
sure that You would catch up with me.
I waited for the familiar whistle
or the pebble on the window-pane.

The poem tells how the Christ of the Gospels called his followers to Him. He broke fishermen's nets, and He performed miracles--casting out demons; indeed the speaker himself becomes a cripple who throws himself at Christ's feet and is able to discard his cane. The imagery of a militant Christianity is invoked, as a serried phalanx of devotees (*faylaqan muwâliyan*) give Him their salute. But Christ turns his back on them and disappears from their sight. Now the crying cannot stop, the speaker says, and it is selfish of Christ to leave his followers so helpless:

li-mâdhâ li-mâdhâ
turîdu walâ'î kullahu
wa-taḥjubu aqalla walâ'ika

Why, why
do you demand my complete loyalty
and yet deprive me of the least part of yours?

Returning to the opening theme the speaker asks Christ to arise again and return; after all, it is a fair exchange:

nâdaytanî qidaman fa-ji'tuka
bi-lâ taraddud
wa-unâdîka aṣrukh astaghîth

In older times You called me and I came to You
without hesitation
Now I am calling you, yelling, pleading...

but there will be no return and no mercy. Instead:

sabt al-ẓalâm hâdhâ
yaqlibu al-usbû^c subûtan
istaraḥta fîhi fî al-azal
wa-ḥaramtanî al-râḥata
li-'l-abad
li-'l-abad

This Black Saturday
turns the week into sabbaths
when You are at rest for all time
while You have deprived me of rest
for ever
for ever.

These two poems that I have selected clearly demonstrate the extent of the inspiration that Ṣâyigh found in a Christian faith that was an integral part of his life and upbringing from his very earliest memories. The imagery and language that Ṣâyigh uses in these two poems may represent some of the more obvious applications of the Gospel accounts and their mythic potential to the broader issues that confronted the modern Arab poet in the decades following the Second World War, but they also provide evidence of the firm base upon which Ṣâyigh was able to craft various combinations of sacred and secular, personal and public, into a unique poetic voice that speaks through a relatively small, yet important, contribution to the modern Arabic poetic corpus. Added to the published diwans in his collected poetry is a poem inspired by a quotation from the great German poet, Reiner Maria Rilke, that was published in five segments in *Ḥiwâr* (1963). Its ending seems to reflect as well as anything he wrote that comfortable, yet ever questioning, relationship that Ṣâyigh established with his Creator:

ilâhatî al-ḥayyah al-lâ-tamût
âsî, ilâhatî, laki

My God, living, undying,
I grieve for You, my God.

POEMS:

(1) Al-Mawᶜiẓa ᶜala al-jabal

English translation [by Tawfîq Ṣâyigh himself] in *An Anthology of Modern Arabic Poetry*, trans. Mounah A. Khouri and Hamid Algar, Berkeley, California: University of California Press, 1974, pp. 218-23.

(2) Arbaᶜ ughniyyât lâ ḥubb

English translation (by Roger Allen):

FOUR SONGS, NO LOVE

My Messiah, entombed, rise again!
Tear off the shrouds,
Colour your cheeks once more,
And forsake the abodes of ice.
You raised up all sorts of people,
You scorned hell's own triumph.
How is it then I see you wrapped
In white flag,
Casting aside weapons
Before being pelted yourself?

Yesterday I did not weep,
for I did not believe.
I saw blood being shed,
yet I knew you as a well-spring of blood.
I saw your mother's tears,
then I recalled her tears
every time you left her for a couple of days

or the elders conspired against you.
In the evening I returned home,
sure that you would catch up with me.
I waited for the familiar whistle
or the pebble on the window-pane.

Yesterday I did not weep,
but today I cannot stop weeping,
in sorrow and fear
and in hatred of you, my Messiah...

Why did you rush into oblivion
when you would walk so slowly towards your devotees?
Why did you embrace the cross
when you did not embrace dozens of people
who longed for such an embrace?
One by one you gathered us to you.

You abandoned us;
No kiss, no smile, no farewell.
Did you gather us together
not so much to assuage a hunger and longing in us,
but rather a hunger and longing in you?
You broke nets,
You removed us from family and homeland,
You cast out demons from us,
You deprived us of memories,
You grabbed us to yourself,
naked and destitute without you.
We raised your flag high
And you marked our brows with your seal.
You reviewed us, a serried phalanx,
Then, our salute received,
You abandoned us and turned toward the foe.

Why, why,
(Just tell me why)
did you draw me to you,
and, when as a cripple I threw myself at your feet,

you gave them wings and broke the crutch?
Why did you shun the past?
On the day you took away memories
and exchanged them for others,
fertile and multicoloured,
never fading or subsiding,
from olden times you took the surest course.
When you were buried, those memories were not buried with you.
Did you not rob me of a trifling threnody
that I could chant to some minor Messiah?

Why, why
do you demand my complete loyalty
and yet deprive me of the least part of yours?
In the abyss of hell itself
You see no corruption.
Why (tell me why)
Do you see no corruption there?
Indeed don't you give yourself a free hand,
breaking new nets,
casting out new demons,
crushing new hearts
that only beat when close to you?
(If only, if only I knew.)

My Messiah, entombed, rise again!
My Messiah, outcast, return.
In older times you called me, and I came
without hesitation
Now I am calling you, yelling, pleading,
yet you deny me the least gesture of your wasting body.
No, you will never return,
(I know)
never return.

Why did you come to me,
why did you take me away,
why did you wound my finger and your own,
why did you thus abandon me of your own volition?

Is it mercy you desire, not a victim?
As a victim you wanted me,
and I was content.
Ah, if only you had accorded me your mercy instead,
but you (I know, I know)
will never accord me your mercy.

Yesterday I did not weep,
but today I cannot stop
nor tomorrow.
If only, if only there were
for you or for me a morrow.
This Black Saturday
turns the week into sabbaths
when you are at rest for all time
while you have deprived me of rest
for ever,
for ever.